PRAISE FOR *UNLOCKIN~*
HIGH PERFORM~

"In *Unlocking High Performance*, Jason Laurit.   ...ets us with a hopeful, affirming message: work can be much better – more challenging and more fulfilling – if we do things a bit differently. He shows how common practices like annual performance appraisals may be holding you back – and how you can improve employee engagement and bring excitement and productivity back to the workplace."
Daniel H Pink, author of When and Drive

"We firmly believe in the power of unlocking human potential and love how the book touches on the value of recognition and appreciation in building high-performance organizations. Jason captures the ways in which organizations can help employees find meaning in their work by building stronger relationship and creating a workplace culture grounded in trust, respect, recognition, and humanity. If you want to inspire and motivate your employees to do the best work of their lives, then you should read this book."
Derek Irvine, Head of Strategy and Consulting, Globoforce

"In a world where the nature of work is changing at a revolutionary pace, continuing to operate in old paradigms can be devasting for organizations and even more harmful for the employees that work there. Jason goes beyond *best* practices and challenges the reader to think about *right* practices. He provides case studies and practical tools to help leaders and practitioners redesign and implement a performance management process that values employees and motivates employees to do their best work and be their best selves – everyday. He reviews the history of performance management and explains why organizations need a more humanistic approach to managing performance that is sustainable, mutually beneficial and helps the organization and employee thrive every day. Jason understands the interworking of even the most complex organizations and cuts to the heart of the matter – life is about relationships and work is no exception."
Ryan Picarella, President, The Wellness Council of America (WELCOA)

"Jason Lauritsen shows you how to deliver on the original promise of performance management. It's not about bureaucratic documentation; it's about making work better and creating better workers."
David Burkus, author of *Friend of a Friend* and *Under New Management*

"Performance management has failed because its view of what makes people successful is far too limited. Jason takes a much more expansive and holistic view and shows how it is truly possible for people to love their work and flourish, so their employers can grow and thrive as well."
Steve Smith, Partner, The Starr Conspiracy

"*Unlocking High Performance* is a field manual for leaders and HR practitioners seeking to create workplaces that attract, retain and develop the talent required by any successful and competitive business. Leaders can always choose to do the hard work to get it right. Reading this book is a great way to either start or remain on that path."
Joni Thomas Doolin, Founder and CEO, People Report and TDn2K

Unlocking High Performance

How to use performance management to engage and empower employees to reach their full potential

Jason Lauritsen

KoganPage

First published in Great Britain and the United States in 2018 by Kogan Page Limited

2nd Floor, 45 Gee Street	c/o Martin P Hill Consulting	4737/23 Ansari Road
London	122 W 27th Street	Daryaganj
EC1V 3RS	New York, NY 10001	New Delhi 110002
United Kingdom	USA	India

© Jason Lauritsen 2018

ISBN   978 0 7494 8329 6
E-ISBN   978 0 7494 8330 2

British Library Cataloguing-in-Publication Data

A CIP record for this book is available from the British Library.

Library of Congress Cataloging-in-Publication Data

Names: Lauritsen, Jason, author.
Title: Unlocking high performance : how to use performance management to
  engage and empower employees to reach their full potential / Jason
  Lauritsen.
Description: London ; New York : Kogan Page, 2018. | Includes bibliographical
  references and index.
Identifiers: LCCN 2018040750 (print) | LCCN 2018042141 (ebook) | ISBN
  9780749483302 (ebook) | ISBN 9780749483296
Subjects: LCSH: Performance technology. | Performance. | Personnel management.
Classification: LCC HF5549.5.P37 (ebook) | LCC HF5549.5.P37 L38 2018 (print)
  | DDC 658.3/12--dc23
LC record available at
https://catalog.loc.gov/vwebv/search?searchCode=LCCN&searchArg=2018040750&searchType=1
&permalink=y

Typeset by Integra Software services
Print production managed by Jellyfish
Printed and bound in Great Britain by CPI Group (UK) Ltd, Croydon CR0 4YY

*To my wife Angie, the best partner
I could ask for, and my three children.
They are the reason for everything I do.*

CONTENTS

About the author xi

Foreword xiii

Introduction 1

SECTION 1
Work is broken and employees
are paying the price 5

01 The shortcomings of 'best practice' and traditional performance management 13
A short history of management 14
The role of human resources 18
References 23

02 Work is a relationship, not a contract 25
The lesson in the data 28
The emotional impact of good and bad jobs 30
Understanding work as a relationship 31
The characteristics of a healthy and positive relationship 33
The relationship test 37
References 39

03 Rethinking performance management 41
Performance management is about employee experience 44
Clarify your intentions 46
Does performance management need a rebrand? 51
Redesigning performance management 53
The three performance processes 54
References 56

SECTION 2

Performance planning 58

04   Creating clear expectations and goals 62

The art of expectations 63

Tools and approaches for expectation setting 67

References 71

05   Defining behavioural expectations 72

What about the employee's expectations? 76

References 80

06   Putting the 'why' and 'how' in expectations 81

Contribution to organizational success 81

World and community impact 82

Personal values alignment 83

Equipping employees with the resources to succeed 85

SECTION 3

Performance cultivation 89

07   Motivation 93

Intrinsic motivators 95

References 102

08   Recognition and appreciation 103

The shout out 105

Recognition programmes 106

Operationalizing appreciation 108

References 109

09   Wellbeing and inclusion 111

The importance of inclusion 115

References 119

10   Removing obstacles 121

Type of obstacles 122

Removing obstacles 123

Reference 125

SECTION 4
Performance accountability 126

11   Fixing feedback 133

Why we hate feedback 134

Making feedback work 135

References 142

12   A new approach to feedback 143

Feedforward 143

Making peer-to-peer feedback work 145

Building skills for receiving feedback 151

13   Measurement and ratings 157

Why ratings failed 158

The three steps of performance measurement 159

References 163

14   The role of reflection 164

Self-review versus reflection 165

Building reflection into performance management 167

References 171

15   Confronting performance issues 172

SECTION 5
Building a sustainable and effective performance management system 179

16   Making immediate improvements 182

Stopping the process 182

Hacking your current processes 184

17   Getting buy-in for change and recruiting a design team 188

Making the case for change 189

Recruiting your design team 192

18   The design process and avoiding the best practice trap 195

Discover and define 199

Reference 203

19   Developing and testing your performance management system 204

Deliver 207

20   Implementing your new performance management system 214

Technology 214

Training 216

Communication and roll-out 219

Track and celebrate progress 221

References 222

Index 223

ABOUT THE AUTHOR

 Jason Lauritsen is a keynote speaker, author and consultant. He is an employee engagement and workplace culture expert whose goal is to challenge you to think differently.

A former corporate human resources executive, Jason has dedicated his career to helping leaders build organizations that are good for both people and profits.

Among his professional experiences, he led the research team for Quantum Workplace's Best Places to Work programme. In this role, he had the opportunity to study the employee experience at thousands of organizations to understand what the best workplaces in the world do differently.

Jason is also the co-author of the book, *Social Gravity: Harnessing the natural laws of relationships*.

He lives on a quiet acreage outside of Omaha, Nebraska in the central United States with his wife (and business partner) Angie, their three children and the family dog.

Connect with Jason at www.JasonLauritsen.com.

FOREWORD

by Cy Wakeman
Drama researcher, New York Times *Bestselling Author of*
Reality-Based Leadership *and* No Ego, *host of the award-winning*
No Ego *podcast, Number 19 on the Top Leadership Gurus List,*
and dedicated conventional leadership wisdom myth buster

I get super-excited about wickedly smart, curious people, questioning the status quo and using great research and experience to write amazing books. And I got really excited when I read this book by Jason Lauritsen.

I must admit, I am rarely able to agree to endorse or write a foreword for new HR/leadership books. Not because I don't believe in supporting my colleagues or in abundance, but because I rarely read a book that resonates with my own research and speaks the truth clearly about what is broken about work with truly applicable ways to fix it. This book makes the cut and it is an honour to provide a few words about its content and its author.

First of all, I am a huge fan of Jason Lauritsen...

We came together years ago when I was a consultant and he an HR leader for what seemed like a simple gig involving the implementation of a standard talent management system. I was a bit of a rebel in HR at the time, preaching some pretty innovative stuff, and Jason was a smart, eager, bright, early adopter willing to play full out to get the best processes in place for his organization. As luck would have it, he was supported by a brilliant young CEO who was all about creating the future. And boy, did we seize the day.

You know those moments in your career where you are convinced that the universe was orchestrating the perfect circumstances for some incredible breakthroughs beyond your wildest imagination? Yep, that is exactly what ensued. Jason and I spent time questioning, thinking, dialoguing, designing, planning, revamping, innovating, and creating some really cool processes and systems to unleash the talent in his organization. It was meaningful, it was a blast, and it was the start of a great relationship and commitment to go forth and make work better.

Some of you who know my work know that I play favourites, and Jason is one of them. While we were working directly together, he showed up highly accountable, great with change and lived as a seeker. He was personally curious and questioning the status quo. He was always on the look-out for ways to be great. He was truly a partner to the business. I even hand-picked him to help me in my own research on how to end entitlement in engagement practices and find ways to actually measure accountability levels in individuals and organizations. He is one of my go-to people for great dialogue and innovative thinking.

Jason and I became partners in crime – disrupting traditional approaches, seeking out new truths, and spreading what we learned throughout the HR community. Jason and I have been friends and colleagues now for years. We both love leadership myth busting, disrupting HR, facilitating better and raucous dialogue about how we lead and how we work. And what I adore most about Jason is that he isn't out there simply disrupting, like so many just pointing out what is wrong, he is out there providing recommendations of what to do and offering solutions on how to fix it.

Back in the day, we seemed to be pioneers, some of the first to speak out – to mention that perhaps the emperor had no clothes. It was exhilarating and at times we both worried that HR might not awaken. But we kept the faith and I am thrilled that we have been joined by many who are now in agreement that our traditional leadership methods and philosophies are not working and haven't been for quite some time. We all feel it, we sense it, and it is time to simply admit it. No harm, no foul, nothing works or lasts forever, time to move on and adopt a modern leadership philosophy.

And it isn't just a feeling. According to my research, drama is increasing, engagement is flat at best, and we are spending ever-increasing amounts on HR systems and leadership development efforts. My conclusion? Our traditional approaches are not working, they are fuelling the drama, not decreasing it. It is time to modernize our approach to leadership and HR.

This seems so simple to me – use a philosophy, measure its success from all angles. 'Does it get the desired results for the business?' 'Does it delight the customer?' 'Does it attract and excite the employees?' And 'Does it facilitate everyone doing their greatest work?' 'Is it sustainable and good for our world?' And when the answers are *No* or *Kinda*, we question, dialogue, create, improve, break-though, find better ways and simply adopt those new ways. This is simply the cycle of co-creation with our world, a key function for leaders.

Simple, yes, but easy, no. Many leaders and HR professionals know our way isn't working and yet so few move on to adopt what's new. Interesting to me. I've asked many leaders what holds them back and their answer is, 'We don't know what to do instead.'

Well, now you do... at least when it comes to unlocking the potential of your talent through a dramatic shift in your performance management practices.

Jason does a fabulous job in this book, helping you understand how outdated and even destructive our current performance management approach is. And in his signature, straightforward, and articulate style, he shows you how to build, piece by piece, a whole new approach to unlocking human potential. This is not a critical book about what is wrong but a hopeful book about how it can be so different.

If you have loved my work over the years, you will love Jason's work. He is presenting a truly reality-based approach to calling your people to greatness. This book adds to your No Ego Toolkit with a comprehensive and modern approach to performance management. Jason teaches how to share accountability as you interact with others to clarify expectations and develop meaningful goals and objective measurements of impact. He shows you how to touch base often to keep performance discussions conversational rather than confrontational. His model is based on self-reflection which is not only the foundation for accountability, but according to my research the greatest drama diffuser.

Jason's recommendations are built on the latest evidence in behavioural health, behavioural economics and motivation theory. His recommendations are a brilliant compilation of the best advice on the market today. And his approach is to recommend brilliant but sometimes subtle updates to our current approaches rather than disruptive calls for blowing up entire systems. And he even shows you how to use technology to support the execution of his suggestions. I am convinced that his recommended approaches when used to work with the willing will create the drama-free, engaging workplaces for which we are all searching.

Enjoy this incredible manual and when you do, buy one for everyone on your team – and then, don't just think about it, execute on it and truly change the way you manage performance in your organization.

Introduction

Twenty years ago, I entered the workforce fresh out of college. I had a newly-minted degree in a discipline that no longer interested me. I had no clue what kind of job would be a good fit for me.

As I sought out advice about what to do next, one person told me to get a job in sales. While I didn't know much about working in sales, it appeared that sales people could make good money if they worked hard and developed their skills. So, I started applying for sales jobs and I got one – selling Minolta Copiers.

It wasn't a good job. The pay was terrible. The day-to-day work was worse. But what really got to me was how I was treated. Some of the managers I worked for were decent people, but at times, it felt like they had a total disregard for how the decisions they made about my job affected me and my life. Worst of all, they kept messing with my pay. So, seven months after my copier sales career began, it was over.

What followed was more sales jobs, none feeling any less dysfunctional than the first. My skills eventually led me to find a job in recruiting. Ironically, I was hired as a sales recruiter. My job was to help my clients find good sales people to hire.

As I began to work with my clients and they'd give me a recruiting assignment, I'd ask questions to understand why the position was open. Why did the last person leave? Why has this position been open for six months? Why do you think you've had so much trouble keeping people in this role?

What I began to quickly realize was that most of these positions were open because of a poor work environment or bad management. In some cases, they had been hiring the wrong type of people because they didn't really understand what they needed. There was dysfunction everywhere I looked.

At the same time, while trying to recruit people for my clients, I'd ask them about their jobs and why they might consider a better opportunity. They would often describe the exact same challenges: bad management, bad environment, unexplained changes to compensation, etc. Dysfunction was pervasive.

To succeed as a recruiter, I learned how to match the right kind of candidate with the right kind of dysfunction. It was a game of pairing people with the opportunity that they were best equipped to survive and maybe even thrive in if they were lucky. It was during my tenure in this job that I became deeply fascinated by the dynamics that exist between people and their work. I wanted to understand this relationship and all of the variables at play.

This was also when I started wondering, why does work have to suck? At first, I thought maybe it was just sales jobs. My jobs had been mostly terrible. My clients were offering up jobs that were awful in a lot of ways, and most of the candidates I spoke with were in jobs that they disliked. Sales didn't seem like a great place to work unless you were making enough money to tolerate the dysfunction.

But it wasn't just sales. Many of my friends and family members were also toiling away in jobs they either hated or that left them feeling unfulfilled. Most of them described surviving their job, rather than enjoying it. At best, they seemed comfortably numb to their work. They showed up, did the work, and went home with hopes of encountering minimal drama each day. It's not that I never found someone who loved their job, it was just rare. I viewed those people as exceptions to the rule. I assumed that it must be accidental that they were having a good experience at work.

While it seemed that work was pretty dismal for most people, I didn't want to believe that it had to be that way. And as someone who has been hardwired since birth to do what I can to make things better, I wanted to work on solving this problem. So I decided to move beyond external recruiting and join the corporate human resources ranks in an attempt to learn how to make work suck less.

I got lucky. I happened to land in an HR management role at a company led by a CEO who believed that work should be a vehicle that allows employees to pursue their dreams. He saw the best in people and was willing to invest in workplace practices to create an experience that was good for the employee. By creating a dynamic and positive workplace where employees were supported in their development, the company thrived. By engaging employees more fully, we literally doubled our revenue per employee (in a company of 800 employees) in a three-year span.

The opportunity to help lead a transformation like this set the course for the rest of my career. While it was still true that work wasn't working for far too many people, I now knew for certain that it doesn't have to be that way. It's because leaders are either choosing or allowing it to be that way. It is a decision, not an inevitability.

About this book

The defining purpose of my career became to help leaders and organizations to make work more human. Work doesn't have to suck. In fact, work can and should be a fulfilling and affirming experience for all involved. When work is designed more effectively around what humans need to thrive, everyone wins. I know this is true because I've seen it and I've experienced it.

If you were raised in the old-school thinking about management, this probably sounds like a bunch of touchy-feely stuff that would interfere with productivity. A lot of this work is about emotion and relationship, so maybe it is a little touchy-feely. But make no mistake, everything in this book is aimed at helping to create a high-performing organization. As you'll discover, creating a more human experience at work is very good for performance.

This book is for those who choose to believe that peak performance is unlocked only when employees can work in a way that feels positive and natural to them. This book is meant to provide inspiration, motivation, and tools to support those who are trying to reshape their organization in this way.

The book is organized in five sections.

Section 1

The first section is dedicated to mindset and understanding. We'll first unpack why our approaches to performance management and employee engagement have failed. This will include a short trip back in time to understand how these practices evolved and persisted. Then, we'll explore what the research and data reveal about how employees experience work. Then, we'll call on insights from the discipline of customer and experience design to illuminate the path forward.

At the end of this section, you'll be motivated and equipped to start the redesign of the work experience at your organization through the vehicle of performance management processes.

Sections 2, 3 and 4

In these middle sections, we will provide the blueprint for building a performance management system that will deliver and sustain a positive employee experience that unlocks performance potential. Each section is dedicated to one of the three key performance management processes. You'll find tools, tactics and case studies to consider as you begin to reshape your management practices and systems.

I've created these middle sections to be a sort of management cookbook. There are a lot of recipes included here. The goal isn't that you'll make every recipe. Rather, my intention is to provide you with a variety of options and ideas to use as you design the approach that's best for your specific organization or team.

Section 5

My hope is that you'll find many tips and insights that are immediately actionable. There are tactics throughout the book that are easy to implement individually. This final section is dedicated to the larger system. Here you will find insights for how to design and implement a sustainable system that helps you make many of the practices in the book the norm for how your organization does work.

In addition, designing a great performance management system isn't of much use if it's not implemented and used effectively. We'll review some approaches and tricks to effective change management, execution and sustainability gleaned from my experiences and those of the people I interviewed for this book.

The final section will help you bring everything together and help you put it into action.

Let's get started.

SECTION 1
Work is broken and employees are paying the price

A friend of mine recently quit his job for a new one. He'd worked for this company for over 20 years of his career. He'd been there so long, it had become part of who he was.

But this transition had been a long time coming. While he enjoyed the work he did for the company, it had been years since he had enjoyed the company itself. Whenever I'd see him, he'd share with me a new story of mistreatment at the hands of his employer.

Sometimes it was personal. Like the third, fourth or fifth time he was passed over for a promotion in favour of someone less experienced from the outside. Or when he was told, again, that he wasn't eligible for a larger raise because he was at the max of his salary grade.

Other times, all employees were impacted. These injustices ranged from arbitrary cuts of their employee benefits to widespread, seemingly annual layoffs of large numbers of staff. All things my friend attributed to gross mismanagement of the organization.

Despite all of this, he kept showing up to work every day. It was as if he'd grown indifferent to all of it and had become more an observer of his life at work than a participant. He was clearly happiest when he had extended time off from work, so I'd ask him why he didn't find a new job. He would reply that he 'should', but that intention was hollow. It was as if he was stuck and couldn't even muster the willpower to break free.

Ultimately, an opportunity found him. A former co-worker who had escaped the bonds of his company had landed at a new one that treated employees very differently. They had a role that was a perfect fit for my friend and, almost in spite of himself, he was finally freed from his 20-plus-year tour of duty at a company he largely despised.

Of all the years I've known him, it was on those days leading up to the tendering of his resignation that he seemed as happy as I had ever seen him. I think he found more joy in one afternoon sharing a couple of pints of beer with me, dreaming up some brazen ways to tender his resignation, than he had at work in many years.

When I asked him about his new job, he shared with me that for the first several days in the office, it felt really strange. It wasn't just because he was in a new company for the first time in decades, there was something more essential than that. Eventually, it hit him. People were smiling. They seemed to be happy working there. It had been so long since he'd been in an environment like this at work, that he didn't recognize it.

So far, my friend is feeling good about his new job and his new company. He wonders why he waited so long to leave.

This story may sound familiar to you. We all know people, probably a lot of people, who are living this same existence. Maybe it was your story.

Most of us have been there, stuck in a job we dislike but having convinced ourselves that we can't leave. We need that pay cheque or the benefits too much. So, we drift through each day, uncomfortably numb, hoping that someday things might get better.

Our employee engagement crisis

This is what a lack of engagement with work looks and feels like. And, according to Gallup's 2017 State of the Global Workplace Report, 'Worldwide, the percentage of adults who work full-time for an employer and are engaged at work – they are highly involved in and enthusiastic about their work and workplace – is just 15 per cent' (Gallup, 2017). This suggests that the other 85 per cent of those full-time employees are having an experience of work something like my friend – showing up each day hoping for something better.

Gallup's data paints a pretty bleak picture of the workplace. Other data, like that from Aon Hewitt's 2017 Trends in Global Employee Engagement report, suggest that over 60 per cent of employees worldwide are engaged. (Aon Hewitt, 2017) The disparity of these two numbers highlights the complexity of measuring the employee experience in a reliable way. I think it's safe to assume that the true number lies somewhere in the middle.

That means that less than half of people working each day around the world are engaged. This is alarming. And what's more alarming is that despite their disagreement about the percentage of employees that are engaged, both Gallup and Aon Hewitt agree that the overall level of engagement isn't trending in a positive direction. If anything, it appears to be getting worse.

What is most alarming about this trend is that I've never met an employee who doesn't want to be engaged. Regardless of age, experience, level in the company or any other differentiating characteristic, every person I've ever had a conversation with about work wants work to be a positive experience.

Many of them have even taken steps of their own accord to try to make that happen. They go out on a limb and try to ask for what they want. They provide their manager with some feedback about what's not working. They go back to school or pursue certifications to create better opportunities for themselves. They want to be engaged.

So, why the disconnect?

I know from spending nearly a decade as a human resources leader that there are a lot of executives and managers out there who still aren't convinced that employee engagement has any merit. In their minds, this is all just touchy-feely stuff that has no place at work. As they see it, people should just be happy to have a job.

Somehow, these people who have been charged with the leadership of other people have forgotten what it feels like to be an employee who's stuck in a bad job or suffering an incompetent (or worse) manager.

Why engagement matters

A number of years ago, I started using a simple exercise to open my management workshops about employee engagement. The goal is to lead participants to a realization of why employee engagement is so important, informed by our own experiences as employees. Here's how it works.

Think back to a time in your life when you were really in love with your job. Hopefully, you have a recent example to call up in your memory. But maybe it was your very first job out of school. If you've worked in your current job for many years, maybe there was a particular time or project that you loved.

Call up the memories of this time in your career. Think about the people you worked with, the work you were doing, and how you remember feeling about work at this point in your career. Now, jot the down the answers to these three questions about this particular time when you were in love with your job:

- How did work make you feel?
- How would you describe the quality of your work? How did it compare to other times in your career?
- How was work affecting your life outside of work? What impact did it have on your personal relationships?

Once you've captured these thoughts, you can let go of those memories. It's now time to travel to another point in your career on the opposite end of the spectrum. Think back now to a low point in your career when you were stuck in a job you really disliked. This can be from any point in your career and, if you are lucky, is in the far distant past.

As before, travel back into your memories to recall the people and experiences of this unfortunate period in your career history. Now jot down your answers to the same three questions:

- How did work make you feel?
- How would you describe the quality of your work? How did it compare to other times in your career?
- How was work affecting your life outside of work? What impact did it have on your personal relationships?

Now compare your responses. What do you notice about the difference between these two experiences? In my workshops, I ask people to discuss and compare their responses in small groups to identify trends and commonalities. Then we share and compare our responses.

What is striking about this exercise is the consistency of the responses regardless of who is in attendance. When people love their job, they feel valued, inspired, appreciated, energized, motivated, and happy. It's almost entirely positive emotion, even when they were working hard or up against a tough challenge.

When people are stuck in a bad job, they feel unappreciated, frustrated, apathetic, disrespected, or worse. It's common to hear mention of the 'sinking feeling in your stomach' on Sunday night when you know you have to return to that terrible place again in the morning. You can actually see the anguish on some people's faces as they recall these experiences. The negative emotions are very powerful. And, they clearly impact our quality of work where a similar polarity of responses is common.

The positive emotions we experience from loving our job means we work harder, are more creative, and feel a greater sense of ownership for the impact of our work. We are more likely to volunteer to help out or contribute extra time or effort without promise of reward. On the flip side, when stuck in a bad job, we do just enough to get by and not get fired because we stop caring as much. We start watching the clock and the calendar, counting down to the time when we don't have to be at work.

It's in this gap that we see the business impact of employee engagement and work experience. When we love our job, we do better work and work harder. When we don't, we orient towards doing the minimum we have to do to survive until something better comes along. This gap is what many refer to as 'discretionary effort' when they are trying to justify the ROI (return on investment) of employee engagement.

When you can get a group of sceptical leaders or managers to participate in this exercise, it often helps them to arrive at an understanding of the value of engagement through their own experience. Everyone who's worked for at least a few years has had both good and bad work experiences and has felt the impact on their own work. This is a powerful insight for a manager because he or she can play a major role in the day-to-day experience of the employees in their charge. By choosing to help shape an experience of work for employees that they love, the manager can unlock better performance.

The impact beyond performance

But the impact of the work experience isn't just about performance. That's why I ask the third question, to prompt some thinking about how work spills over into our personal life. While it's convenient to believe that there is a tidy separation between our work and personal lives, we all know that isn't true. What happens at work affects us personally and what happens to us personally affects our work.

When people love their job, they report feeling more energized and present in their relationships outside of work. Because they feel positive about work, they feel that their positivity rubs off on their friends and family. On occasion, some will argue that there can be negative impacts to loving your job, like working too hard or becoming overly obsessed with it, but that is certainly not representative of the majority of responses. When work is good, people report being better spouses, parents, friends, and neighbours.

Figure 1   Discretionary effort explained

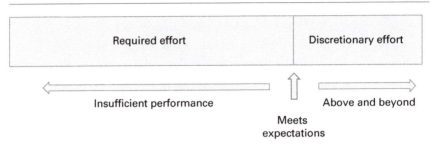

When work isn't going well, the impacts can be pretty severe. As with the positivity of the good experience, the negativity of a bad experience travels home and spreads across our personal lives. It's common to hear people talk about how they would go home after work and complain to their loved ones about it. They also recognize that they became more impatient and short in communicating with their spouses and children. And that's the least of the damage.

A bad job experience doesn't just impact the individual and their performance. And the damage isn't even confined to the workplace. It hurts families and friends. My own experience reinforced how painfully true this can be.

Many years ago, I remember arriving home from work on the day that I had tendered my resignation from a job that felt like it was crushing my soul. To those on the outside looking in, it was a big job at a big company with a big pay cheque: everything that's supposed to equal happiness at work. But I was miserable and had been for some time.

But the misery was finally coming to a close. I had accepted a new job after months of searching and the transition had officially begun. Shortly after arriving home, my wife poured us each a glass of wine and made a toast to a new beginning.

That evening, as we were sitting around the dinner table eating with the kids, she looked across the table and said something to me that I will never forget. She said, 'It's so good to see you smile again.' It still breaks my heart a little bit every time I think about it.

As things had become worse and worse at work, I had convinced myself that I was keeping my work separate from my personal life. As someone who studies employee engagement and the dynamics of work for a living, I was confident that I could compartmentalize the experiences until I found my way to something better. I thought I was shielding my family from this negative thing that I was experiencing.

I was so wrong.

As it turns out, it wasn't me who was protecting my family, it was them who were protecting me. My wife shared with me how much of a change there had been in me as my work situation deteriorated. I had no patience with my kids. I was tired all of the time. I had been drinking too much and eating too much. Generally, I'd become much less fun to be around.

And my family was carrying that load for me. My wife knew it was temporary, so she toughed it out for me and did what she could to be supportive. And I didn't even realize that it was happening. My story is just one example of the unintended damage caused when employees are disengaged and suffering through an unfulfilling work experience. The impacts were pretty obvious to me.

In contrast, I've also witnessed the power of great work experiences on employees. For three years I worked for Quantum Workplace, an employee feedback software provider. During that time, I had the opportunity to lead the Best Places to Work team. Quantum Workplace is the research and technology partner behind nearly 50 'Best Places to Work' programmes across North America.

One of the perks of my job was the opportunity to attend the awards events in cities around the United States, where the winners of these contests were announced and celebrated. The organizations being recognized often brought groups of employees along to share in the recognition. In some cases, videos of employees were shared during the awards presentations.

Some of the Best Places to Work winners were truly exceptional organizations. You could feel the energy, passion and commitment that their employees had for their organization and for each other. It was common to hear things like, 'I love working here' and 'It feels like family here'. The emotion was contagious.

When work is good, it injects positivity into our employee's lives. When work is bad, our families, friends, and communities pay a price. In other words, the stakes are high when it comes to the type of work experience we create for our employees.

So, why do so many organizations keep getting this wrong? Why do we continue to see over half of employees in our workplaces not fully engaged?

I've wrestled with this question for most of my career. It's hard to fathom how an organization built by people can work so poorly for people. At the heart of the problem is a major disconnect between the mindset of many employers about work and the way employees actually experience it.

References

Aon Hewitt (2017) Trends in Global Employee Engagement [Online] http://www.aon.com/engagement17/ [Last accessed 24 April 2018]

Gallup (2017) State of the Global Workplace [Online] http://news.gallup.com/reports/220313/state-global-workplace-2017.aspx [Last accessed 24 April 2018]

The shortcomings of 'best practice' and traditional performance management

01

'Those who cannot remember the past are condemned to repeat it.'

GEORGE SANTAYANA

I remember hearing a story many years ago about a young woman preparing to host a holiday dinner for her family. As newlyweds, she and her husband were hosting the holiday meal for the first time.

As they were working together in the kitchen, the husband observed as his wife cut off both ends of the ham before putting the ham into the baking pan. This struck him as unusual. So he asked, 'Why do you cut the ends off the ham before you bake it?'

To which she responded, 'I'm actually not sure. That's just what my mom always did.'

This made them both curious, so they decided to call her mother. When asked the same question, the mother's response was surprisingly the same.

'Well, that's what my mom had always done, so that's what I did.'

Now the young couple was really curious, so they decided to call her grandmother to see if they could solve this mystery.

As they explained why they were calling and that they must know why she cut the ends off of the ham, the grandmother started chuckling. When they finished, they asked why she was laughing.

'My dear, the reason I cut the ends off of the ham is because my pan was too small.'

I've never forgotten this story because it's a perfect reminder of how easy it is for bad practices to become standard practices within organizations.

We are quick to assume that simply because someone with authority or positional power does something a particular way or believes something strongly, then it must be the right way. The mother in this story had probably been cutting the ends off of hams for years. It is a wasteful and unnecessary practice and she had no idea why she was doing it.

This story also illustrates how best practices can become dangerous. Cutting the ends off of the ham made perfect sense for the grandmother with the small pan. It was a smart practice for her, but assuming the mother was using a bigger pan, it made absolutely no sense for her. But she treated it as a 'best practice' for ham preparation. And, years later, her daughter almost adopted this same wasteful practice.

Except she didn't.

She asked why. And by understanding the context behind the practice, she could make an informed decision about whether that practice made sense for her given her current circumstances.

This chapter is dedicated to exploring the 'why' behind some common management and human resources practices. Specifically, we'll explore the origins of traditional performance management practices like the annual appraisal. When stepping back to consider the bigger picture, it becomes clear that we may be cutting the ends off a lot of hams unnecessarily. Taking a different approach may be long overdue.

A short history of management

The birth of what we would today call 'management' as a discipline and profession can be traced back to the Industrial Revolution, which began in Britain in the mid-18th century and spurred a period of mass industrialization that lasted into the early 20th century. During this era, the economy shifted from one dominated by agriculture and individual artisanship to one of mass production. It also represented the development of large urban centres as people migrated to where these new industrial jobs resided (Investopedia, nd).

Perhaps the most significant invention of industrialization was the 'factory system'. This was a system of manufacturing based on the use of powered machines and division of labour, a means of task specialization designed to increase throughput. These new factories created jobs in which relatively unskilled workers could assemble goods faster and cheaper than had ever been possible in the past.

While these factories represented a substantial gain in terms of the efficient production of goods and creation of many new jobs, the effects weren't all positive. Most of these workers had in the past been independent craftsmen who owned their own tools and set their own hours. Many of these new unskilled jobs could be done equally well by women, men or children, which drove down wages because of the supply and availability of workers. Factories also 'tended to be poorly lit, cluttered, and unsafe places where workers put in long hours for low pay' (Encyclopædia Britannica, 2014).

The terrible working conditions and imbalance of power between owners and workers gave rise to the trade union movement and the rapid growth of organized labour (Encyclopædia Britannica, 2014). Trade union membership in the UK grew from 100,000 in 1850 to nearly a million by 1874, almost a 1,000 per cent growth in less than 25 years (Trade Unions, 2018). In the United States, in the four decades from 1877 to 1917, there were reportedly 1,500 strikes each year, involving 300,000 workers (Licht, 1988). These strikes became contentious and often included violence. The chaos and unrest were powerful motivation both for government action and more civil collective negotiations between employers and employees for improved working conditions. This was a key development in the evolution of management and human resources practice as it formalized the 'contractual' approach to work that still pervades our thinking about employment today.

These new factories also revealed a need for the role of people management. Prior to this time, most people worked as individual craftsmen or farmers. Even businesses who produced goods like textiles did so using a system called the 'putting-out system', where those being asked to create goods worked independently, not unlike how independent contractors work in today's economy (Encyclopædia Britannica, 2017). The practice of management as we know it today wasn't needed at scale until factories brought together large groups of employees who needed to be supervised.

Management guru Gary Hamel argues that management is the most important invention of the past century. He describes management as the set of methods used to bring people together, and the mobilization and organization of resources towards productive ends. Hamel describes how, in the period from 1890 to 1915, a majority of modern management practices were created. This included pay for performance, task design, and divisionalization. In his view, most modern management practices were created before 1920 and we still rely on many of those same practices in today's enterprises. In other words, we still look to leaders and thinkers from a century past to guide our practices yet today (Hamel, 2011).

We keep cutting the ends off the ham even though today's management problems are very different than those of the early 1900s. Consider the challenges that management faced in operating these new factories. The majority of factory jobs required workers to complete routine, repetitive tasks over and over for long hours. This does not naturally align with the innate curiosity and desire for novelty that humans possess. It was unnatural work. Hamel characterizes that management's primary problem to solve during its period of invention was this: 'How do we turn human beings into semi-programmable robots?'

This probably feels a little harsh as you read it. But it's hard to argue that it doesn't describe the circumstance accurately. Knowing that this was the problem that these early management thinkers and business owners were trying to solve is important to understanding both why they approached things as they did and also why those approaches are outdated given today's very different management challenges.

You are probably familiar with some of these early management innovators from your history or management classes. One of the most famous was Frederick Taylor, who is often credited as the creator of 'scientific management'. He recommended that managers should scientifically measure performance and set high targets for workers to achieve (*The Economist*, 2009). On the surface, Taylor's approach seems reasonable. Setting high goals and measuring performance scientifically are good practices. It's when you dig a little deeper that you find context that should cause us to raise some questions.

Taylor's approach (frequently referred to as 'Taylorism') was motivated by trying to solve a problem in the factories they described as 'soldiering'. This word was used to describe the belief that a significant amount of workers were taking as long as they could to produce the minimum amount of work. In other words, these workers were thought to be taking advantage of the system. Taylor articulated four principles of scientific management which he felt would combat soldiering and maximize productivity in the factory:

1 use scientific methods to determine best way to do a work task;

2 select and train individual employees for specific tasks;

3 provide very clear and detailed instructions for each task to employees and closely supervise their performance of the tasks;

4 create a separation of work between management and the workers where management 'scientifically' plans the work and the workers do it.

Inherent in these principles is the advancement of task specialization that was so central to how factories operated. This also appears to be the invention of what we would today describe as 'micro-management', where the manager is hyper-involved in every detail of day-to-day work. Taylor wanted to remove all possible 'brain work' from the factory floor in favour of turning as much work as possible over to the machines (Taylor, 1911/1986). According to

The Economist, Taylorism was the first big management idea to reach a mass audience (*The Economist,* 2009). In an era of unprecedented management innovation, this may have been one of the biggest. Other innovators of the time built on the foundation he laid.

Another prominent and important management thinker of the time was German sociologist and political economist Max Weber. It is Weber's Bureaucratic Theory that has had lasting impacts on the field of management. In short, he believed that a bureaucracy was the most effective way to run the 'modern' organization. From his perspective, it was the setting forth and abiding by rules, laws and other formal administrative structures that allowed the organization to operate best. He describes necessary features of a bureaucracy in this way (Weber, 2015):

1 A rigid division of labour is established that clearly identifies regular tasks and duties of the particular bureaucratic system.

2 Regulations describe firmly established chains of command and the duties and capacity to coerce others to comply.

3 Hiring people with particular certified qualifications supports regular and continuous execution of the assigned duties.

It's easy to see the appeal of this structure to businesses that were scaling and growing their factories. When you are asking a majority of your employees to perform tasks that are contrary to their nature for long hours each day, being able to lean on a strong system of rules and hierarchy is valuable. What's surprising is that so many of today's organizations still lean on bureaucracy as their method of organization, considering how much has changed.

So, let's recap some of what we've learned about the birth of modern management. The problem that management was designed to solve was how to turn human beings into semi-programmable robots to power factory production.
The solutions conceived and implemented to solve this problem included:

- remove as much 'brain work' as possible;
- measure everything so employees cannot take advantage of the system;
- micro-manage the workers to ensure maximum productivity;
- use division of labour to simplify work through task specialization;
- leverage a bureaucracy of rules and hierarchy as the most efficient means for organizing work.

This history is important to understand if we are to move beyond outdated processes and replace them with new, more relevant approaches for our current environment. My hope is that it makes you uncomfortable to realize how many of these early solutions can still be found today, alive and well in a variety of forms in our organizations.

But our history lesson doesn't end here. We need to talk a bit about human resources.

The role of human resources

In the early evolution of management as described above, the key roles were owners, employees, and manager or supervisor. Today, any conversation about management or the work experience of employees will almost certainly involve a discussion of another role, that of the human resources (HR) function.

Many of the processes and structures that we associate with present-day management are 'owned' by the HR department. HR handles management training and development. HR oversees the selection and promotion of managers. And, perhaps most importantly, HR creates and maintains the formal policies, procedures and tools used by management in the execution of their roles. Processes like performance appraisals, policy manuals, progressive discipline and job descriptions are all examples of the control exerted by HR over management practice within most organizations.

The human resources function systematized management through this structure – a well-intentioned application of bureaucracy. While it can be argued that all of this structure and process is in the interest of supporting management and making the job of management easier to execute with consistency, it has also made the practice of management more resilient and resistant to change. And I believe this helps explain why we see so many outdated and ineffective management behaviours yet today. HR has played a lead role in perpetuating the practices of early factory management into today's workplace. As with management, it's helpful to understand a little bit about HR's inception as a way to better understand where we find ourselves today.

The earliest origins of what we know as HR today are also tied to the rise of the labour unions in the late 1800s and early 1900s. As unions began to force owners to negotiate with them for improved working conditions and better wages, roles were created to manage these affairs. In Britain, they were called 'Welfare Workers' because their focus was on the welfare of the employees. In fact, when it was created in 1913, the original name of CIPD, one of the largest HR associations in the world, was the WWA (Welfare Workers Association) (CIPD, 2018). The profession later became known as Labour Relations to reflect its role in negotiating working conditions with collective employee groups.

The evolution of the HR function over the following century is tied closely to the passing of employment laws and regulations that governed the role and responsibility of the employer to the employee. As new laws were passed that dictated the treatment of employees or protection of civil rights, the HR department adapted to meet these needs (Salvator, Weitzman and Halem, 2005).

It's valuable to remember that HR's roots are set in a history of two primary purposes:

1 negotiating agreements with labour on behalf of ownership;

2 adapting the organization for legal compliance and risk reduction.

In other words, HR's role started with ensuring the existence and enforcement of a fair 'contract of employment' with employees while minimizing legal exposure and risk. As the discipline of HR expanded to include the acquisition and development of talent and other more strategic functions, echoes of this heritage in compliance can still be found throughout much of what we still consider today to be standard HR best practice.

Redesigning the work experience in a way that best unlocks an employee's full potential is going to require breaking the shackles of our past, both in management and HR. It means asking why, early and often, to understand the context surrounding how and why 'best practices' were created to ensure we aren't perpetuating an approach or belief that is no longer best given our current circumstances.

To illustrate, let's look to an example of a practice that, until very recently, was treated as a best practice and nearly universally adopted by organizations around the globe for decades.

The annual performance appraisal

A number of years ago, when I was leading the corporate HR team for a large regional bank, my team and I decided, after hearing complaints for years about our annual, ratings-based performance appraisal process, that we'd do some investigating. Before deciding how to fix or change it, we wanted to gain a deeper understanding of why the process existed and what about the experience was generating so many complaints.

Figure 2 Example of appraisal ratings distribution

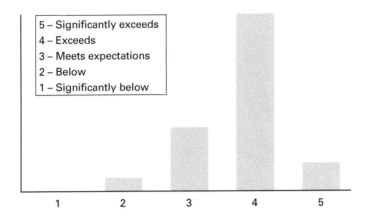

We first started with the question, 'Why do we have the performance appraisal process?' For this organization, there were two answers to this question. First, it was intended to improve and recognize performance. So we ran some analysis to see if this was indeed the case.

When we charted out the distribution of individual ratings across the organization, the curve had the shape of a standard distribution curve, except it was very narrow and centred on the four of a five-point rating scale.

Only a small percentage of ratings scattered to either side of the centre of the curve and very few fell below the three, a rating defined to signify 'meets expectations'. These findings wouldn't have been problematic if all employees in the organization were performing above expectations. That was not the case.

It was also clear, based on this analysis, that the process could not be differentiating performance in any meaningful way. When everyone is a four, there's not much room to recognize truly exceptional performance. Another failure of the process.

The second reason for our performance appraisal process was to provide a framework for employees and managers to discuss performance feedback and clarify expectations. To investigate if it was effective, we formed a task force of managers and leaders from across the organization and asked them to collect some feedback on the process. We asked that they each talk to at least 10 employees in different roles and at different levels to learn about their experiences with the process.

The feedback was clear and consistent. Employees hated the process. It filled them with anxiety and dread. While many of them expressed a desire for improved clarity regarding their performance, they felt this process was wholly ineffective. And, unsurprisingly, managers also hated the process. It felt to them like a burden that added little or no value to their supervision of employees.

We had a broken process on our hands, one that was both failing to deliver on its stated objectives (to improve and recognize performance) while at the same time creating an experience for employees and managers that was highly demotivating. What's more, our process wasn't unique. It was a pretty standard annual performance appraisal like those used in most organizations at the time (and still used by many today).

The context of the broken appraisal process

How could a management 'best practice' be so terribly ineffective? It seems to make no sense until you remember our history and dig a little deeper.

The early roots of what we today think of as performance management can be traced back to the famed US businessman and philanthropist, Andrew Carnegie. In his book *Talent on Demand* (Cappelli, 2008), Peter Capelli of The Wharton School describes how Carnegie build his steel empire in the early 1900s by expanding and introducing management practices he'd first observed working in the railroad business. There were many innovative practices he translated to the factory workplace that had significant impact, but 'especially the notion that standards of performance could be created for every job and that every individual should be held accountable for his job performance'.

Carnegie created what many would describe as a meritocracy, evaluating employees based primarily on the strength of their individual performance. This was transformative. But it fails to explain how we started with such good intentions and transformed them into the ineffective, universally disliked, annual process of the performance appraisal.

It seems that we may have the government and military to blame for making the process sterile and bureaucratic. The use of formalized forms and ratings tied to rewards was given credence in US workplaces as laws were passed mandating it for governmental entities (US Office of Personnel Management, 2018). This appears to be when the tide started turning towards performance management being a mandatory form to complete or an annual box to be checked off.

Also consider that during this period, work and management were highly influenced by the presence of labour unions. As a result, organizations learned to treat work as a contract with the employee because in many cases it was through collective bargaining. In this model, work is purely a transactional experience. The employer offers a salary and agreed-upon working conditions. In exchange, the employee does the work assigned to an agreed-upon standard. In this view of work, the employer's primary concern is getting what they are paying for from the employee – ensuring compliance with the contract.

It's not hard to see how performance management practices like the annual appraisal evolved. The primary purpose underlying this approach is to create documentation of employee performance to legally support compensation and promotion decisions as well as punitive employment actions like demotions and terminations. It is a process motivated by contract compliance and risk mitigation.

It also follows that a formal 'appraisal' of employee performance should be completed once per year when annual compensation decisions are expected. This all looks to management like a tidy process for ensuring compliance with the contract of employment they maintain with employees. Hence, the annual performance appraisal became a staple of organizational management.

It shouldn't be terribly surprising that the annual appraisal is so unpopular with employees. It was designed, after all, almost entirely for the benefit of the organization.

When looking back at how processes like the performance appraisal evolved, it's easy to see how we got here and why smart, reasonable people created these processes. The context of the time warranted it.

It also becomes painfully obvious that change is far overdue. It's time to stop cutting the ends off our hams.

In the next chapter, we'll explore how work has changed over the past century to arrive in an era where employee engagement is craved and yet continually elusive. In addition, we'll look at what we've learned from decades of employee sentiment research about how employees actually experience work. And, spoiler alert, it's got nothing to do with a contract.

Key takeaways

- Best practices are context-dependent. It is important to understand the context driving the creation of any practice to responsibly decide if it might be best for you. Otherwise, we may end up 'cutting the ends off our hams' unnecessarily.

- The role and practice of people management as a discipline was born in the late 1800s as we evolved to an industrial economy that replaced agricultural and trade jobs with urban manufacturing jobs.

- Management's purpose upon creation was, as Gary Hamel described, to turn human beings into semi-programmable robots who could complete rote, repetitive tasks over and over for long periods of time.

- Organized labour rose in response to the poor working conditions and low wages provided during early industrialization. As unions became more powerful, they began to negotiate contracts with owners to improve the working experience for employees.

- Human resources was born out of the labour movement as an organizational representative to oversee and enforce labour contracts. As a result, HR began to systematize management processes like the performance appraisal to aid managers in enforcing and ensuring compliance with negotiated contracts with employees.

- These early best practices were largely designed to protect the organization's interests, sometimes at the expense of the employee. Many of these practices still persist today despite a very different economic context.

References

Cappelli, P (2008) *Talent on Demand: Managing talent in an age of uncertainty*, Boston, Mass: Harvard Business Press

CIPD (2018) The History of the CIPD [Online] https://www.cipd.co.uk/about/who-we-are/history [Last accessed 27 April 2018]

The Economist (2009) Scientific management [Online] https://www.economist.com/node/13092819 [Last accessed 27 April 2018]

Encyclopædia Britannica (2017) Domestic system [Online] https://www.britannica.com/topic/domestic-system [Last accessed 27 April 2018]

Encyclopædia Britannica (2014) Factory system [Online] https://www.britannica.com/topic/factory-system [Last accessed 24 April 2018]

Hamel, G (2011) Reinventing the technology of human accomplishment (Video) [Online] https://www.youtube.com/watch?v=aodjgkv65MM&feature=youtu.be [Last accessed 27 April 2018]

History.com (2009) Industrial Revolution [Online] https://www.history.com/topics/industrial-revolution [Last accessed 24 April 2018]

Investopedia (nd) Industrialization [Online] https://www.investopedia.com/terms/i/industrialization.asp [Last accessed 24 April 2018]

Licht, W (1988) How the workforce has changed in 75 years, *Monthly Labor Review*, pp. 19–25 (February)

Salvator, P, Weitzman, A and Halem, D (2005) 50th Anniversary HR Magazine: How the law changed HR, *SHRM* [Online] https://www.shrm.org/hr-today/news/hr-magazine/pages/0550thhowlaw.aspx [Last accessed 27 April 2018]

Taylor, F W (1986) *The Principles of Scientific Management*, Harper and Brothers, originally published 2011, reprint, Hive Publishing Company

Trade Unions (2018) The Growth of Trade Unions, *Weebly* [Online] https://industrialrevolution-tradeunions.weebly.com/the-growth-of-trade-unions.html [Last accessed 30 April 2018]

US Office of Personnel Management (2018) Performance management, overview & history [Online] https://www.opm.gov/policy-data-oversight/performance-management/overview-history/#url=Historical-Chronology [Last accessed 27 April 2018]

Weber (2015) in *Weber's Rationalism and Modern Society*, edited and translated by Tony Waters and Dagmar Waters, New York, Palgrave Macmillan, p. 76

Work is a relationship, not a contract

02

As we have seen in the previous chapter, one legacy of our management heritage that still shapes the workplace today is the contractual model of work. For the most part, employers structure work transactionally as you would if it were governed by a clear contract. This is almost certainly a holdover from the early days of unionization. In some cases, work is governed by a formal contract between the employer and employee. But even when there is not a formal contract, most organizations behave as though there is.

This contractual mindset about employment is pretty simple. The employer provides salary and other benefits in exchange for the employee's time and effort. It's a basic, transactional value exchange between two parties.

Many of our modern management and human resources systems are designed to ensure employee compliance with this contract of work:

- Job descriptions are used primarily to document the duties and requirements of a role to ensure the organization offers competitive compensation for that role. These descriptions also establish a baseline expectation for performance with their role against which an employee may be held accountable.

- Policy manuals and employee handbooks put forth a list of rules and regulations for what is allowed and expected of each person under this contract of employment. Violation of any of these rules may put your contract of employment in jeopardy.

- Progressive discipline procedures are internal 'due process' for dealing with behavioural or performance problems (potential breaches of the contract). These are typically informed by legal precedents with the intent to reduce risk and create documented justification for firing someone (terminating the contract).

- Time tracking is used to monitor the amount of time worked to ensure the fair exchange of time for money. It's also used to monitor paid vacation and sick leave days away from work to ensure that the employee is only taking the amount of 'time off' they are afforded. It's a method to ensure the employer is getting their money's worth when it comes to amount of time worked by the employee.

- Performance appraisals, as illustrated earlier, are used to evaluate if the employee lived up to their end of the contract in the previous year and as a justification for compensation adjustments.

When put in the context of early management processes and how they evolved early on in an era of work defined by unionized manufacturing factories, it's understandable how and why these processes came to exist. Creating and maintaining a fair contract of work was a defining issue in these early days. The employees of that era needed and demanded a contract to protect them from terrible working conditions and inadequate wages.

As it should be with any good legal contract, these early contracts were designed in the interests of both parties, with protections for both as well. These early contracts were important, particularly since the nature of the work being done in these factories wasn't enjoyable or fulfilling. There wasn't a lot of intrinsic value to be found at work in those days. It was about doing what you needed to do to survive.

But work has changed a lot in the past century. Beginning in the late 1960s, both the nature of work and our understanding of the employee's relationship with work began to shift.

Many management historians will point to Douglas McGregor's 1960 book, *The Human Side of Enterprise*, as a critical inflection point in our thinking about management. In it, McGregor puts forth his often-cited Theory of Motivation, which argues that there are actually two competing theories about how to motivate workers: Theory X and Theory Y.

Theory X assumes that a person's natural instinct is to avoid work at all costs. This view of work assumes that people are inherently lazy and unmotivated to do work, thus requiring a management approach constructed to continuously counteract this lack of motivation through prodding, micromanagement and rewards for work completed.

It's easy to imagine how a Theory X mindset about employees might evolve and flourish in an era defined by work that, by all accounts, was largely unpleasant. As a supervisor charged with managing people who are building a railroad or working in an iron factory, where the work is hard and conditions are unpleasant, it would be easy to attribute the workers' lack of motivation as inherent rather than as a by-product of the work or environment itself. The work has to be done and the conditions are hard to change, so it's far easier to assume it's the people who are the problem.

In stark contrast to this way of thinking, Theory Y is built on a very different assumption that people are in fact self-motivated to succeed at work as a means to fulfill their individual needs. Based on this assumption, management behaves quite differently, perhaps adopting a more participative and trusting approach. Under Theory Y, the constant prodding and micro-management that forms the basis of Theory X management is no longer viewed as productive or helpful (*The Economist*, 2008).

It's common to hear McGregor's theories referenced today, some 50-plus years later, because they so powerfully cut to the heart of the issue of why work wasn't a rewarding and fulfilling experience for employees. And they are rooted in the core beliefs of owners, leaders, and managers about human motivation. A majority of leaders in the time when McGregor's book was published operated on a Theory X mindset that shaped everything about how work was managed within their organizations.

Getting those leaders to abandon a Theory X belief system is challenging, not only because it represents letting go of some control, but it also represents a major shift in accountability. In Theory X, when performance or production is down, it's clearly because the workers aren't working hard enough. The solution is to tighten control and add more prodding. But, with Theory Y, we have to assume that employees are self-motivated. So, when performance is down, it's likely because of something that management or leadership has done (or not done) that's creating the problem. The friction becomes clear pretty quickly. It's in the best interests of managers to preserve a Theory X approach because productivity issues will never be seen as their fault.

The distinct differences between Theory X and Theory Y beliefs likely represent why the evolution of management has been so slow. Instincts of human preservation on the part of management and ownership are a powerful force to hold them firm to a Theory X view of people. Theory Y has always been a courageous choice.

The shift in thinking represented by McGregor's work was amplified by a shift in the very nature of work. It was during this same time his book published that a new kind of work was emerging based on technologies designed for the production and dissemination of knowledge and information. This new era became known as the 'Knowledge Economy' and represented a significant shift from the Industrial Economy it began to replace (Powell and Snellman, 2004).

The knowledge economy grew for decades and was ultimately accelerated as computers and the internet became available (Powell and Snellman, 2004). This changing economic landscape had many effects, but among the most significant was a change in how employees created value at work. This rise of 'knowledge work', which management guru Peter Drucker first described in 1959 as a shift to creating value with your mind instead of your muscle, further reinforced the need for a new approach to management. For the first time, the employee's ability to be creative, problem-solve and process information had become a core part of how the employee produced work output.

As a result, the following decades represented an expansion of efforts both in academia and in business to better understand work and employee motivation. This included studies of goal setting, intrinsic motivation and job satisfaction (Psychology, 2018). In 1990, William Kahn at Boston University published a research paper in which he is credited for coining the term 'Employee Engagement' (Kahn, 2017; Burjek, 2015). Since then, the concept of employee engagement has increasingly represented the quest to create workplaces that fully embody the ideas of Theory Y that McGregor imagined so many decades ago.

One result of this pursuit of employee engagement has been pervasive research and data collection about the employee's experience of work. Employers have been conducting employees surveys for decades. Add to that the massive amount of data collected through 'Best Place to Work' programmes and other employee survey efforts and what results is a mountain of employee opinion data that begins to paint a robust picture of the complexity involved with motivating and managing employees in a constantly changing world of work.

The lesson in the data

One thing that these decades of research has shown clearly is that when employees feel emotionally connected with their work, they perform better in a variety of ways.

Below are five crucial elements that drive the feeling of engagement:

- *Feeling valued.* When employees feel valued by their employer at work, they are significantly more likely to be satisfied with their work experience and to be motivated to do their best work. In addition, feeling valued increases the employees' perceptions of growth and development and reduces the likelihood that they will report feeling stressed at work (American Psychological Association, 2017).

- *Trust.* Research has repeatedly revealed the importance of trust in the employee's experience at work. When an employee trusts their employer, they are more likely to feel motivated to do their best work and to recommend their employer as a great place to work (American Psychological Association, 2017). Empirical studies have also revealed a strong relationship between employee trust and workplace performance (Brown et al. 2015). The linkage is so powerful that the Great Place to Work Institute, the global gold standard for awarding 'best places to work' honours, uses their 'Trust Model' as the definitive measurement of the quality of the workplace experience for employees (Great Place to Work Institute, 2018)

- *Caring.* According to Gallup's employee research, which stretches back several decades, the employee's relationship with their supervisor is critical to their overall feeling of engagement with work. Their research revealed that great supervisors are those who genuinely care about the people with whom they work. They curate a relationship with each employee, treating them as individuals and trying to understand their individual needs (Gallup, 1999).

- *Recognition and appreciation.* Another consistent finding of employee survey data is the importance of recognition. In their 2001 book, *How Full is Your Bucket?,* Don Clifton and Tom Rath argue that their research suggests that the main reason people leave their job is a lack of appreciation. Other recent research revealed that when employees agree that they receive recognition for good work, they are more than twice as likely to rate their overall employee experience as positive (IBM Corporation and Globoforce Limited, 2017).

- *Belonging.* While the research about the impact of belonging in the workplace is more recent, the importance of belonging as a fundamental human need has long been acknowledged by those in the field of psychology (Ben-Zeev, 2014). So, it shouldn't be surprising to learn that a feeling of belonging at work is highly correlated with overall engagement with work and even more so for members of under-represented groups within the workplace population (Chu, 2016).

If you've spent much time trying to improve employee engagement, it shouldn't be surprising to see any of these things on the list. It has been common to see these things as top drivers of employee engagement on most employee surveys I've administered or analysed over the years. And in the majority of cases, these were also areas where improvement was needed.

The emotional impact of good and bad jobs

These things are the heart of what makes for a good employee experience. It's easy to recognize these things in our own work experiences, particularly the times when they were missing. During my 10 years working in corporate roles, I had experiences at both ends of the spectrum, some that felt really good and others that felt really bad. In every case, these were the kinds of jobs that most people would consider 'good'. I worked for good, stable companies and had jobs with fancy titles, nice offices and big pay cheques.

In some cases, I loved my work. In others, it felt completely soul-crushing. The difference for me boils down to whether I felt truly valued and like I belonged. In the job I loved the most, I felt like I was on a righteous quest with people who I truly cared about and who I believed cared about me. We were truly a team and even when there was conflict, it was never personal. I felt like my contribution really mattered and was valued by others as I valued theirs. I felt truly connected in this role.

In contrast, the role in which I experienced the most pain was an even bigger role in a bigger company with a bigger pay cheque. The longer I worked in that role, the more miserable and unhappy I became. It wasn't the job itself that was the problem, it was the way I felt working at this organization.

From the very beginning, I wasn't a good 'fit'. I was hired, in part, because I was different. And this difference in style, thinking, and approach meant that a true sense of belonging was hard to come by. I just couldn't assimilate in the way that was expected. This led to increasing feelings of both isolation and alienation. Even when the results of my work and that of my team were positive, it never felt truly valued because I had likely accomplished it in a way that wasn't the cultural norm. This disconnect contributed over time to diminishing trust and ultimately to my departure.

When it was finally over, it felt like a break-up at the end of a long and strained relationship. Despite only being in this job for two-and-a-half years, I was emotionally damaged and needed time to heal.

As we explored at the beginning of the book, the most powerful impact that our job has on us individually is emotional. While work may get treated like a contract by the employer, it sure doesn't feel like a contract when it's happening to you as an employee.

Common drivers of employee engagement

- feeling valued;
- trust;
- caring;
- recognition and appreciation;
- belonging.

When you consider the drivers of engagement, they clearly do not sound like contractual language. In fact, it's quite the opposite. Everything on this list is relational and emotional. They describe a desired feeling that comes from how we are treated by others.

Understanding work as a relationship

When I was leading the Best Places to Work team at Quantum Workplace, one of the things my research team was responsible for each year was to do a macro-level analysis of the hundreds of thousands of employee survey responses we had collected the previous year to identify trends and insights that could be shared.

In analysing which factors were most strongly correlated to overall high engagement, these same factors were always near (or at) the top of the list. After seeing these outcomes a few years in a row, it suddenly hit me. These are the same things we look for in any important relationship in our lives. The five things taken together would be what we might describe as 'being loved' if it wasn't in a work context.

The implication of this insight would be that what people are looking for in a great work experience was love. This was an uncomfortable realization because 'love' isn't something often discussed in a workplace context. But, as I began to pay more attention, I started noticing that it wasn't uncommon to hear employees who worked for Best Place to Work organizations invoke the word 'love' when talking about work. I'd hear things like:

'I love working here. It's the best job I've ever had.'

'My coworkers are amazing. I love working with them. It's like family.'

'I love our owners. They really care about people.'

Once I started listening for it, the word seemed to be everywhere I looked within organizations that were really committed to creating a great work experience for employees.

Love is an emotion that only exists within a relationship with someone or something. It represents a strong sense of attachment and commitment. If we were to talk about how we know someone loves us, we'd probably talk about things like trust, appreciation and care. These are the reasons that my marriage is so fulfilling and healthy. I also know that my wife and I accept each other for who we each are – good, bad and ugly. We belong in this relationship in a fully authentic way.

Whether it's a relationship with our significant other, our best friend, or a close family member, we want to feel valued, trusted, cared for, appreciated and to truly belong. These things form the glue of any strong, healthy relationship.

When you consider all of this, it becomes clear that for employees, *work isn't a contract*. For employees, *work is a relationship*. When we accept a job and join an organization, we aren't looking for an efficient, transactional value exchange as the contract might govern. We actually show up looking to be loved, cared for, and for an expanded sense of our identity by joining together with the organization.

And work isn't just another relationship for an employee – it's often one of the most important. Most of us spend more time with work than we do with anyone else in our lives. We often derive our sense of security, purpose and identity from work. This work relationship is critical to our overall sense of wellbeing. When it's healthy, we are free to do some great work. When it's not, it's a struggle.

This is a major clue to solving the crisis of employee engagement. Employees view work as a relationship and expect to be treated as such. It's an emotional experience. The employer, on the other hand, views work as a contract to be honoured. They treat it as a legal transaction.

Imagine being in a marriage where your partner rarely shows you affection or attention and never expresses any sentiments resembling love. But he (or she) reminds you regularly of your 'marital obligations' and frequently tells you how you are falling short of those requirements.

That's a recipe for divorce. And yet, this is the day-to-day reality for far too many employees. They come to work every day, craving to be treated as if they matter in this relationship, only to be reminded of their contractual performance obligations. It should be no surprise that employee disengagement and retention continue to be such a challenge. Why would we expect employees to stay in a relationship like this?

One place this disconnect between employer and employee is most obvious is in how organizations approach their performance management processes. Everything from performance appraisals to one-on-one meetings are treated as compliance exercises designed to ensure the employee is living up to their end of the deal.

Creating a more human-friendly workplace where employees can truly engage and unlock their performance potential requires redesigning the work experience to feel like a healthy relationship for all employees.

The characteristics of a healthy and positive relationship

We've all had healthy relationships – the best friend we could talk with for hours, or the significant other we couldn't imagine life without. And we've all had unhealthy relationships – the inconsiderate sibling, or significant other who seemed incapable of intimacy.

If we are to design a work experience for employees that feels like a healthy relationship, we need to have a clear understanding of the elements that differentiate a healthy relationship from an unhealthy one.

For help, we can turn to the field of psychology, which is dedicated to the study of what makes us human. One helpful model comes from the work of Dr Will Meek at the University of Portland (Meek, 2013). He outlines the eight keys to a healthy relationship:

1 Taking interest. People in healthy relationships are curious about one other. They desire a deeper understanding of the other person and show an interest in their wellbeing.

2 Acceptance and respect. The best relationships are built upon a foundation where each accepts the other for who they are, including each other's differences.

3 Positive regard. When a relationship is healthy, both parties choose to see the other in a positive light. They assume positive intentions of each other. When negative things happen, they view them as honest mistakes, not flaws in the individual.

4 Meeting basic needs. As humans, we have basic needs in any relationship (Meek, 2012): belonging, affection and emotional support. In healthy relationships, both individuals commit to understanding and satisfying these needs for the other person.

5 Positive interactions. While this may seem obvious, research (Rath and Clifton, 2004) from John Gottman, Gallup and others illustrates how important it is to tend to the balance of positive to negative interactions within a relationship. When we achieve a ratio of at least five positive to one negative interactions, we will have created a positive, satisfying relationship.

6 Solve problems. Every relationship has its problems. Strong relationships are defined by a mutual commitment to resolve the problems they can and minimize the impact of those they can't. This requires a willingness to participate in some constructive conflict.

7 Rupture and repair. The ability to quickly and effectively repair damage to a relationship is critical. In too many cases, ruptures to the relationship are left unattended to fester. Those in healthy relationships push past their discomfort to have the hard conversations needed to make necessary repairs.

8 A healthy relationship is never one-sided. It only occurs when both parties are fully committed and working actively on the relationship. It's this shared commitment to one another that ultimately makes or breaks the relationship. And, as we saw earlier, it is broken for far too many employees.

It becomes quickly clear why some of our traditional performance management practices have failed us. The annual performance appraisal, for example, doesn't feel like a relationship-building exercise. My personal experiences of this process were largely coloured by angst, anxiety, frustration and confusion. When your value to the organization is boiled down to a subjective evaluation by another person, it can feel devoid of any care or concern of the individual being 'appraised'. In particular, the basic needs of belonging, affection and emotional support are absent in the process. The one-way nature of the experience also often completely lacks reciprocity.

Even the manager-employee one-on-one meeting, which should be a positive experience, can become a relationship liability when it's turned into a compliance-driven update meeting rather than a robust conversation. An effective one-on-one meeting, as we will discuss later in the book, can have an enormous positive effect on the employee's engagement when it incorporates all eight of these keys.

One thing not explicitly noted in Dr Meek's model is the importance of time. Almost everything on this list requires a commitment of time and focus. To take and express interest in someone, for example, requires that you spend time with them. There is no shortcut.

A few years ago, when my daughter was seven years old, I asked her how she knew if someone loved her. She paused for a moment to consider the question. Then she responded, 'I know someone loves me if they give me lots of hugs and kisses. And, they spend time with me.' Even as children, we recognize that time is the most valuable thing anyone can give you if they truly care about you.

Without the intentional investment of time, there can be no relationship. This is an inconvenient reality because much of the focus of management over the past few decades has on been the pursuit of efficiency. The quest for optimal efficiency led organizations to invest in Lean Six Sigma, Kaizen, and other process improvement efforts.

From the employer's contractual view of work, maximizing efficiency is getting the most out of the contract with the employee by making every moment count. In other words, it's about maximizing productivity. In the traditional, industrial management way of thinking, the more 'productive' the employee becomes in every minute they are at work, the more the employer benefits. Corporate profitability over the past 60 years shows that this focus on productivity has paid dividends for owners and shareholders (Trading Economics, 2018a; 2018b). But at what cost? During the period from 1958 to present, the average lifespan of a company on the S&P 500 index has gone from over 60 years to less than 20 (Sheetz, 2017).

Relationship building is rarely efficient because it requires a consistent investment of time over months and, sometimes, years. It looks unproductive when viewed through the contractual lens so most of the time required to create a healthy relationship with employees has been engineered out of the system. And that's likely a big reason why employee engagement continues to suffer and people continue to change jobs frequently in search of a better experience.

CASE STUDY Merck one-on-ones

In early 2015, the management team at Merck's vaccine manufacturing facility in Durham, North Carolina decided to invest in relationship building as a strategy to improve employee engagement within their facility. Their approach was simple. Each month, employees should have at least one opportunity for a one-on-one meeting with their supervisor.

This expectation was set and communicated to both managers and employees. Despite operating a manufacturing facility where time literally is productivity, they made this commitment with a long-range aspiration that managers would come to spend up to two hours per month in a one-on-one setting with every employee. The team crafted a simple framework for these meetings to help provide a starting point for the conversations.

The recommended format for these conversations was simple:

- discuss recent work experience and progress on objectives;
- share feedback in both directions (manager to employee and employee to manager);
- review career goals and development progress.

The primary goal was to get the manager and employee together in a conversation to either form or strengthen the relationship. For the first two years, managers reported when these meetings had been completed and employees were surveyed for the same purpose – to ensure the conversations were happening.

Their bet was that the strengthened relationship between manager and employee would translate to improved engagement while maintaining or improving performance. And they were right. In the two years following implementation of these one-on-one meetings, they saw an overall average increase of 15 per cent in employee engagement scores, including improvements of up to 24 per cent in some teams. This contributed to improved quality and performance metrics over the same period, all catalysed by investing in relationships using the one resource that seems to be in shortest supply in most organizations: time.

It may be both your biggest challenge and biggest opportunity to help your organization succeed by designing the time into work to allow for the culti- vation of the elements of a healthy relationship. If you succeed, you can create an employee experience that feels good to employees and, as a result, unlocks their potential for high performance.

The relationship test

The balance of this book will be dedicated to how we can redesign our approaches to performance management as a way to both create a more human-friendly experience of work and to improve performance. The foundation of this is the understanding that work is a relationship for employees and that to unleash their full potential, it must feel like a healthy one for each of them.

The process of transforming your organization in this way will be one that requires time and intention. As you navigate through the book, you'll find everything you need to take that journey. But, if you are impatient and want to get a head start now, there is a shortcut I'd like to share with you to help you start identifying areas where you can make some immediate impact.

I call it the 'Relationship Test'.

It is a simple thought exercise. For any process or interaction in the workplace, you simply consider how that same approach would work if you used it in your relationship with someone who is important to you like your best friend or significant other. You can either apply the process to a circumstance outside or work or you can just assume that your best friend or spouse happens to work with you. Either way will work.

As you consider using this work approach with this person who you care for, ask yourself this question, 'Does it harm or help the relationship?'

If it helps or preserves the relationship, then it is probably okay to leave it alone for now. It passes the relationship test.

If using this particular approach would harm the relationship, then it fails the test and needs to be changed. This quick shortcut forces us to confront the fact that we somehow rationalize treating people at work in a way that we'd never treat someone in our personal lives, particularly not someone we care about.

Let's try an example together. Imagine what it would be like if we approached the beginning of a new romantic relationship in the same way we approach new employee onboarding.

Imagine this. You've been on a few dates with this person and things have gone well. You enjoy each other's company, you like spending time together, and you share several interests. You both agree to enter a committed, exclusive relationship.

You decide to invite your new significant other over to your home on Saturday morning to get the relationship off on the right foot. For the first hour together, you review a variety of papers, including your emergency contact information, medical information, and your usual weekly schedule. Upon finishing this, you spend the next two hours providing an overview of your personal history and values. Then, in the last hour, you might review your expectations of your new partner to equip them to be the very best partner they can be.

At this point, I'm guessing this new relationship may be well on its way to being a past relationship. It feels awkward at best, arrogant and insensitive at worst. This experience is entirely one-sided and ignores the fact that there are two participants in the relationship.

It fails the relationship test. If we wouldn't do this to someone in our personal life, why would we do it to employees? The next step would be to think about how to redesign the onboarding process so that it accomplishes the objectives of the process, but does it in a way that builds a relationship instead of harming it.

The relationship test helps us quickly identify where our behaviours and actions might not be as human-friendly as we'd like and reminds us to ask questions that move us towards progress. What about this experience damages the relationship? How might it look different if we designed it with the relationship in mind?

The relationship test is a useful tool to use as a rule of thumb to evaluate the impact of our interactions and processes at work. But if we are to create an overall work experience that feels like a healthy relationship to employees, we need to think in a bigger way about how to systematically make relationship building an integral part of what we do. In the next chapter, we'll explore how performance management can be reimagined as the system to make it happen.

Key takeaways

- The legacy of 'work as a contract' continues to shape the employee experience through current HR and management practices such as performance reviews, job descriptions, and employee handbooks.

These practices exist primarily to protect the interests of the organization, sometimes at the expense of the employee.

- The contractual model of work is frequently paired with a legacy management mindset which assumes that employees are inherently lazy and must be coerced and closely monitored to comply with the contractual expectations of work.

- A shift in understanding about the nature of work was sparked by Douglas McGregor in the 1960s and ultimately led to the understanding and measurement of employee engagement which assumes employees are self-motivated to pursue success at work.

- Measurement of employee sentiment has revealed that employees experience work in the same way they do any important relationship – needing to feel valued, trusted, appreciated, cared for, and a sense of belonging.

- To unlock the full performance potential of employees, work needs feel like a healthy relationship. The relationship test is a tool that can be applied to make some immediate progress in that direction.

References

American Psychological Association (2017) 2017 Work and well-being survey, *Center for Organizational Excellence* [Online] http://www.apaexcellence.org/assets/general/2017-work-and-wellbeing-survey-results.pdf?_ga=2.82923862.1359115985.1512314246-2101083144.1512314246 [Last accessed 27 April 2018]

Ben-Zeev, A (2014) Why we all need to belong to someone, *Psychology Today,* 11 March [Online] https://www.psychologytoday.com/us/blog/in-the-name-love/201403/why-we-all-need-belong-someone [Last accessed 27 April 2018]

Brown, S et al. (2015) Employee trust and workplace performance, *Journal of Economic Behavior & Organization, ScienceDirect* [Online] https://www.science-direct.com/science/article/pii/S0167268115001365 [Last accessed 27 April 2018]

Burjek, A (2015) Re-engaging with William Kahn 25 years after he coined term employee engagement, *Workforce* 14 December [Online] http://www.workforce.com/2015/12/14/re-engaging-with-william-kahn-25-years-after-he-coined-term-employee-engagement/ [Last accessed 27 April 2018]

Chu, H (2016) New technology industry diversity & inclusion report 2017, *Culture Amp* [Online] http://hello.cultureamp.com/diversity-and-inclusion?

utm_campaign=Blog%20Link%20Campaigns&utm_source=Blog&utm_medium=Belonging_importance [Last accessed 27 April 2018]

Clifton, D and Rath, T (2001) *How Full is Your Bucket?* Gallup Press

The Economist (2008) Theories X and Y, 6 October [Online] https://www.economist.com/node/12370445 [Last accessed 27 April 2018]

Gallup (1999) Item 5: my supervisor cares about me, *Business Journal* 19 April [Online] http://news.gallup.com/businessjournal/493/item-supervisor-cares-about.aspx [Last accessed 27 April 2018]

Great Place to Work Institute (2018) Survey, analyze and improve your culture, *Great Place to Work* [Online] https://www.greatplacetowork.com/culture-consulting/survey-analyze-improve-your-culture [Last accessed 30 April 2018]

IBM Corporation and Globoforce Limited (2017) The employee experience index, *IBM,* July [Online] https://www-01.ibm.com/common/ssi/cgi-bin/ssialias?htmlfid=LOW14335USEN [Last accessed 30 April 2018]

Kahn, W (2017) Psychological conditions of personal engagement and disengagement at work, *Academy of Management, 33* (4) [Online] https://journals.aom.org/doi/abs/10.5465/256287 [Last accessed 27 April 2018]

McGregor, D (1960) *The Human Side of Enterprise*, McGraw-Hill

Meek, W (2012) Basic relationship needs [Blog] *Will Meek PhD*, 16 December [Online] http://www.willmeekphd.com/relationship-needs/ [Last accessed 29 April 2018]

Meek, W (2013) 8 keys to healthy relationships, *Psychology Today* 28 October [Online] https://www.psychologytoday.com/us/blog/notes-self/201310/8-keys-healthy-relationships [Last accessed 27 April 2018]

Powell, W and Snellman, K (2004) The knowledge economy, *Annual Review of Sociology*, 30, pp. 199–220 [Online] https://web.stanford.edu/group/song/papers/powell_snellman.pdf [Last accessed 27 April 2018]

Psychology (2018) Industrial-organizational psychology history, *Psychology Research and Reference* [Online] http://psychology.iresearchnet.com/industrial-organizational-psychology/i-o-psychology-history/ [Last accessed 27 April 2018]

Rath, T and Clifton, D (2004) The big impact of small interactions, *Gallup*, 14 October [Online] http://news.gallup.com/businessjournal/12916/The-Big-Impact-of-Small-Interactions.aspx [Last accessed 29 April 2018]

Sheetz, M (2017) Technology killing off corporate America: average life span of companies under 20 years, *CNBC*, 24 August [Online] https://www.cnbc.com/2017/08/24/technology-killing-off-corporations-average-lifespan-of-company-under-20-years.html [Last accessed 29 April 2018]

Trading Economics (2018a) United Kingdom corporate profits, *Trading Economics* [Online] https://tradingeconomics.com/united-kingdom/corporate-profits [Last accessed 29 April 2018]

Trading Economics (2018b) United States corporate profits. *Trading Economics* [Online] https://tradingeconomics.com/united-states/corporate-profits [Last accessed 29 April 2018]

Rethinking performance management 03

In the last chapter, we learned that work is a relationship for employees. Understanding this reality is a great first step towards reshaping the employee's experience of work for the better. But it is only the first step on a long journey towards rethinking and redesigning the work experience for employees.

It will be a rewarding journey. But it will be challenging at times. Human relationships are complicated. Creating a lasting, healthy relationship of any kind is incredibly rewarding but rarely easy. Recognizing that work is a relationship helps to illuminate why it's so challenging to fully engage employees. Becoming fully engaged in any relationship takes time and consistent effort.

As I reflect on conversations I've had over the years with friends about their experiences in romantic relationships, they sound a lot like the conversations we have about employee engagement in the workplace.

Two people come together hoping to find a relationship that makes them happy and meets their needs. At first, both people work really hard to impress the other and they get caught up in the excitement and 'newness' of it all. The excitement of this new relationship means they might pretend to like things they don't or overlook things that might generally be a deal breaker. They see what they want to see, overlooking the rest.

But as time passes, they stop trying so hard. Both parties start revealing more and more about who they are to the other. As this process of revealing themselves unfolds, they start to make silent decisions about the other that lead them to either give more of themselves to the relationship, becoming more committed and vulnerable, or to pull back, closing themselves off.

Each of these silent decisions represent a 'moment of truth' for the relationship, a small fork in the road. The sum total of these moments of truth leads either to a stronger relationship or an eventual break-up. It's rarely one single decision that builds or ends a relationship, but the culmination of many, many small decisions made over time.

When my wife and I first met, my impression of her was of a beautiful, strong, funny woman: all things I was very attracted to. Thankfully, she was attracted enough to me to share her phone number. That first meeting, our first and critical moment of truth, went in my favour. This was followed by a first date where we began getting to know each other.

In those first conversations, I learned that my future wife was a divorced single mother with full custody of her son. As a single guy in my late twenties, I was looking for a serious relationship, but I wasn't sure I was ready yet for the responsibility of a child and the complexity that added to a relationship. This was another major moment of truth early in our courtship. Obviously, I decided I was open to the idea, but we agreed that we should first explore how serious our relationship was before I met her son.

Several weeks later, the time arrived for me to meet my future stepson. He was a spunky, borderline-obnoxious, blonde-haired five-year-old who decided to really test me out that day. Our first experience together was awkward and uncomfortable. He was testing me, I was studying him, and my future wife was evaluating how I showed up in that situation. This was another critical moment of truth in our relationship for each of us. You know how the story ends, so clearly we all made the decision to keep moving further into the relationship.

My marriage, like every relationship in our lives, is an ongoing shared experience between two people defined by these moments of truth. While the nature of these moments has changed for us over the years, they still happen all the time. Do we say we are sorry even when we don't want to? Do we choose spending time together over time doing something else? Do we prioritize the other's needs over our own? Each moment of truth represents an opportunity to make a decision about the relationship. These moments are still as important to our relationship today as they were in the early going.

When you consider your own personal relationships, it's easy to start identifying the key moments of truth that separate your best relationships from the rest:

- How do they treat you?
- How do they make you feel when you spend time with them?
- How do they treat others you care about?

- Do they show up when you need them?
- Do they have your back (even when it's inconvenient for them)?
- Do they keep your secrets?

It is these 'moments of truth' that define the experience of the relationship. With each moment of truth, you become more or less engaged in the relationship. Each moment of truth either strengthens or weakens your feeling of connection with the other person.

As your connection with the other person increases, your commitment to the relationship increases and you become more likely give of yourself to the other. There's nothing I wouldn't give of myself for my wife, but that's an extreme example from one of the most intimate and important types of relationship.

On a less extreme level, I have a few friends for whom I would willingly give up my weekend to help build a shed in their backyard despite having a lot of other things I'd rather do with my time. The sole reason I'd give up my weekend for them is due to the type of relationship we've built over the years. We make relationship decisions like this every day. The stronger our level of connection or 'engagement' in the relationship, the more willingly we will sacrifice and invest of ourselves in the other person.

This is why the conversation about employee engagement has turned more towards employee 'experience' in recent years. As in any relationship, the quality and nature of our experience drives our level of connection. This level of connection, in turn, drives our willingness to invest of ourselves in the relationship.

Put in workplace terms, experience drives engagement. And engagement drives performance. Unlocking higher performance starts with the employee experience.

While the concept of experience might be new when applied to the employees in the workplace, it's not a new concept. The fields of marketing and product design have been studying and designing customer experiences for years. The importance of experience seems almost intuitive when considered through the lens of personal shopping or dining.

Figure 3 How employee experience drives performance

EXPERIENCE   ENGAGEMENT   PERFORMANCE

Think about the last time you had a great experience as a customer in a shop/store, restaurant, or even online. How did it feel? Would you recommend the organization that created that experience for you?

Now consider the last really bad experience you had as a customer. The difference between the two is stark. A great experience leads to repeat business and referrals. A negative experience can mean a lost customer, negative reviews, and a potential wildfire of negative comments on social media.

Experience can make or break a customer relationship even more quickly than it can a personal relationship. As a result, there are fields of work dedicated to applying design principles to the customer experience or, as it's often referred to in software development, user experience (UX). Broadly defined, customer experience design is a practice of designing products and services with an intentional focus on the quality and thoughtfulness of the experience of the user. This involves shaping every customer interaction to align to the brand promise (Longanecker, 2016).

In experience design, these customer interactions with the product or brand are often referred to as 'moments of truth'. As we learned with personal relationships, each moment of truth represents a decision point that ultimately shapes our commitment and investment in the relationship. Because of their importance, experience designers strive to identify these moments of truth to ensure that each one results in a positive impression of the product or brand (The Interaction Design Institute, 2018a).

Performance management is about employee experience

The key to unlocking employee performance is to apply the discipline of experience design to shape the moments of truth for employees each day. The goal is to ensure that each of these key moments contributes to building the feeling of connection and relationship for the employee. This is the essence of employee engagement. And improved engagement goes hand in hand with improved performance.

Every meaningful interaction an employee has at or related to work can be a moment of truth, an experience that strengthens or weakens the relationship. Some moments of truth are simple and happen every day. For example, how your co-workers greet you in the hallway is a small moment of truth. When you have a question about something at work, your ability to find an answer can be a moment of truth. Even the quality and comfort of your workspace can be a daily moment of truth. In each case, a positive experience draws you into a better relationship while an experience that falls short might cause you to disconnect a little bit. If you've ever worked in an uncomfortable office setting or work environment that made it challenging to do your best, you understand how much damage that daily moment of truth can do to your engagement level at work.

There are also many higher-stakes moments of truth, those that might have a more profound and immediate impact on the employee's relationship with work. These tend to be moments that strike at the heart of a healthy relationship: communication, trust, feeling valued, appreciation, and the others outlined in the last chapter.

High-stakes moments of truth include:

- any one-on-one interaction with your manager or a leader;
- evaluation of job performance and feedback;
- recognition of meaningful effort;
- discussions of salary or career path;
- meetings;
- leadership response to bad news;
- expectation setting;
- interviews and new hire onboarding;
- communication about significant change;
- support for a personal crisis outside of work.

These are just a few of the more obvious significant moments of truth. These interactions happen for employees all day, every day within your organization. What silent decisions are employees making based on their experience in each of these moments? And, more importantly, are you thinking about how to make each of these moments of truth one that builds a relationship with the employee rather than harming it?

Traditional performance management, for example, with its annual appraisals and ratings-driven salary increases is a high-stakes moment of truth for both employees and managers. Even in its best form, there is minimal consideration of the employee experience in the annual appraisal. It is an event-based process designed to check employee outcomes against expectations. Not only is it not usually concerned with experience, the near-universal dislike of the process suggests that it may be creating negative moments of truth, damaging the employee's relationship with work and, by extension, their performance over the long run.

It is far past time to reinvent performance management. In the future, it should be a system for creating and maintaining an employee experience that fuels engagement and unlocks each employee's full performance potential. To achieve this, performance management can no longer be an event-based, check-the-box activity. Instead, it must become a mindset and approach to shape each moment of truth in the employee experience to foster a strong relationship and sense of connection with their work.

Performance management will no longer be an HR programme defined by forms and policies. It must be a system for how work happens within the organization. If humans are the 'hardware' of the organization, then performance management must be the software that programs how we individually and collectively create work. Like any effective software, it's value will be based on its utility and effectiveness at achieving desired results. And, like software, design is the difference between the tools that we love and those we hate.

Fortunately, we can borrow lessons from customer and user experience design methodologies to give us a head start in this work.

Clarify your intentions

The first lesson is found in the definition of customer experience shared earlier. Experience design is about creating interactions that reinforce the brand promise. A brand promise is an articulation of what a customer can expect from their interactions with the organization (MBA Skool, 2018). This promise creates clarity for the type of experience that the organization designs and creates through its products, services and interactions with customers.

Amazon, one of the largest and most admired companies in the world, has an exceptionally clear and powerful brand promise to provide the earth's biggest selection and be the earth's most customer-centric organization (Davis, 2016). While that seems like a pretty ambitious promise to make, it certainly clarifies how and why Amazon does business as it does. If you have shopped on Amazon or interacted with their customer service team, does your experience measure up to this expectation? As a frequent Amazon customer, it wasn't surprising to me to read their brand promise for the first time because it accurately describes my experience of the company.

Another example of clarity comes from the BMW brand promise: the ultimate driving machine (Leifer, 2015). While BMW is a very different kind of company from Amazon, the clarity of their promise sets some clear expectations for the type of experience you should expect of their products and services. In both cases, they have articulated clearly and boldly what their customers should expect from them. Armed with this clarity, they can design a customer or product experience that delivers on that promise. Clarity of intention is a necessary input for good design.

The first step in reinventing your performance management system is to find clarity about the type of experience you are promising to your employees. You may have already done some of this work in the form of organizational values, culture, employer branding, or employee value proposition. These represent the variety of ways you might approach gaining clarity about your intended employee experience. The particular process you choose isn't critical as long as it helps you create the equivalent of a clear brand promise that describes the employee experience you are intending to create.

When you've achieved clarity, you will be able to answer these two questions:

- What kind of work experience are we trying to create for employees?
- Why is creating this experience important?

The examples of brand promise from Amazon and BMW are short, concise statements that capture the high-level aspiration of the brand. Obviously, these short statements are only the start of creating the clarity needed to craft the customer experience. At companies of this size, there are entire teams dedicated to further defining and executing on these promises.

For the workplace, the equivalent of a brand promise is culture. Some companies have gone to great lengths to clearly define their culture in a way that clarifies the kind of employee experience they desire to create. This clarity also invites the employee to co-create that experience with the organization.

Hubspot, a developer of software for inbound marketing and sales, has something they call their culture code. The code, shared below, is explained in detail in a 128-page slide deck that the company has published online for both employees and non-employees to view. The code paints a clear picture of what it's like to work at Hubspot. And, by publishing the deck online, they invite their employees (and customers, investors, and others) to hold them accountable to their intentions.

Hubspot Culture Code (Shah, 2017)

1 We commit maniacally to both our **mission** and **metrics**.

2 We look to the long term and **Solve For The Customer**.

3 We **share openly** and are **remarkably transparent**.

4 We favour **autonomy** and take **ownership**.

5 We believe our best perk is **amazing people**.

6 We dare to be **different** and question the status quo.

7 We recognize that **life is short**.

Another company that has committed to clarity of the employee experience is the financial insights and analysis company, The Motley Fool. Instead of a culture deck, they have used an unlikely tool to create clarity: the employee handbook. But this isn't the boring employee handbook that is today's norm. This employee handbook isn't really a handbook at all, but an interactive website published online for all to see at www.thefoolrules.com. Within the first few pages of the handbook, you find the organization's purpose and core values clearly stated and explained. Based on this foundation of clarity, the rest of the handbook explains and outlines how the organization creates an experience that aligns.

The Motley Fool – purpose and values

Purpose: 'To Help the World Invest – Better'.
Core values: 'Be Foolish'.

- Collaborative – do great things together.
- Innovative – search for a better solution. Then top it.
- Honest – make us proud.
- Competitive – play fair, play hard, play to win.
- Fun – revel in your work.
- Motley – make foolishness your own!

Both of these examples demonstrate the kind of clarity that enables the design of an aligned employee experience. With this clarity, it's possible to start defining a performance management system to ensure that key moments of truth are positive and strengthen the relationship.

If it feels a little overwhelming to think about how to create this kind of clarity for your organization, you're not alone. My experience is that the majority of organizations lack clarity of intentions, which contributes to a poor and inconsistent employee experience. For insight into where to start, we can turn again to customer and user experience design.

A necessary ingredient of the design process is a deep understanding of the customer and how they interact with the product, service or organization (The Interaction Design Institute, 2018b). Applied to the workplace, this suggests that we must have deep understanding of our employees, how they interact with the organization, and what interactions they view as most important.

If you are just beginning this process, the simplest way to gain insights about your employees related to these questions is to ask them. Depending on the size of your organization, an online survey or some focus groups might be a great place to start. If your organization is smaller, sitting down one on one or in small groups with employees for a conversation is powerful.

The goal is to uncover how the employee views their experience with the organization, and to uncover ideas for how to strengthen the employee relationship with their work while delivering on the organization's purpose and objectives.

Here are some examples for the types of question you might want to explore:

- When do you feel most energized by your work?
- When do you feel most fulfilled by your work?
- When you have a good day at work, what happens to make you feel like it was a good day?
- When you have a bad day at work, what happens to make you feel like it was a bad day?
- If you could change or eliminate something from your weekly work routine, what would it be and why?

It might feel tempting to skip this research and discovery phase because it can be time-consuming and arduous to undertake. Don't do it. The process of design, whether applied to experience, software or architecture, begins with discovery and research (Design Council, 2018). To create something with intention, you have to understand who you are designing for and why.

It is also tempting to assume that you already understand what your employees need and want. Unless your organization is very small or is relentless in creating ongoing conversations and feedback loops including the types of questions listed above, your assumptions are almost assuredly at least partially wrong. Even after decades of working in and around employee research, I'm still amazed to this day how surprised most leadership teams are when presented with the results of a survey or focus groups. It's almost always the case that the day-to-day reality for employees is very different from what leaders assume it to be. It is this gap of understanding that must be closed to really design employee experience with intention.

Your success in creating the type of experience you intend will be dependent upon a deep knowledge of your employees needs and preferences. Equipped with this foundation, you can start to make decisions and clarify the kind of experience you can create that both motivates your employees and delivers on the purpose of the organization. You can see this synergy reflected in the examples from Hubspot and The Motley Fool.

It is in the alignment of employee experience with organizational purpose that magic happens. And there is no formula that can be borrowed from one company and applied to another. The employee experience within a banking organization with a purpose of creating a feeling of safety and stability for customers should look very different from the experience within a technology start-up or a fine dining restaurant. The key is in discovering the right formula for your organization. A great example of this is Menlo Innovations.

CASE STUDY   Menlo Innovations

Menlo Innovations is a software development company headquartered in Ann Arbor, Michigan, and has been a role model for how to intentionally design and create a positive work experience. Menlo's approach garnered so much interest from other companies that their CEO, Richard Sheridan, wrote the book, *Joy, Inc.* to share the key inner workings of their culture. The culture at Menlo is designed to create a 'joyful' experience by being 'open and transparent, collaborative, and democratic' (Menlo Innovations, 2017). Those words represent a clear idea of the type of experience that employees can expect when they come to work at Menlo.

When you peek inside Menlo and talk to those who work there, you quickly discover that everything about the Menlo work experience has been designed to create positive moments of truth that reinforce those intentions. There are cards on the wall within the factory (what they call the office) where anyone can see what anyone else is working on during any given day. On another wall is a sort of chart that shows where every employee is in terms of career progression relative to their current role. Working teams follow a process to gather feedback and offer promotions to their teammates without any traditional leadership or management involvement.

It's important to note here that Menlo's approach to software development is unique. All of their work is done in pairs. Two developers, one keyboard, writing code and building software. They also give customers more direct influence and input during the process of development and employ 'High-Tech Anthropologists' in the process as well. Their culture and employee experience are designed to support and sustain their model of software development. It's all intertwined into what I would describe as their system of performance management.

Menlo's approach to work is unique and trying to apply what they do directly to your organization is probably the wrong answer. Menlo has clearly defined its intentions related to the employee and work experience and has aligned everything about the day-to-day work experience and environment to support that. Only once you have achieved such clarity can you then design your own system with the specific processes and tools that make the most sense for your organization.

Does performance management need a rebrand?

As we've collectively woken up to the failures of the traditional approaches to performance management, one of the side effects has been a backlash against the very idea of 'managing' performance. In fact, there's such a disdain for annual performance appraisals that some have argued that we shouldn't even use the term 'performance management' any longer.

Some have argued for performance motivation (Comaford, 2016) and performance conversations (Gandhi, 2017). The arguments for new language are compelling and easy to agree with because they suggest that a new and different approach is needed. After years of suffering the old system, anything new sounds good.

Inherent in most of these rebranded approaches to performance management is a common theme that the new process should help create a more 'human' workplace. After decades of treating employees as replaceable cogs in a machine, we crave a process that treats people like people. So, these new replacement processes are named to reflect the more human approach by invoking words like 'motivation' and 'conversations'.

But there are some who are rightly cynical. Like it or not, the concept of performance management has become deeply ingrained in how we think about managing work. When we suggest humanizing work and replacing 'performance management' in favour of approaches with different names, it can feel pretty dangerous to leaders. As we saw last chapter, the traditional model of work has in recent decades produced some pretty impressive results in terms of profitability for stakeholders. As the old saying goes, 'if it ain't broke, don't fix it'.

The need for performance management is intuitively obvious. After all, performance is why organizations exist. Performance is the measure of how effectively an organization delivers on its purpose.

Every organization has a purpose (or several). Businesses create stakeholder value by meeting a market need. For example, Adidas creates clothing and gear for athletes. If people stop buying those products, Adidas would need to find a new purpose or be out of business.

Nonprofit organizations have a different kind of purpose. They exist to serve the needs of a particular group or cause. As an example, CARE International works to end global poverty. If poverty was eradicated globally, CARE International would no longer need to exist.

Performance success at the organizational level is generally determined by the organization's ability to consistently perform over time. Adidas sells enough product to drive up the value of its stock. CARE International helps reduce poverty so they can continue to raise support and funds to continue their work.

Performance is the lifeblood of the organization.

To achieve success, organizations need employees to work in concert to produce individual outcomes. The performance of one individual often enables or supports the performance of another. When one performance link fails, it affects the whole chain.

At the same time, as the individual's performance improves, it can have a positive impact on everyone that person's work enables or affects. In this way, unlocking each individual's full potential for performance can have an exponential amplification effect on the performance of the organization.

It's been my experience that most leaders intuitively understand the critical significance of individual performance. And that's why they rightly believe that its management is a key priority.

Performance management makes sense to leaders. The goal of managing performance is the right one when considering that it's why the organization exists. What's broken about performance management has never been its aspiration. It's the outdated and ineffective methods we've applied that are the problem.

Our objective should not be to replace or rename performance management, but to redesign it to finally achieve its aspiration of fully unlocking human performance to power organizational performance.

Redesigning performance management

Earlier, I introduced the idea of performance management as the software of the organization. If we stick with this analogy, the software version we are running in many organizations today is equivalent to the first word processing programs in the early days of personal computers. These programs were essentially a digitized typewriter with very few features other than being able to replace typing on physical paper with 'digital paper'. At the time, the ability to type and edit a document electronically (mainly to fix spelling or typing errors) was an amazing breakthrough.

Now think about that early technology in contrast to today's document creation tools like Microsoft Word or Google Docs. These tools foundationally do the same thing. They allow us to type up and edit documents electronically. But these modern tools have evolved and changed as technology and people have changed over the past few decades.

Today's tools can automatically fix your typos and improve your grammar. You can format your document with seemingly endless font, colour, and appearance options. It might automatically save your work so you never lose anything. Files can be easily converted to different content types and are easily shareable without ever printing. And, if that's not enough, most of these new tools allow multiple people to work together collaboratively on the same document at the same time, even if they are hundreds or thousands of miles apart.

The original word processor served the needs of the time. As time passed, it has been designed and redesigned repeatedly to keep up with a changing landscape and shifting user needs.

Performance management requires the same kind of upgrade from a rudimentary, stand-alone program to a system designed for how work and the worker have evolved. A well-designed performance management system, like well-designed software, will make work easier and more enjoyable for everyone involved, while feeling easy and rewarding to use.

As you consider where to begin the work of redesigning your performance management system, there is some good news. Even though the annual performance appraisal system wasn't particularly effective or popular, it was built around some of the fundamentals of effective performance management: goal setting, measurement and evaluation of progress. The capabilities your organization has developed in these areas will be valuable as you design your system; they just aren't nearly enough on their own.

The three performance processes

I grew up in a small rural community surrounded by farmers. It could be argued that farmers are in the business of performance management. After all, their livelihood is dependent on how well their crops grow and perform. The more successfully they manage the performance of their crops, the bigger the reward they reap at harvest time.

Obviously crops and humans are very different. But I think there are some lessons we can learn from the farmer. Farmers have specific goals for the crops they plant each year and they also closely monitor and measure progress throughout the seasons. They track how well their crops performed according to their expectations. All of this is valuable, but they will tell you that the really important work of farming is what they call 'cultivation'.

Cultivation in farming is about removing obstacles and adding supportive elements that enhance growth (ie performance) of the crops. They may irrigate to provide water. They likely add treatments to ward off weeds or pests that would hinder performance. And that's just the beginning.

Farmers recognize that they can't force their crops to grow and they don't need to. Each individual plant is genetically programmed to grow on its own. The farmer instead works within what they can control to create the conditions that best optimize growth. They are trying to unlock each plant's full potential for growth and performance. Cultivation is the difference between an average versus a bountiful harvest.

In my experience, cultivation is almost entirely missing from traditional performance management, both in terms of practice and mindset. Traditional performance management, informed by its compliance-based legacy, was created to control and coerce performance. This is the opposite of cultivation. It's the equivalent of trying to force the plants to grow.

A mindset of cultivation recognizes that each person has a natural desire and potential for performance to be unlocked. And it assumes that growth and performance is just as natural for the person as it is for any living thing. Like the farmer, we should focus on what we can control to cultivate an experience and environment that optimizes human growth and performance.

An effective performance management system is designed to create an intentional employee experience that unlocks each person's potential for performance. It recognizes that each employee experiences work as a relationship and is designed to build and strengthen their feeling of connection with their work.

Performance management consists of three ongoing and interrelated processes that manifest in different ways based on the organization's purpose and intentions:

1 planning;

2 cultivation;

3 accountability.

Figure 4 The performance management processes

In the upcoming sections, we will further define and break down these three processes, including sharing some examples from successful organizations as models and inspiration. We'll also outline a variety of approaches and tools for you to consider as you design the system that's right for your organization.

Key takeaways

- Designing work as a relationship is challenging because relationships are complicated. Every relationship is made up of a series of 'moments of truth' that either build or harm the relationship. A healthy relationship is created by consistently creating more positive than negative moments over time.

- An employee's experience of work is a series of 'moments of truth' that either build or harm the relationship. To unlock an employee's performance potential, we must intentionally create an employee experience rich in positive moments of truth.

- Customer experience design provides a model for employee experience design. It starts with clearly articulating your intentions based on a deep knowledge of employee needs and preferences.

- Performance is the lifeblood of any organization and management of performance is vital. Performance management has failed due to faulty practices and it's in desperate need of innovation, not a name change.

- Performance management consists of three ongoing and related processes: planning, cultivation, and accountability.

References

Comaford, C (2016) Why performance management is dead and performance motivation is here to stay, *Forbes*, 22 October [Online] https://www.forbes.com/sites/christinecomaford/2016/10/22/why-performance-management-is-dead-performance-motivation-is-here-to-stay/#478f5e772dfe [Last accessed 29 April18]

Davis, S (2016) How Amazon's brand and customer experience became synonymous, *Forbes*, 14 July [Online] https://www.forbes.com/sites/scottdavis/2016/07/14/how-amazons-brand-and-customer-experience-became-synonymous/#335951473cd5 [Last accessed 29 April 2018]

Design Council (2018) The design process: What is the double diamond? [Online] https://www.designcouncil.org.uk/news-opinion/design-process-what-double-diamond [Last accessed 29 April 2018]

Gandhi, V (2017) Managers, get ready for ongoing performance conversations, *Chief Learning Officer*, 31 May [Online] http://www.clomedia.com/2017/05/31/managers-get-ready-ongoing-performance-conversations/ [Last accessed 29 April 2018]

The Interaction Design Institute (2018a) The moment of truth: build desirable relationships with users and customers [Online] https://www.interaction-design.org/literature/article/the-moment-of-truth-build-desirable-relationships-with-users-and-customers [Last accessed 29 April 2018]

The Interaction Design Institute (2018b) Customer experience (CX) design: what is customer experience (CX) design? [Online] https://www.interaction-design.org/literature/topics/customer-experience [Last accessed 29 April 2018]

Leifer, K (2015) The best brand promise examples we've seen, *Stella Service*, 24 April [Online] https://stellaservice.com/the-best-brand-promise-examples-weve-seen-2/ [Last accessed 29 April 2018]

Longanecker, C (2016) Customer experience is the future of design, *UX Magazine*, 19 February [Online] https://uxmag.com/articles/customer-experience-is-the-future-of-design [Last accessed 29 April 2018]

MBA Skool (2018) Brand promise, *Disqus* [Online] https://www.mbaskool.com/business-concepts/marketing-and-strategy-terms/7506-brand-promise.html [Last accessed 4.30.18]

Menlo Innovations (2017) Our culture. Available from: http://menloinnovations.com/our-story/culture [Last accessed 29 April 2018]

Shah, D (2017) The HubSpot culture code: creating a company we love, *Hubspot*, 4 December [Online] https://blog.hubspot.com/blog/tabid/6307/bid/34234/the-hubspot-culture-code-creating-a-company-we-love.aspx [Last accessed 9 April 2018]

Sheridan, R (2015) *Joy Inc.: How we Built a Workplace People Love*, Portfolio

SECTION 2
Performance planning

It's 1 pm and you've just finished lunch. When you open your email to see what you've missed you find an e-mail from your boss.

Subject: *Today*
Message: *I need to see you in my office today before you leave.*

That's it. No other details provided.

How do you feel when you read this e-mail? What do you immediately assume about why your boss needs to see you?

You've probably received e-mails like this in the past. And if you are like most people, just reading it makes you feel anxious. Despite the fact that there is no detail in this e-mail, we tend to assume that something bad is about to happen.

We feel like we are in trouble. We assume we did something wrong. Depending on where we work or our past experience, we might even assume we're being fired – even if we have absolutely no evidence to support that idea.

The actual content of the e-mail is vague and neutral. There's nothing to suggest whether the meeting will be positive or negative. So, why do we almost universally assume that it's more likely negative?

It's because the e-mail leaves us feeling uncertain. And our brain hates uncertainty.

Neuroscience has helped us gain a scientific understanding of the impact of uncertainty on our brains and none of it is good. Research has revealed a distinct linkage between perceived uncertainty and both anxiety (Grupe and Nitschke, 2013) and stress. In a 2016 study, researchers found that stress responses are 'tuned to environmental uncertainty' (de Berker et al. 2016). In other words, the more uncertain you feel, the higher your stress response.

One reason for this is that when we are faced with ambiguity, it triggers a threat response in the amygdala region of our brain (Rock, 2009). The amygdala is often referred to as the alarm system of the brain, responsible for our fear response to danger (Edwards, 2005). This is more commonly referred to as our 'fight or flight' response. When confronted with uncertainty, our brain reacts similarly to how it does when we are in real physical danger. As a result, our brain treats uncertainty like pain – something to be avoided (Rock, 2009).

The brain likes to feel certain. In fact, when we experience certainty (ie things happen as we expect them to happen), our brain actually experiences a sense of reward much like when an addiction is satisfied. This pleasure sensation drives us to crave certainty, even when it's not in our best interests to do so. (Rock, 2009) Fortune tellers and online horoscopes exist in part because of the human desire for certainty about a future that is unknowable. This is but one example of where our craving of certainty can make us vulnerable to potentially negative influences.

Our brain commonly reacts to uncertainty by filling in the missing details as a way to satisfy its desire for certainty. If we don't know the full story, we make it up. And, when we fill in those details, as we hinted at earlier, we usually assume the worst. When that ambiguous e-mail from our boss comes in, we don't assume we are getting promoted. We assume we are in trouble or worse.

We've all had this experience many times in our lives. When your spouse or child is late coming home, you might start thinking that they have been in an accident or had some other trouble. When you get a note from your child's teacher requesting a meeting, you assume that you're going to hear some bad news that reinforces insecurities about how you are failing as a parent somehow. When someone you're newly dating doesn't return your text message immediately, you assume it's a lack of interest.

This automatic response to assume the worst seems to be driven by our 'flight' response to reduce the pain of uncertainty and negative experiences. Additional research has revealed that uncertainty actually makes a bad event feel even worse (Lampert Smith, 2009). When we expect something bad to happen and it does, our emotional response to it is less severe than when we are uncertain. So, by assuming the worse when faced with uncertainty, we're protecting ourselves from the potential worst-case scenario. If we assume the worse and it happens, at least we were somewhat prepared for it. When we are surprised by it, the experience of it is more intense.

To sum it up, our brain craves certainty and tries to avoid uncertainty in the same way it actively avoids physical pain. And when we experience uncertainty, our brain react automatically in ways that almost universally generate negative emotions like stress, anxiety, fear and angst.

It seems clear, then, why uncertainty is toxic to relationships. Strong relationships are fuelled by positive emotions and killed by negativity. So, when working to create an employee experience that feels like a strong, healthy relationship, uncertainty is the enemy. The negative emotions generated by uncertainty are powerfully toxic when left unchecked.

This could lead us to the conclusion that we should focus on creating more certainty for employees at work. But trying to create total certainty for employees is a fool's errand. In an environment of perpetual and accelerating change, certainty isn't achievable.

It is equally impossible to eliminate all uncertainty from any relationship. The key is to focus on reducing the amount of uncertainty as much as possible by creating greater clarity. This means actively working to help employees have a clear understanding of everything that impacts their work experience.

Clarity is achieved when transparency meets context. It implies that I can not only see what's happening, but that I can understand it as well. When my leader shares the strategic plan for the organization with me and then we accomplish a goal or objective from that plan, my brain gets that hit of certainty it craves. This also builds trust and consistency into my relationship with work. Clarity is vital to a healthy relationship.

Using performance planning to create clarity

In this chapter, we'll explore planning, the first of the three performance processes we'll cover in this book. Planning is at its essence about creating clarity. As we just highlighted, one way we experience a greater feeling of certainty is when things happen as we expect. By investing the time to create clear and consistent expectations, we reduce the opportunity for uncertainty at work.

Performance planning is made up of the processes and approaches that clarify the what, why and how of the work experience:

- What is expected?
- Why does matter?
- How will I succeed?

Planning isn't just about reducing uncertainty, however. It also provides the roadmap that guides our efforts and decisions each day towards a desired end result. When planning is effectively done, it provides focus and alignment for both the employee and manager in terms of day-to-day work and what is most important.

While planning is an ongoing process that should occur throughout the year, its foundational importance is why we start with it. The plan makes your intentions and aspirations actionable. If you are leaving for vacation without first doing any planning, it's far less likely that you'll end up where you hoped and have the experience you desire. Nor would you attempt to build a house without first having a blueprint drawn.

In the following three chapters, we'll do a deep dive into the core processes of performance planning and share examples of each in practice:

- Chapter 4 sets the foundation with the art and practice of expectation clarity including an exploration of a variety of approaches for effective goal setting.

- Chapter 5 provides you with tools for the often overlooked step of clearly articulating behavioural expectations.

- Chapter 6 shows you how to amplify the power of clear expectations by connecting them with purpose and ensuring employees are equipped to succeed.

References

de Berker, A O et al. (2016) Computations of uncertainty mediate acute stress responses in humans, *Nature Communications*, 29 March [Online] https://www.nature.com/articles/ncomms10996 [Last accessed 29 April 2018]

Edwards, S P (2005) The amygdala: the body's alarm circuit, *The Dana Foundation*, May [Online] http://www.dana.org/Publications/Brainwork/Details.aspx?id=43615 [Last accessed 29 April 2018]

Grupe, D W and Nitschke, J B (2013) Uncertainty and anticipation in anxiety: an integrated neurobiological and psychological perspective, *Nature Reviews, Neuroscience*, 14 July, pp. 488–501 [Online] http://doi.org/10.1038/nrn3524 [Last accessed 29 April 2018]

Lampert Smith, S (2009) Future angst? Brain scans show uncertainty fuels anxiety, University of Wisconsin-Madison, 17 August [Online] https://news.wisc.edu/future-angst-brain-scans-show-uncertainty-fuels-anxiety/ [Last accessed 29 April 2018]

Rock, D (2009) A hunger for certainty, *Psychology Today*, 25 October [Online] https://www.psychologytoday.com/us/blog/your-brain-work/200910/hunger-certainty [Last accessed 29 April 2018]

Creating clear expectations and goals

04

In one of my first management roles, I learned the power of clear expectations. As someone who valued development and learning, I would regularly create 'lunch and learn' opportunities for my staff. We'd each bring our lunch as we gathered in a conference room to watch a webinar together or discuss a particular article.

Overall, these lunches were well received by my team with one exception: one member of my team was conspicuously absent from these discussions. It was incredibly frustrating to me that she wasn't attending and taking advantage of this opportunity. I thought I had expressed their importance in my team communications.

But, as I learned, I had also communicated that these lunch and learns were optional. And this particular employee valued her free time at lunch over the learning opportunity I was offering. If anything, this only increased my frustration with the situation, which seemed out of place because she wasn't breaking any rules or doing anything wrong based on what I had communicated. Her behaviour was perfectly within stated expectations.

I know in hindsight that I unfairly projected my frustration on her and it created a strain on our relationship. What I eventually realized was that I had not accurately communicated my expectations to my team. An expectation I had, but hadn't communicated, was that you should take advantage of every opportunity to learn and grow. Because this was a core belief for me, I was projecting that on my team but had never communicated it to them. When I finally did, it became clear that the training wasn't optional in my mind. And, if it was to be required, it needed to be moved into regular work time instead of over the lunch hour.

This is just a small example of how a lack of clarity can create negative moments of truth for both manager and employee. In this case, there were two failures of expectations. First, my communicated expectation was inconsistent with my actual expectation as the manager. This created confusion and frustration for both the employee and me. Then, there was also the lack of explicit communication of my true expectations to the team. Once my true expectation was shared with the team, we were able to discuss the implications for all of us. This clarity of communication eliminated the confusion and uncertainty almost immediately.

Clarity of expectations is critical to fostering a positive work experience, but despite its obvious importance, we have not historically done a great job of creating it. In my experience, most employees have at least some level of uncertainty about what's expected of them at work. It's a key reason the annual performance appraisal is nerve-wracking for so many. A lack of clarity about expectations creates massive uncertainty about how you are being evaluated.

The art of expectations

When we think of expectations at work, among the first things that come to mind are goals and policies. As employees, we crave a clear understanding of workplace rules and the measures that will be used to evaluate our performance. But we also want greater clarity in expectations about how the work is supposed to get done. Even when objective measures of performance are defined, behavioural and communication expectations that play a major role in performance are often left undiscussed.

Creating clear expectations is one of the most powerful ways to reduce uncertainty at work. And it's important to remember that we must approach setting expectations in a way that strengthens the feeling of being in a healthy relationship for the employee. How you go about setting expectations can be just as powerful as the expectations themselves. Below are three practices that will help you ensure that your efforts have the biggest positive impact.

1 Check your own expectations first

In 1965, Harvard professors Robert Rosenthal and Lenore Jacobson conducted research to identify the effect of teacher expectations on student achievement. As part of the experiment, a group of elementary school teachers were told that a percentage of the students in their class had been identified as 'growth spurters' based on a new measure of intelligence. In reality, these students had been chosen at random. It was a simple experiment designed with the purpose of determining if the students from whom more intellectual growth was expected actually experienced more intellectual growth than the other students who had not been singled out.

The results were so significant as to be startling. For some age groups, the average gain in intelligence for the randomly selected 'growth spurter' students was over double the average for the class. The conclusion of the study was that the expectation of one person about another, teachers in this case, can have a significant impact on the other's behaviour or performance. They described this phenomenon as the 'Pygmalion Effect' (Rosenthal and Jacobson, 2012).

Over the past several decades, researchers have replicated the results of the Pygmalion Effect in environments beyond the classroom with people of all ages. Others have researched its corollary, the Golem Effect (Wikipedia contributors, 2018; Psycholo Genie, 2018), which suggests that low expectations have an equally powerful effect on lowering performance.

The incredible insight in this research is that people tend to live up or down to our expectations of them. As managers or leaders of people, this means that we must be keenly aware of how our own beliefs or experiences of others might be impacting the expectations we place upon them. Our expectations of others can be affected by a variety of things. Sometimes our natural biases affect us in ways we aren't even aware of.

For example, we might automatically assume that someone with more experience or education would perform at a higher levels than others. Or that someone who has been at the company longer would have better ideas than a new person. In performance specifically, we often suffer from something called the recency effect (Psychology Research and Reference, 2018) where we place a higher weight on what you've done more recently over performance in the past.

Each of these are beliefs that could negatively influence the expectations we have of others. It's important to be self-aware in expectation setting to eliminate this impact. To remind myself of the importance of this, I use this rule of thumb: *People will live up or down to your expectations of them. Use them wisely.*

2 Invite input and feedback

When setting expectations, the goal is to reduce as much uncertainty as possible. Since the clarity of an expectation can only be assessed by the individual it's intended for, the only way to ensure its effectiveness is through their feedback and input. This means that employees should participate actively in expectation and goal-setting processes.

There are several reasons for encouraging participation. Research supports that when employees participate in goal setting, they have a higher level of commitment to the goal (Li and Butler, 2004). In providing input, the goal is co-created by the manager and employee (or the team) and this creates a feeling of ownership that doesn't exist when it is created and assigned by someone else.

This is a good example of where applying the relationship test from Chapter 2 can be helpful. If you wanted to set a meaningful goal in a personal relationship, how would you approach that process? For example, how would you approach setting a major financial goal for your family if you were married? I'm guessing the process would start with some conversation with your spouse about why the goal is needed. Then you both might share what you think a good goal would look like. If you didn't have immediate alignment, you'd discuss and negotiate any differences in your perspectives until you landed on a goal you could both support. It would be a collaborative process.

Why not apply the same approach to setting goals and expectations at work? Granted, the manager and employee relationship is a bit different, but the overall steps might look the same. The objective should be to create a conversation about the expectations that clarifies the what, why and how. This ultimately leads to agreement and buy-in by everyone involved.

3 Write everything down

This may seem too obvious to need inclusion here, but my experience has been that many well-intentioned managers skip the step of committing expectations to paper. When speed is a priority, putting down in writing things that have been discussed can feel like wasted time. This, however, is not the case.

As I just highlighted, it's a good idea to discuss and negotiate expectations. Conversation is a valuable tool in this process. But there's no substitute for the clarity that comes when forced to write something out. When you write out expectations and goals, it removes a lot of the space where misunderstanding occurs. And, the act of committing something to writing also makes it feel more formal and official. This motivates most people to treat the words more seriously.

A practice I picked up over the years was to create a set of written, behavioural expectations for my teams. I'd generally write a draft of expectations to act as a starting point for conversation and feedback. The team would then ask questions, provide feedback, and suggest items that were left off the list. There was no set number or format for items. We just kept working on it until it felt complete.

Here's an example of a set of expectations I created with one of my teams:

- Do great work. Never settle. If there is a better way, find it.
- When you hit an obstacle you can't get around, move it. If you can't, find someone who can. Asking for help shows strength.
- Take risks. Don't be afraid of mistakes. Learn quickly.
- Be accountable. No excuses.
- Communicate fiercely. Be open. Be honest. Be candid. No pulling punches.
- Make clarity your responsibility. If you aren't clear, keep asking questions until you are.
- No surprises. Good news or bad news should always be old news.
- Assume positive intent.
- Forgive quickly. We don't have time to carry baggage.
- Give and seek feedback often. Feedback is our rocket fuel.
- Work with intention. Know why we do what we do.

There's no magic to this particular set of expectations. It was calibrated to this particular group of people. The magic was in the shared understanding and commitment to it. This list helped to clarify what I expected of them and what they should expect from me and of each other.

Without committing this to writing, there's no way we could have achieved this clarity. No number of meetings can replace the impact of writing down goals and expectations; plus, there's a bonus to doing this. According to some research, simply writing down goals makes you significantly more likely to accomplish them. The concreteness of written content moves the exercise from a right-brain (imaginative, creative) activity only, to a full-brain activation by inducing the logic-based left brain in the process (Morrissey, 2017). While this is true at an individual level, I've also observed it in groups. When a group clarifies a goal together in writing, it aligns the collective efforts towards its achievement.

The bottom line is, if it's important, put it in writing.

Tools and approaches for expectation setting

There are many ways to approach expectation setting; so many, in fact, that it would impossible for me to list them all here. Instead, I'll share some of the more common and interesting practices I've found through my research and work with organizations. As you review these practices, remember that the objective is to reduce uncertainty and bring greater clarity to the employee's relationship with work. It's important to find the right mix of approaches and tools for your organization and culture.

At the heart of clear expectations are well-defined goals and objectives. A goal is simply an articulation of the desired outcomes of our actions. As in sports, the achievement of 'goals' is often how overall success is measured.

S.M.A.R.T. Goals

There are a variety of proven techniques to apply to the creation of goals. One of the most commonly applied is the S.M.A.R.T. goal approach. (Mind Tools Content Team, 2018) When creating goals, this method reminds you that an effective goal meets five criteria:

- S – Specific. The intent of the goal is crystal clear, no ambiguity.
- M – Measurable. It should answer the question, 'How will I know if I succeed?'
- A – Achievable. A goal can stretch your capabilities, but shouldn't feel impossible.
- R – Relevant. The goal should be connected to a bigger objective or aspiration.
- T – Time-bound. There is a time by which the goal should be achieved – a finish line.

The S.M.A.R.T. approach is helpful in the articulation of goals because it reminds us of the elements that help create clarity. Consider the example of the goals below for a customer success coordinator:

Ambiguous Goal: Improve my customer feedback scores.
S.M.A.R.T. Goal: Improve my average weekly customer feedback scores by 10 per cent before 1 July.

Any stated goal is better than no stated goal. But when you consider the difference between these two goals, it's obvious that the second goal removes far more uncertainty about what is specifically expected.

Objectives and key results (OKRs)

In recent years, the OKR approach to goal setting was popularized through Google's use and evangelization of it, although they credit former Intel CEO Andy Grove for its creation (re:Work with Google, 2018a). The advantage espoused for using the OKR approach is that it encourages larger, more aspirational expectations than traditional goal setting alone.

In the OKR approach, objectives tend to be more ambitious and aspirational than a traditional goal. Objectives should feel challenging and represent a stretch of capabilities. They should still be specific in describing the state or endpoint to be achieved, but don't need to meet the same standards of measurability as a S.M.A.R.T. goal.

Staying with the customer success example used above, examples of objectives might be:

- become a world-class customer success coordinator;
- delight every customer, every time.

Both of these objectives are aspirational and feel almost as if they are beyond achievement. According to those who use the OKR approach, the benefit in stretch objectives is that even when an objective is not fully attained, it represents significant achievement. Google's guidance to management is to set objectives at a level where 70 per cent achievement would be a success (re:Work with Google, 2018b). This is a powerful application of the Pygmalion Effect. These objectives communicate to employees that management believes each person and team is capable of more than they might believe is possible themselves.

In the OKR approach, the objectives are paired with approximately three *key results* that represent how progress will be measured. The key results articulate the measurable milestones to be achieved along the path towards achieving the objective. The key results look in many ways like S.M.A.R.T. goals. Keeping with our example, the key results for our customer success coordinator might be:

- achieve an average customer feedback score of 4.25 for Q1;
- achieve an average customer feedback score of 4.5 for Q2;
- achieve an average customer feedback score of 4.75 for Q3.

When they key results are paired with one of the objectives listed above, 'Become a world-class customer service coordinator', this OKR paints a picture of what needs to be accomplished throughout the year. It could feel overwhelming to pursue an objective aimed at becoming 'world class' in your role by itself. Pairing the objective with key results makes it feel manageable and provides clarity on where to start. If key results are created correctly, their achievement propels an individual or team toward meeting its objective.

Rocks and traction

CASE STUDY Rocks at South Dakota State University

Several years ago, leaders of the Facilities and Services Department at South Dakota State University realized they needed a better way to align and set expectations for their nearly 200 employees. Given the fact that this department needed to balance day-to-day objectives like keeping the campus clean and beautiful with large collaborative building projects, ensuring that work was well-planned and coordinated had significant performance implications.

The solution they implemented is based on an approach set forth in Gino Wickman's book, *Traction* (Wickman, 2012). The key element of this approach is the use of an idea called 'Rocks'. Rocks represent priorities (or goals) that must be accomplished in the upcoming quarter. These priorities are set at the department, leader and individual levels.

At SDSU, department leadership holds offsite meetings to calibrate and agree upon their collective Rocks for the upcoming quarter. Each leader brings to this meeting what they see as the Rocks for their area. The team then puts all of these Rocks up on a board in front of the room for all to see. Once the full picture is visible, the leaders participate in a process they call 'keep it or kill it', where they sort and clarify the department priorities.

Items are 'killed' if it's agreed that they don't rise to the level of being a priority for this quarter. This might be because of timing or because the other priorities simply happen to be more important or pressing. It might also be that the goal or project being proposed doesn't have a broad enough impact to be considered a department-level Rock. These might then be considered as a Rock for one of the leaders. Or, it may simply get shelved for possible consideration in the future.

The proposed Rocks that make the 'keep it' cut are then prioritized by the leadership team, putting the most important Rock at the top. Then, a leader is assigned ultimate accountability for each of the prioritized Rocks. This step is seen as critical because while many of the Rocks require broad participation and collaboration across many of the teams in this department (ie preparing campus for Homecoming), one person is responsible for ensuring that everything gets done.

The Rocks are then added to a scorecard which is shared across the department and updated weekly with a red, yellow, or green light depending on progress. The department-level Rock prioritization process and scorecard aligns the efforts of the entire department on what is most important for that quarter. Individual employees also work through a similar process with their manager to clarify their own performance Rocks each quarter.

Rocks, OKRs and S.M.A.R.T. represent three different approaches to achieving clarity with regard to goals. These are just a few approaches of many that you could adapt for your organization. Any one of the goal-setting approaches can be highly effective if it's done with intention and it fits your organization's way of working.

In the next chapter, we'll focus on how to create clarity with regard to how work gets done through behavioural expectations.

Key takeaways

- Clarity of expectations is critical to fostering a positive work experience, but despite its obvious importance, we have not historically done a great job of creating it.

- People will live up or down to your expectations of them. Use them wisely.

- To create greater ownership for the achievement of goals, collaborate with employees in the goal-setting process, allowing for conversation and feedback.

- When it comes to expectations, if it's important, put it in writing.

- There are many processes for effective goals setting including S.M.A.R.T., OKRs, Rocks and others. Find an approach that works best for your organization and commit to its consistent use. This will create greater clarity for employees about what is expected.

References

Li, A and Butler, A (2004) The effects of participation in goal setting and goal rationales on goal commitment: an exploration of justice media-tors, *Journal of Business and Psychology* [Online] http://www.jstor.org/stable/25092885?seq=1#page_scan_tab_contents [Last accessed 29 April 2018]

Mind Tools Content Team (2018) SMART Goals: How to make your goals achievable, *Mind Tools* [Online] https://www.mindtools.com/pages/article/smart-goals.htm [Last accessed 29 April 2018]

Morrissey, M (2017) The power of writing down your goals and dreams, *Huffington Post*, 14 September [Online] https://www.huffingtonpost.com/marymorrissey/the-power-of-writing-down_b_12002348.html [Last accessed 29 April 2018]

Psycholo Genie (2018) Psychology behind the golem effect and consequences of the same. Available from: https://psychologenie.com/psychology-behind-golem-effect [Last accessed 29 April 2018]

Psychology Research and Reference (2018) Recency effect, *Psychology* [Online] http://psychology.iresearchnet.com/social-psychology/decision-making/recency-effect/ [Last accessed 29 April 2018]

re:Work with Google (2018a) Learn the (abridged) history of OKRs, *Google*, [Online] https://rework.withgoogle.com/guides/set-goals-with-okrs/steps/learn-the-abridged-history-of-OKRs/ [Last accessed 29 April 2018]

re:Work with Google (2018b) OKRs and Stretch Goals, *Google*, [Online] https://rework.withgoogle.com/guides/set-goals-with-okrs/steps/understand-moonshots-vs-roofshots/ [Last accessed 29 April 2018]

Rosenthal, R and Jacobson, L (2012) Pygmalion in the classroom, *The Urban Review*, pp. 16–20 [Online] https://www.uni-muenster.de/imperia/md/content/psyifp/aeechterhoff/sommersemester2012/schluesselstudiendersozialpsychologiea/rosenthal_jacobson_pygmalionclassroom_urbrev1968.pdf [Last accessed 29 April 2018]

Wickman, Gino (2012) *Traction: Get a grip on your business*, Benbella Books

Wikipedia contributors (2018) Golem effect, *Wikipedia* [Online] https://en.wikipedia.org/wiki/Golem_effect [Last accessed 29 April 2018]

Defining behavioural expectations

05

Goals are important, but they represent only a part of what is expected of employees each day. The way we go about achieving our goals can, at times, be as (or more) important than the outcome we achieve.

I learned this lesson quickly through my first experiences of the infamous annual performance appraisal. My first corporate job was as a manager of recruiting for a debt collection call centre company with nearly 1,000 employees. Prior to accepting this job, my career had consisted of sales and entrepreneurial roles where I had worked very independently. These prior jobs taught me to be laser focused on results. In sales, it's helpful to have a 'do whatever it takes to close the sale' mindset. The only thing that mattered was closed deals.

I carried this same approach with me into my new corporate job. I had inherited a function that was wildly underperforming, and my job was to fix it as quickly as possible. And I did. Over the course of my first year, I led the transformation of this function. All the metrics that matter to recruiting performance had moved significantly in the right direction. I thought that I was performing exceptionally well.

Then came my performance appraisal. As my boss shared her assessment of my performance with me, the overall rating was much lower than I had expected based on the measurable improvements I'd achieved. She shared that she was pleased with those results and that I was doing a great job in that area. But there was a problem.

As the Manager of Recruiting, I was a part of the HR management team, something I'd honestly paid very little attention to. In my focus on delivering on my goals, I was mostly ignoring the fact that I even had teammates. And this had become an issue for my boss. I learned that my peers had expressed concern that I wasn't investing time in developing relationships with them or being a supportive teammate. The longer I was there, the more my behaviour was creating drama within the team. This was creating a headache for my boss.

While it may seem to you that it should have been obvious that I was part of a team and should have behaved accordingly, at that time in my career, with the experience I'd had in the past, it wasn't obvious to me. I was doing what I thought I was expected to do. My performance on my goals was exceptional, but there were clearly other expectations in play that weren't clear to me until it was too late. I learned through my performance appraisal that my boss expected that we work together and support each other as a team. She also expected us all to get along and exist in harmony with one another without the drama I'd been fuelling through my behaviour.

I was angry about the feedback, mostly because I wasn't aware of it until after the fact. Had the expectations been clear to me, even if I didn't like it, I would have at least had the opportunity to adjust my behaviour accordingly.

These unspoken expectations are harmful to the employee's relationship with work. If something is important enough to affect how my performance is evaluated, it should be explicitly communicated and explained to me. When expectations like these are not shared, it creates uncertainty. And uncertainty is hard on relationships.

In the previous chapter, I shared a list of behavioural expectations that I once created with my team. The process I used to create that list was simple. Reflect and write down my expectations. Share those with the team for feedback, discussion, additions, and negotiation. Revise and review again until the list feels complete. At a team level, a simple exercise like this can create tremendous clarity.

At the organizational level, this same gap in clarity can exist regarding behaviours versus goals. A majority of organizations can clearly communicate their organizational goals and their overall performance is relative to those goals. If the organization has a goal of growing revenue by 25 per cent in the upcoming year, that goal is known to most employees. The CEO talks about it in employee communications. The CFO posts financial results. And for a goal this big, most departments and individuals are likely aware of how their own goals contribute to achieving this bigger goal. Big organizational goals get a lot of attention and air time.

At the same time, many of these same organizations have a mission and values written down or hanging on the wall somewhere that claim to define how the organization goes about pursuing its goals. But while many of the employees could recite the big revenue goal, they are far less likely able to recite the values, much less explain what they mean or specifically how those values should inform their individual behaviour. Clarifying these expectations and connecting the dots between individual behaviours and what the organization values is a powerful way to enhance the work experience for employees.

One organization that has done this exceptionally well is Farm Credit Services of America (FCSAmerica), a 1,700-employee financial services organization that serves farmers and ranchers across the Midwest in the United States. FCSAmerica has propelled itself to exceptional growth over the past decade by creating an award-winning culture and work experience for their employees. FCSAmerica espouses an approach of 'creating culture on purpose'. They have gone to great lengths to intentionally understand and document their culture.

FCSAmerica's culture is communicated most concisely through a set of 'We are' statements:

- We are teammates.
- We are leaders.
- We are adaptable.
- We are innovators.
- We are experts.
- We are values driven.
- We are servants.

Each of these 'we are' statements is supported by a paragraph that explains the deeper intent. Take for example how they further define what it means to be 'servants' at FCSAmerica:

> *We are servants.*
>
> *The farmers and ranchers we serve are the reason we exist. They are also part of our extended family. Every day, we focus our talents, technologies and passions toward serving the people who are feeding the world.*

If you were to read through all of the 'we are' statements, you'd gain a pretty clear picture of the culture at this organization and what it might be like to work there. This kind of clarity is important, but the team at FCSAmerica didn't stop there. They realized that in order to ensure that these pillars of their culture were lived out and reinforced every day, they needed to be translated into specific behaviours. To do this, each statement was translated into four explicit behavioural expectations.

Here are two examples of how they translated 'We are servants' into behavioural performance expectations.

Identifies and anticipates requirements, expectations and needs of others. Continually searches for ways to improve customer and teammate experience (including the removal of barriers and providing solutions).

They have taken the aspirational statement, 'We are servants', and made it clear and tangible in a way that empowers employees to choose their behaviours intentionally to align with the culture. These expectations are then used for coaching conversations and performance feedback discussions at FCSAmerica. The clarity they've created makes it much easier for leaders and employees to engage in meaningful conversations about both performance and growth.

Achieving this kind of clarity is no small undertaking. It's required a significant amount of time and resource investment over many years, but the payoff has been dramatic for FCSAmerica. The organization has grown its assets 300 per cent and net income over 400 per cent in the past 13 years with high employee retention. Impressive results by any standard.

CASE STUDY DirectPath's good to great behaviours

DirectPath, a leader in personalized benefits education and enrollment services and health care transparency, is also taking steps to make behavioural expectations clear and compelling for employees. The leaders at DirectPath embraced from the beginning that their product is dependent upon the quality and engagement of their people. Culture here has always been treated as critical. It seems to be paying off. They have grown 1,000 per cent in the past five years and show no signs of slowing down.

As their growth accelerated, they recognized the need to invest even further in culture by taking the definition of behavioural expectations to the next level. They wanted to ensure that employees had clarity on what was most important in how they pursued their goals each day. To accomplish this, they engaged in a process that resulted in the identification of four 'Potential Factors' they believe were central to performance at DirectPath.

For illustration, one of their four potential factors is '*Genuine*', which they define in this way:

Life moves fast at DirectPath. We don't have time to figure out complex people, so we seek out teammates who are trustworthy, authentic and transparent.

This definition is compelling and aspirational, but not terribly specific or instructional. For example, what exactly does it look like to be authentic or transparent in your work? There are many ways one could interpret that definition. So, they took the step to outline the specific behaviours that reflect what it means to be Genuine at DirectPath. In fact, as fans of Jim Collins' *Good to Great* book and concept, they decided to define the behaviour on two levels: good and great. Below is how they define these levels for Genuine.

Good:

- You are trustworthy. You can treat confidential information as confidential and you don't broker in gossip.

- What we see is what we get. You're authentic and don't change your personality much from meeting to meeting or across conversations with teammates.

- You can be counted on to be transparent at all times, seeking to make sure your teammates have all the information they need to be successful.

Great:

- All items in the good category, plus these additional items.

- You've respectfully stuck to your convictions on work-related matters even if it caused some disagreement.

- You're able to dial the authenticity up and down for the audience in question, remaining genuine while not antagonizing people around you.

These behaviours and those for the other potential factors are used as the basis for ongoing check-ins and coaching between managers and employees. They are also integrated into performance review processes along with their more tangible, quantitative goals.

The DirectPath team believes that the investment it took to create this kind of clarity is critical to maintaining the consistency of their employee experience and, by direct extension, their client satisfaction. This operationalization of behavioural expectations into performance management processes is a key step in supporting their continued and future growth.

What about the employee's expectations?

In conversations about expectations, much of the emphasis is placed on what is expected of the employee by the organization or team. Achieving this clarity is empowering for employees both as they make choices about their behaviour and even before that, deciding if they even want to be on this team in the first place.

But we must also remember that employees are individual, unique human beings who each bring with them a set of expectations for how they expect and want to be treated. Each individual has preferences for how they like to work, what kind of communication works best, and the approach to feedback that works best for them. While many people may not be aware of exactly what works best for them, if you ask them, they can likely give you a list of what doesn't work.

It's nearly impossible to treat someone in the way they ideally want to be treated without some inside information from them about their expectations. And yet, we tend not to take steps to clarify and document these expectations individually for the benefit of our peers and supervisors. Instead, we leave this process to trial and error based on our interactions with others, hoping we slowly come to understand how to work better together over time.

Personality assessments

One way to close this gap is through the use of personality, work style and strengths assessments. These tools are valuable for a variety of reasons. First, an assessment can reveal things about an individual's style and preferences that they may not even be aware of or able to articulate in a helpful way. For example, your assessment may reveal that you have an intense drive related to pace, meaning you are naturally low in patience. This could help you realize why you get frustrated with long meetings or any type of communication that isn't fast-paced.

These assessments also provide valuable insight and guidance for how to work more effectively together. An objective assessment of your natural behavioural and personality drives can foster an understanding of stylistic differences that may diffuse some potential conflicts and make it easier to work together with others. If your manager or teammates know you are naturally low in patience, they are more likely to forgive you when you get frustrated with how long something is taking. They would also know when communicating with you one on one to get to the point quickly if they want to keep you engaged.

As another benefit, if you know that you are naturally driven by a faster pace and have a low level of patience, you can be more aware of how this influences your approach with others. If you need to work on a project with someone who is more comfortable working at a more deliberate, consistent pace of work, the two of you could talk about your varied styles and identify ways to mitigate the tension it might create.

There are literally hundreds of assessment tools on the market today. It's less important which tool you use than how you use it. Make sure you understand what the tool measures and how to use it. From there, the key is to apply it in a way that facilitates improved self-awareness of personal styles and preferences. This will create a foundation on which employees can more clearly understand and articulate their own expectations about how they'd like to be treated at work.

Individual user manual

An approach that seems to be gaining momentum recently is to create a personal 'user manual' to be shared with others you work with as a way to help them understand you and how you work best (Kessler, 2017). It's an ingenious idea when you consider it. We expect a user manual for nearly everything we interact with in our life that's complicated and hard to understand at first – our smartphones, cars, appliances, etc. A good user manual quickly and easily helps us understand how to have the best experience possible with this device or vehicle.

As humans, we are far more complicated and difficult to understand than any of these things. That alone seems to warrant the creation of a user manual. By creating clarity for others of our individual needs, quirks, and preferences, we could make it significantly easier for others to engage with us and vice versa.

Aaron Hurst, CEO of the 'purpose activation' technology company, Imperative, is among the leaders who have adopted the user manual approach. He originally wrote his own user manual when serving as the President of the Taproot Foundation, a non-profit that helps mobilize professionals to offer pro bono services to other non-profit organizations. He describes that he originally undertook writing his own user manual to help his employees understand his 'flavour of craziness'. He wanted to make it easier for his staff to work with him. It worked. The exercise was so successful that they adopted the practice for all employees and he even published his own user manual on LinkedIn as a template for others to learn from (Hurst, 2013).

The idea of the user manual is to help others understand what is most important about working with you, particularly those things like preferences that are difficult or impossible to know without being told. There is no single best template or format for a user manual. For Hurst, these are the questions that should be answered in a user manual (Imperative, 2017):

- What is your style?
- When do you like people to approach you and how?
- What do you value?
- How do you like people to communicate with you?
- How do you make decisions?
- How can people help you?
- What will you not tolerate in others?

These questions lean a bit more toward leadership and management behaviours and maybe aren't as relevant to everyone, depending on the nature of the work being done. Use those that fit and not those that don't.

Other questions you might want to consider:

- What do I love to talk about that's not work?
- What makes me feel the most appreciated?
- What do people usually misunderstand about me?

The best way to determine what should be included for your team is to ask them. What do they want to know or wish they knew about each other? Using their feedback will ensure you create a template of questions that have the most impact for your team.

Equipped with the template, it's now a matter of getting employees to thoughtfully complete their user manual and then share it with others. Based on my experience, it's best to share the assignment with the group in a team meeting where everyone can hear it and ask questions about it together. Then, provide some time for people to reflect and work on it individually.

If your team has used personality or other assessments as described earlier in the chapter, that information can be a great resource in completing this exercise. Once written, the next step is to share and socialize. The goal of the user manual is to help others understand how to work best with you, so sharing is a critical step. Some teams might share and discuss them as a group. Others might decide to do it one on one. Either can be effective if it's done in a spirit of understanding and collaboration.

Key takeaways

- Unspoken expectations are harmful to the employee's relationship with work. If something is important enough to affect how performance is evaluated, it should be explicitly communicated and explained as an expectation.

- Creating clarity of behavioural expectations can happen in a variety of ways. Putting values up on a wall isn't enough. Values are often aspirational and vague. They must be defined to the level of individual behaviours that demonstrate each value in action.

- Behavioural expectations go in two directions: the employer's expectations of the employee and the employee's expectation of how they'd like to be treated at work.

- Two ways to create greater clarity of individual employee expectations of work are through personality (and other behavioural) assessments and the creation of an 'individual user manual'.

References

Collins, J (2001) *Good to Great: Why some companies make the leap and other don't*, HarperBusiness

Hurst, A (2013) Do you have a user manual? *LinkedIn*, 28 January [Online] https://www.linkedin.com/pulse/20130128234025-201849-do-you-have-a-user-manual/ [Last accessed 30 April 2018]

Imperative (2017) Creating your personal user manual, *Imperative* [Online] http://blog.imperative.com/post/87802616741/creating-your-personal-user-manual?lipi=urn%3Ali%3Apage%3Ad_flagship3_pulse_read%3B%2BJ42ZL MqQ%2Fahv522FE4leQ%3D%3D [Last accessed 30 April 2018]

Kessler, S (2017) Writing guides to our work styles helped my team bond, *Quartz*, 29 December [Online] https://qz.com/1168218/management-exercise-creating-user-manuals-helped-our-team-understand-one-another/?mc_cid=3b5967a681& mc_eid=ff668b618c [Last accessed 30 April 2018]

Putting the 'why' and 'how' in expectations

06

Another element of performance planning is helping individuals to find meaning and purpose in what they are being asked to achieve. If we think of expectations and goals as mapping out the performance journey, then this step is about clarifying why you are taking the trip in the first place.

Attaching meaning and purpose to a goal can make a dramatic difference both to how you feel about the goal and how motivated you are to achieve it. Consider the difference between making a long gruelling trip to visit someone you love versus making the same gruelling trip for work without understanding why it's even necessary. Same trip, but your experience of and feelings about the trip are completely different because of its purpose.

Contribution to organizational success

Connecting goals to a purpose can happen in a variety of ways. What most easily comes to mind is to put goals in context of contribution to organizational goals and mission. Employee engagement surveys have long included questions that measure the degree to which an employee understands how their job contributes to the organization's success. The implication being that if we know why our work matters to the bigger picture, we will feel more fulfilled and motivated in doing it. Feeling like our efforts don't matter is highly disengaging, regardless of the type of work.

While this is probably the easiest path to connecting an individual's goals to some sense of purpose, it also comes with a caveat. For this approach to be effective, the larger objective or goal of the organization to which the individual's goals are being anchored must be something the employee feels is meaningful. As an individual, helping me understand how my goals contribute to a larger goal I don't care about does nothing to attach a sense of purpose to that goal. It may actually make the goal feel even less purposeful.

World and community impact

Another way to connect goals to purpose is by communicating an organizational purpose connected to having a broader impact on the world. It feels good to be a part of an organization that's contributing in a positive way to the community or the world around it. When my employer is having that impact, I feel that I am part of making that impact possible.

Some organizations like TOMS Shoes and Warby Parker have created a business model that very tangibly and directly connects business success with making an impact on the world. In both cases, when a customer purchases a product from either company, it immediately pays forward to someone in need of help somewhere around the world. Buy a pair of shoes and someone in need gets a pair of shoes. Buy a pair of eyeglasses and someone in need gets one too. Regardless of where you work within those organizations or what your goals are, it's not hard to understand how the achievement of your goals is having a true impact on the world.

This model doesn't work for everyone. And to cast a broader purpose doesn't require a change in business model. In some cases, it's a matter of understanding what kind of impact your organization can have and creating some intention around that. For several years of my corporate career, I worked for debt collection companies. As you might imagine, on top of the fact that debt collection is really challenging work that often feels thankless, there's a serious social stigma attached to being a debt collector.

The CEO of the company had deeply rooted beliefs about the importance of this work and how we did it. He shared and communicated regularly his conviction that debt collectors helped keep the economy healthy. He also believed that while people didn't look forward to talking to collectors, when we treated debtors with dignity and helped them to pay their debts, we were helping them improve their lives as well. When we could help a new collector see their work through this lens, it changed both how they approached their work and how they felt about it.

In these cases, the purpose or 'why' behind the goals is found externally to the organization by articulating or creating a positive impact. While this can be a powerful strategy, other organizations are focusing their efforts on helping individuals connect their work to what's most important to the employee individually.

Personal values alignment

The Motley Fool, a financial and investment information company mentioned in Chapter 3, is committed to creating a work experience for their growing workforce to support their commitment to an 'employees for life' mantra. They intend for employees to come to work at the organization and never want to leave. To accomplish this, they have several tenets about work. At the top of the list is that people come to work to connect to a purpose they believe in.

If you visit the company's publicly published and lauded employee handbook at thefoolrules.com, within the first few pages you will find a page that shares and explains the company's purpose: 'To Help The World Invest – Better'. This is a good example of a clearly articulated, compelling purpose. But it's what you find on the following page that's more interesting.

The page lists out the company's core values. Among them is 'Motley – Make Foolishness your own!' The core value 'Motley' is actually meant to represent the most important core value of the individual. The company is explicitly communicating to employees that, at its core, it values whatever is most important to each employee with the same commitment as the company's other values. Each employee at the company is asked to develop and articulate their 'Motley' as a way to ensure that their work remains connected to and supportive of what they value most, regardless of whether that value is Connection or Exploration.

CASE STUDY Personal values at Ansarada

Ansarada, an Australia-based technology company, also believes that there's real power in connecting work with the employee's personal values. As a rapidly growing technology firm with 200 employees and counting, creating a culture that people want to be a part of and one that helps them perform at their best is a top priority. From the first day, Ansarada's founders believed that the organization existed for more than just profits. They were always committed to creating a great workplace where people can grow and develop themselves personally and professionally.

To accomplish this, they adopted a servant-leader philosophy for all people managers. The primary role of the leader is to serve their people and to help them succeed. To succeed, they found that this requires a solid foundation of trust in the relationship and an informed knowledge of what's truly important to the employee. They have found that when you can help an employee align their personal and professional goals with what they value the most, it amplifies the potential in that person.

They introduced a process by which managers and employees can discover and share their top five personal values. Graham Moody, People and Culture Manager, explained that during the onboarding process, once the manager feels a baseline level of trust exists, the values exercise is introduced to the employee. In addition to sharing the invitation with the employee to participate in the process, the manager shares with the employee their own values and the stories behind why they are important. This step, 'the leader goes first', is critical to establishing vulnerability-based trust with the employee and setting the example to demonstrate the importance of the process.

The actual exercise is called a 'values card exercise'. The individual is given a deck of cards, each with a different value and definition on it. The first task is to sort the deck into two piles, one for those that the employee feels are important and one for the rest. Then, the challenge is to take the important pile of cards and narrow it down to the 10 they feel are most important to them. The last step is to take those 10 cards and narrow them down to their five most important values.

On the surface, the process sounds simple. Moody shared that for some people the process is incredibly challenging and sometimes emotional because values can run pretty deep and be connected to emotional moments in their lives. This is why employees aren't forced to complete or share this exercise. They are invited to do it. And the employees decide when they are ready to share and discuss the outcomes. If they aren't willing to participate or share, it's viewed as a signal that more trust building is still needed to make the process feel safe.

Managers have been trained on this process to ensure they use it in a positive way to build their relationship with the employee.

Once personal values have been identified and shared, it makes the process of aligning both goals and work experience with meaning much more tangible. For example, managers are trained to ask employees periodically, 'When am I at my best in the context of your values?' and 'When am I at my worst?'. These questions often lead to rich conversations that create alignment and reduce gaps between the employees' work and their values. Through this alignment, they believe that they foster high engagement and commitment that leads to great performance.

When thinking about how to help employees connect their work to purpose, it's wise to consider multiple approaches. Each individual is motivated differently, so offering a variety of opportunities can be powerful. To excel at this, it's wise to follow the lead of The Motley Fool and Ansarada, who recognize that they have to understand what the employee values most in order to ensure that it's included in their work. When both the organization and the employee are clear about their purpose, aligning becomes much easier.

Equipping employees with the resources to succeed

The last element of performance planning is to consider what resources are needed to support success. To continue with my earlier example of taking a trip, if clear expectations are the map and connecting it to meaning is the reason for the trip, this step is about preparation and determining what you need to pack for the trip.

Addressing the necessary resources can be a relatively simple process when expectations are clear. The most common and effective tool for identifying what's needed for this performance journey is a structured conversation using a few key questions. This conversation can happen between the employee and their manager or as a team, depending on the nature of the expectations.

What obstacles should we anticipate facing?

Start by calling out and making visible those things that are real or perceived obstacles. When you set challenging goals, the reasons they feel challenging have a lot to do with the obstacles you expect to face. Obstacles can take on many forms and can show up as large or small. Examples can range from relatively simple obstacles like competing priorities or a feeling of insufficient time, to more complex ones like economic slowdowns or changes in the political landscape.

Once you've identified the obstacles you consider to be real, discuss both how likely and how disruptive you expect those obstacles to be. For those that you deem most significant, you must decide what to do about them. Can the obstacle be removed or avoided? If not, how can you minimize its impact by taking action now?

Whose support will be critical to success?

In today's working world, a very small percentage of work is done truly independently. Our success is increasingly intertwined with others. Successfully meeting expectations will depend on the support, collaboration and cooperation of other people. By identifying those people up front, you can engage them in a conversation about how you can best work together. And, if you anticipate that you will need support from someone in the future, you can start investing in that relationship in advance to increase the likelihood of gaining their support when you need it.

What will you need to know or learn this year?

In the pursuit of both personal and professional goals that stretch us, we are almost always challenged to learn new things or find new information that we hadn't needed in the past. As you consider the expectations that have been set, where will learning or growth be most needed? This conversation can reveal several kinds of learning needs:

- Training: will a new skill or expertise be needed (ie learning a new product or discipline)?
- Coaching: will new behaviours be needed (ie learning to provide supervision to others)?
- Mentoring: will I have to up my game (ie presenting to higher-level executives or more sophisticated customers)?
- Networking: are there people I will want to know (ie external peers or experts) or who can teach me things I can learn internally?

These are important questions to consider to ensure that a plan is in place to provide the employee with the know-how to succeed. The bigger the goal, the more likely the individual or team will need some significant learning to prepare them to make it happen.

What resources will we need that you don't already have?

Much like the previous question, this one is a check-in to explore if there are any tangible resources missing that could become a barrier to achieving success. Several years ago, a marketing coordinator on my team had proposed an idea to create and launch a newsletter for our customers as a way to support our team goals. It was a good idea. We set some goals for what success of this new newsletter would look like and gave her the green light to proceed.

As she dove into the work of actually launching it, she realized that she lacked the graphic design tool she'd need to create a quality newsletter. In her view, this was a critical piece of the project because the tools she currently had available to her were not sufficient. Choosing not to get her a better tool would certainly have hampered her ability to achieve the goals of the newsletter. And it would have left her feeling frustrated about this new project instead of excited about the opportunity. So we found and purchased for her the resource she needed.

This particular question is simple but incredibly powerful. If you've ever been in a situation at work where you lacked a tool you needed to do your job, you know how frustrating it can be. When we have everything we need, we don't even think about resources. We can focus on the quality and impact of our efforts. When we lack essential tools or resources, it can become the main thing we focus on. That is never good for performance.

This shouldn't be interpreted as 'give employees anything they ask for', but rather as ensuring that they aren't legitimately hindered by the lack of any critical tools. There will be things identified that aren't hindering performance but might enhance it or simply help the employee feel happier doing the work (ie a new laptop). In those cases, you can talk it through and decide if the positive benefit is worth the investment.

While it's important to have the conversation about these questions when goals and expectations are being set, it's equally important that they continue throughout the year. The circumstances that exist when goals are set can change quickly. New obstacles arise that couldn't be anticipated which give rise to new learning, support or resource needs. By incorporating these questions in to regular one-on-one check-ins throughout the year, you can be sure that you will overcome these obstacles successfully.

Key takeaways

- Attaching meaning and purpose to a goal can make a dramatic difference both to how you feel about the goal and how motivated you are to achieve it.

- Helping employees feel a sense of purpose for their goals can be accomplished in several ways including aligning individual goals to organizational objectives. Another method is to create or highlight ways that the organization has a positive impact on the community or world around it.

- Another way to add purpose to goals is by discovering what is most important to employees and what they value, then helping them find linkage between these things and the achievement of goals at work.

- With clear and purposeful expectations in place, the next important step is to ensure that the employee or team has everything they need to succeed. This is accomplished through structured conversations that explore the potential obstacles, learning needs, resources, and support needed so that gaps can be discussed and addressed.

SECTION 3
Performance cultivation

Growing up in a farming community, you get put to work at a pretty early age. Neighbours and friends always had work that even someone as young as 11 or 12 years old could do. When I was that age, I had my first experience of work doing something call 'picking rocks'. It was the simplest of the farm jobs and literally involved riding around on a trailer pulled by a tractor through a field and picking up any rocks we saw. Not exciting work, but it was motivating at that age to go home with some cash in my pocket.

Eventually, I grew into some of the more interesting jobs. The one I remember most clearly was a task called 'walking beans'. Before soybean plants were being genetically modified to be resistant to herbicides to make it easy to kill invasive weeds, those weeds had to be dealt with directly. If weeds were allowed to grow unchecked in a field, they would choke out the bean plants and have a catastrophic impact on the quality of the farmer's harvest.

One approach to dealing with the weeds was to literally take on the weeds, one by one. It sounds crazy now, but we would carry either garden hoes or corn knives (think machete) and walk back and forth across large fields cutting out the weeds one at a time. It was gruelling, boring work but it had to be done to give each soybean plant the best opportunity to grow fully and produce its maximum yield of beans.

Farmers go to great lengths to create the best possible conditions for their crops to thrive. As I referenced in Chapter 3, in farming this is called cultivation. Farmers cultivate the growth of their crops in a variety of ways. Removing or combatting weeds is one important step, but there are many others.

Farmers prepare the ground in different ways depending upon the crop they are planting. They often add to the soil the nutrients and fertilizers that are most required by the crop being planted there. Depending upon the climate or location of the field, they might have irrigation systems to ensure there's enough water. Other times, they will bury tile under the field to drain water away. And, beyond fighting weeds, they also have to combat insects who eat and destroy crops.

Cultivation in farming is about using deep knowledge of the plants to affect every controllable factor to create optimal growth conditions for that crop. Successful cultivation is proactive and involves taking action informed not only by knowledge of the plant but also of the surrounding environment and external conditions.

As I alluded to earlier in the book, I think there are some powerful lessons we can learn from farming about how to create a more nourishing and fulfilling employee experience for the people we employ. While humans are infinitely more complex than plants of any kind, the mindset and approach of cultivation is just as relevant to human growth as it is to crops.

The cultivation mindset

When we break it down, there are several lessons we can learn and apply from how farmers approach cultivation.

Knowledge of what impacts and hinders growth. The farmer invests in having a deep knowledge of their crops and what most affects growth and performance. As a leader or manager, we should be equally invested in gaining a deep understanding of human beings and what affects their growth and performance. Over the past few decades, the fields of psychology, sociology, behavioural economics and, increasingly, neuroscience have revealed powerful insights about human nature and motivation that should inform our decisions about work. Humans have core needs that, when left unsatisfied, can dramatically hamper their capacity for performance.

Growth and performance are the default. Since farmers are working with plants, they can operate with perfect confidence that when they put a seed in soil, it will grow unless something interferes. Plants are genetically programmed for growth. The farmer never questions this. As a result, when plants don't grow or are struggling, they know it's because a need isn't being met or a barrier is present. This way of thinking can be applied to humans as well.

If you have children or have been around many, you know that growth is natural to them. They are curious and absorb information without any prompting. Schools are designed around this assumption that children are naturally designed for learning. In my experience, people are also naturally motivated for performance. I've never met someone who, given the choice, wouldn't choose succeeding over failing. Adopting a mindset of cultivation means that we choose to view humans in the way that farmers view their crops. Growth and performance is the default mode. When it's not happening, it's should be viewed as a failure on the part of the leader or organization, not the person.

Removing barriers and meeting needs is the work of management. The farmer serves the needs of the plant. If the ground is dry and the rains aren't coming, they irrigate to provide the needed water. They don't waste energy arguing over whether they 'should have to' irrigate or lamenting about why the plants need water, they just do whatever is within their control to get the crop some water. If they don't, the performance of the crops will suffer and harvest will fall short of expectations.

If we are to cultivate performance with humans, we need to adopt the same mindset. Our work is to ensure that the motivating needs of each person are met so that they can perform to their full potential. Some people will need more communication than others. Some will need more encouragement or instruction than others. If we are to optimize performance, our opinions about what any given employee 'should need' is irrelevant. When we leave needs unsatisfied or obstacles unaddressed, it's like failing to get water to the crops. Performance will suffer. And that's on us, not the employee.

Cultivation is ongoing and adaptive. As plants grow and mature, their needs change and evolve. The farmer adjusts their approach as the plants progress through their life cycle. Fighting weeds is very important early on, but less so as the plants are fully grown. In the same way, adopting a mindset of cultivation at work requires understanding and regularly monitoring growth and development. What an individual needs as a new employee is different than when they've been around for five years. In the same way, the needs of someone early in their career is different than later and also in different types of roles. Cultivation of growth and performance requires that we be attentive to each individual's evolving needs. This requires ongoing conversations and check-ins throughout the employee's career to understand and adapt to their evolution.

In my experience, cultivation is the missing piece in most performance management processes. Cultivation, at its essence, is about creating the employee experience that meets those core human and relationship needs to unlock their full potential. As in farming, there are several dimensions to cultivating human performance.

Figure 5   Performance cultivation processes

In the following chapters, we'll explore the key dimensions of cultivation: motivation, obstacle removal, recognition, wellbeing, and inclusion. For each, we'll explore why it's important and share processes and approaches from successful organizations to illustrate how it happens in practice.

Motivation 07

Perhaps the most complex element of performance management is motivation. Motivation is simply our desire to do things. Without motivation, even the clearest expectations will have little impact. We know from personal experience that setting a goal like getting a new job or running a marathon is hollow without a drive to do the real (often hard) work to achieve it. Effectively managing performance requires an understanding of how humans are motivated in order to move them to action towards the achievement of their goals.

Psychology tells us that we have two sources of motivation: intrinsic and extrinsic (Ryan and Deci, 2000). Richard Ryan and Edward Deci at the University of Rochester provide these definitions.

- **Intrinsic motivation** is defined as 'the doing of an activity for its inherent satisfactions rather than for some separable consequence. When intrinsically motivated, a person is moved to act for the fun or challenge entailed rather than because of external prods, pressures, or rewards.'

- **Extrinsic motivation**, on the other hand, is 'a construct that pertains whenever an activity is done in order to attain some separable outcome.' For example, an extrinsic motivator could be the promise of a financial reward, developmental opportunity or promotion upon completion of a work task or project. (Ryan and Deci, 2000)

Organizations have historically focused on motivating employees by using extrinsic motivations such as merit increases, financial bonuses, and other 'earned' incentives. Even a performance rating falls in this category since it is used traditionally to inform compensation decisions. This legacy of extrinsic motivators makes sense given the historical context we explored in Chapter 1. For decades, it was assumed that workers were inherently lazy and required external intervention to get work done. Given this mindset, offering up external rewards in exchange for task completion makes perfect sense. Intrinsic motivation wasn't even a consideration.

In recent years, many have begun to argue that the key to sustaining higher levels of employee performance is to help them find intrinsic motivation associated with their work. Intrinsic motivation occurs when we find personal satisfaction or value from the work itself, independent of any promise of reward or threat of punishment.

Author Dan Pink researched and wrote about this shift in his influential book, *Drive: The surprising truth about what motivates us*. Pink presents what he discovered by reviewing decades of research about human motivation.

According to Pink's research, humans have a complicated relationship with extrinsic financial rewards, including our salary level and incentive compensation like bonuses. The research reveals that offering a financial bonus as an incentive to increase performance works effectively when the work is rote, routine, or mechanical, such as you might find in a traditional manufacturing facility. But when the work requires problem-solving or creative skills (as most jobs do in our current economy), these same incentives actually have the opposite effect. For example, offering up a big bonus in exchange for more creative ideas tends to produce more stress than it does positive results. Trying to coerce creativity is a losing battle.

To better understand the relationship of pay to motivation, we can turn to the research of psychologist Frederick Herzberg during the 1950s and '60s. Herzberg was interested in understanding the impact of attitude on employee motivation and satisfaction. He interviewed employees and asked them to describe times when they felt really good about their jobs and times when they felt bad.

He concluded that there were two very different sets of factors driving the two different experiences. In his view, there were 'motivating factors' that were drivers of satisfaction at work, and then there were 'hygiene factors', which mitigated dissatisfaction at work. Herzberg viewed hygiene factors as extrinsic. These included things like company policies, working conditions, compensation, and job security. All things that when absent or insufficient can create dissatisfaction but when effective, aren't necessarily motivating. Motivating factors, on the other hand, are intrinsic and Herzberg viewed them as central to motivation. This included things like achievement, responsibility and recognition.

In this model, the opposite of satisfaction is not dissatisfaction but rather no satisfaction, the absence of satisfaction. The same was true for dissatisfaction. The implication to leaders and organizations is that creating satisfaction and reducing dissatisfaction are actually two separate bodies of work. Reducing dissatisfaction, in many cases, does not produce satisfaction or motivation.

Herzberg concluded that salary was a hygiene factor. In his model, this would suggest that salary, when perceived as insufficient, could be a dissatisfier for the employee that could decrease motivation and attitude at work. Alternatively, when salary and compensation is working well, it will achieve an absence of dissatisfaction, but not result in satisfaction or motivation (Mind Tools Content Team, 2018). This is what Dan Pink was echoing in his book.

The takeaway from this research is that compensation is important to motivation, but probably not in the way you once thought. People should be paid enough to take money off the table as a primary concern, to eliminate any dissatisfaction with pay. Once you do this, offering more money won't produce greater motivation. Instead, it is intrinsic motivators that are the key to unlocking higher performance.

Intrinsic motivators

In his book, Pink outlines three specific motivators that research points to as most important: mastery, autonomy and purpose. Additional research from Kenneth Thomas reinforces these and adds a fourth: progress (Thomas, 2009).

1 *Mastery* is the desire to improve our skills and competence in areas that are important to us. Mastery requires that we have the ongoing opportunity to learn, grow and find challenge in our work.

2 *Autonomy* is the desire to be self-directed and have choice in how our work gets done. Autonomy requires the opposite of micromanagement by providing people with the freedom to make decisions related to how their work gets done.

3 *Purpose* is the desire to do work that has greater meaning and a broader impact than simple task completion. Purpose can come in a variety of ways, from a dynamic company vision to a philanthropic mission. The key is that each employee has visibility to how their work has meaning and impact beyond themselves to those around them.

4 *Progress* is the desire to move forward toward an improved future or realization of your individual purpose. We achieve a sense of progress when we achieve meaningful milestones, recognize personal growth, or help our team succeed.

If you reflect on your own career, it's likely that you can identify when these factors were present for you and when they weren't. During my tenure in my first corporate job, I remember a stretch of about 18 months when I felt like

I was on fire professionally. We had gained approval from the executive team to execute a culture branding project. The project felt like my baby and my boss trusted me enough to let me largely run with it on my own as part of a team with some colleagues in marketing and communication (autonomy).

Through the project, we were blazing new trails and I felt like I had to learn new stuff every day, just to keep up with the work we needed to get done (mastery). The energy around this project was incredibly high because if done right, it could have a huge impact on our employees, prospective employees and customers (purpose). And, since it was an organic, discovery-based process, there were many checkpoints along the way where we were getting validation from our employees and executives that we were on the right path (progress). To this day, I still get a small jolt of energy and motivation when I think about that work. In hindsight, it's obvious why the project was so motivating, since it delivered on all four of these motivating factors.

As I profiled organizations during research for this book, it was common to find these factors woven into their practices and thinking. In many cases, they might not have called these factors out explicitly or intentionally, but they clearly understood their importance.

Mastery

At The Motley Fool, one of their beliefs is that they are hiring people for life. This sounded unbelievable when Lee Burbage, Chief People Officer for the organization, said it in our interview. But I came to realize that this was a very real intention that drove how they architected the work experience for employees there. They recognize that to keep people for the long run, work has to be incredibly motivating and meaningful.

To accomplish this they have articulated four core 'tenets' about work that they use to create their work experience. These tenets describe why they believe people are motivated to come to work each day.

The Motley Fool Tenets

1 A purpose they believe in.

2 A challenge every day.

3 To work with people they love.

4 Autonomy.

It should come as no surprise that they are fans of and believers in the research of Dan Pink, as described earlier, since mastery, autonomy, and purpose are all central parts of their tenets, along with commitment to the importance of relationships.

Burbage shared how they operate with a perpetual nagging thought that everyone in the company is in the wrong job or is under-utilized. This creates a sense of urgency within the organization to be constantly thinking about development and growth. One way this plays out is that the organization is a project-based culture. They were early adopters of the Agile method, and this has led to a method of organizing work where an employee might be working on five or six different projects at any one time. Projects end and begin frequently, so employees are constantly challenged with new opportunities to learn and build mastery.

To further cultivate a motivating work experience, they employ a team of internal coaches whose role is to meet with employees throughout the year to help them clarify individual goals and aspirations and then build plans for how to achieve them. These coaches take on this role voluntarily in addition to their regular role as a way to support and build the culture. Coaches can also identify obstacles or barriers that need to be confronted or removed and can help to make that happen.

Autonomy

Autonomy is an increasingly important ingredient as technology has made work more portable than ever before. In the past, autonomy would have been largely focused on having influence over 'how' the work got done. In today's environment, autonomy has taken on a much broader meaning. Not only might employees expect autonomy in how work gets done, but also where and when.

At employee benefits consulting firm, SIG, they have adopted ROWE (Results Only Work Environment) as a way to create autonomy for their employees. This management approach was created by Cari Ressler and Jody Thompson in 2003 (GoROWE, 2016). At SIG, ROWE means that the employees can work when and where they want, as long as their work gets done. This creates the freedom for employees to shape their workday around what works best for them.

Ironically, moving to ROWE has actually made coming to the office more attractive for many employees at SIG. This autonomy for employees puts a heightened focus on making the work environment at the office a place where employees want to come. Plus, when employees do work from the office, it's because they've chosen to be there, not because they have to. Both of these factors have contributed to further reinforcing the positive work environment facilitated by the company's CEO, Richard Silberstein.

Technology firm, Hudl.com, recently opened the doors on a new headquarters location in Lincoln, Nebraska. Since Hudl is in the business of sports, the office is impressively sports-themed throughout, down to the detail that each employee has their own locker (just like those you might find in a locker room, absent the pungent odours). But that's not what makes this new office location notable. Hudl doesn't have a policy dictating where you should work. Instead, there's a general expectation in place that you should work where and how you can be most productive.

What stands out about Hudl's offices is the variety of space available. Hudl employees don't have assigned workspaces, they simply have a locker in which to store the things they bring or keep at the office. Each day, when employees come into the office, they can find a space that best suits their needs that day. There are open, collaborative spaces with tables and chairs. There are smaller areas with desks. There are small and large conference rooms. There is space that feels like a coffee shop and another like a sports bar. There's a cafeteria. Whatever kind of space you are needing, it probably exists here. Hudl has created a dynamic workplace where you can find whatever space you need. But if you just need to be away, you can do that too.

Autonomy is increasingly taking the form of flexibility. This is particularly true for the small accounting services firm, Patke and Associates, who designed their entire culture around creating maximum flexibility for its employees. To both attract and retain talent as a small firm, they recognized that they needed to differentiate the work experience. One way they could do that was through flexible work arrangements.

At Patke and Associates, most employees work from home in various places across the United States. As with SIG, employees have tremendous freedom to decide when and where they do their work. Accomplishing this flexibility, however, wasn't simply about changing a policy or expectation. The type of work and clients that Patke and Associates serves require responsiveness and a sense of urgency in follow-up. To create the desired flexibility, ironically, the creation of some structure was essential to ensure that quality of work and responsiveness didn't suffer.

For starters, each employee understands that they are required to work a minimum number of hours per week. They can make decisions about when they work those hours, but they must all be tracked and reported on a weekly report (a standard practice within this industry). Beyond that, they learned that they needed to set a standard expectation for responsiveness to both customer and internal communication. They ultimately agreed to a specified time within which both e-mails and phone calls should be returned. In addition, they have formal processes in place to audit work for quality, which creates an accountability to not only get work done, but to do it right. While this kind of structure might not feel necessary within your organization, it makes sense for the team at Patke. They see it as a small trade-off to make in exchange for the autonomy they enjoy. The lesson to take from this is that most organizations can create greater autonomy for their employees but how it works will likely be very different from one organization to the next.

Purpose

Earlier in the book, we reviewed the role that purpose can play in expectation setting. Purpose is, perhaps, the most powerful of the intrinsic motivators. When we know how a goal matters in something that matters to us; the goal is more meaningful. And, as a result, we are more driven to achieve it. This is the power of purpose.

CASE STUDY Antis Roofing's journey to purpose

Purpose can motivate us on a variety of levels. This is made incredibly clear through the story of Charles Antis and his company, Antis Roofing. Charles Antis is a leader who radiates purpose. But, by his own admission, it wasn't always that way. He started his roofing business in southern California in 1989, and recalls his first realization of the importance of purpose to his business from the early days.

As someone trying desperately to keep his business afloat and growing, every phone call that came in as a lead needed to be converted into a new customer. On one particular morning, the phone rang and on the other end was a woman inquiring about a roof repair. Charles eagerly took down the address of the house and agreed to come out to give it a look. Another potential new customer to serve.

It wasn't until he arrived at the address to find what he can only describe as a 'shack', that he realized that this wasn't at all what he'd had in mind. His first thought was to immediately turn around and leave, but he had promised this woman he'd come out. So, he knocked on the door. When it opened, a thick smell of mildew struck his nostrils and he was again overcome by the urge to get out of there. But, as he was about to say that he probably couldn't help and leave, a five-year-old little girl appeared beside him with a bright smile and took his hand. She was excited to show this visitor around her home. So she led him into the house.

She led him through the living room and down a crowded hallway. She was most excited to show Charles her room. Upon stepping into the small bedroom, he noticed the mildew smell had intensified. On the floor lay four mildew-covered mattresses where this little girl and her siblings were sleeping. It was at that moment, looking at this little girl and her mother, knowing that they were in pain, that Charles knew what he had to do. He was going to help.

So, he climbed up on the roof to look it over. It was beyond repair. It had to be replaced. And, he was going to figure out how to do it for free because it was the right thing to do. The following weekend, because he didn't have any employees yet, he rounded up seven volunteers and they put a donated roof on that house so that little girl and her family didn't have to continue living in an unhealthy and unsafe home.

This moment changed Charles's life and his perspective on business. While he didn't realize it at the time, it was the first time he had put people before profit. This would ultimately become a guiding principle for how he would build his business. He committed that at his company, 'we could never let someone have a leaky roof just because they didn't have the money to pay'. Over the past several decades this has led to innumerable donated roof repairs and replacements, including donating every roof for all homes built in their area by Habitat for Humanity, a non-profit house-building organization, since 2009. The company donated the equivalent of over 5 per cent of total revenue in 2017 while growing the business by over 70 per cent in a single year.

On the surface, it would seem that a company that is so committed to a purpose of helping the community and individual people would surely be incredibly engaging and motivating to employees. And for some that is true, but Charles discovered along the way that it was actually demotivating to some employees. Since most of the donations being made by the company were either roof replacements or repairs, that had downstream impact with the company on those who had to do the actual work. A donated roof might feel great for the person who gets to give it away, but it simply feels like more work to the teams who have to do the work. As a result, there was some tension within the company over the value of these donated projects.

To compound that tension, much of the money being spent by the company was external, to both attract and entertain customers. In hindsight, Charles realized that his priorities weren't aligned. He was generous to a fault with both the community and customers, but the employees were often getting overlooked.

He came to eventually realize that while he was personally very connected to this bigger purpose, it wasn't shared with all his employees. Purpose is something that each individual must connect with on an individual level. This was a lesson Charles learned as he conducted one-on-one conversations with every employee in an attempt to better understand their individual values and motivating purpose. Hearing each of their stories and gaining an understanding of what mattered to them, he and his team began transforming the organization into one powered by purpose both at organization and individual levels. They engaged with Imperative, a purpose-activation company, to get the training and tools needed to help each employee identify their own motivating purpose and use it to find more meaning in their individual work.

The story of Antis Roofing is both inspiring and informative. It illustrates how purpose can exist on many levels within the organization, but that the true motivational power of purpose is only fully unlocked when it's personal and individual. As an employer or manager, a powerful first step is to help employees to identify and connect with a sense of purpose that is meaningful to them. The personal values sort at Ansarada or defining your 'Motley' at The Motley Fool are examples highlighted in the last chapter of how you might approach this. Once you've named your purpose or core values, it's much easier to align your work to create greater meaning and make it more motivating.

Progress

A sense of progress is the fourth intrinsic motivator. It's easy to identify with the impact of this motivator when you reflect on a time in your career when you felt stuck or were struggling to see any real impact of your work. Psychologically, progress creates a feeling of momentum and positive energy.

Progress is closely related to purpose because the most powerful progress is that made in the pursuit of our purpose. This is why putting goals and expectations the in context of our individual purpose and values is so effective in motivating us to achieve our goals. In the next section of the book about accountability, you'll find a variety of examples of processes that create visibility and a feeling of progress through feedback and measurement.

Key takeaways

- The most complex element of performance management is motivation. Without motivation, even the clearest expectations will have limited impact.

- There are two types of motivation: intrinsic and extrinsic. Traditionally, organizations have relied heavily on extrinsic motivators like incentives and bonuses. These motivators work for rote, routine work but are less effective for knowledge and creative work.

- Pay is a hygiene factor. People need to be paid enough to remove money as a primary consideration. After that, intrinsic motivation is most effective in unlocking higher performance.

- The most powerful intrinsic motivators for employees are mastery, autonomy, purpose and progress. Every job can be designed to include more of these factors but it will look different depending upon the role and context.

References

GoROWE (2016) What we do [Online] http://www.gorowe.com/what-we-do-1-1/ [Last accessed 30 April 2018]

Mind Tools Content Team (2018) Herzberg's motivators and hygiene factors: learn how to motivate your team, *Mind Tools* [Online] https://www.mindtools.com/pages/article/herzberg-motivators-hygiene-factors.htm [Last Accessed 30 April 2018]

Pink, D (2011) *Drive: The surprising truth about what motivates us*, Portfolio

Ryan, R and Deci, E (2000) Intrinsic and extrinsic motivations: classic definitions and new directions, *Contemporary Educational Psychology*, **25**, pp. 54–67 [Online] http://repositorio.minedu.gob.pe/bitstream/handle/123456789/2958/Intrinsic%20and%20Extrinsic%20Motivations%20Classic%20Definitions%20and%20New%20Directions.pdf?sequence=1&isAllowed=y [Last accessed 30 April 2018]

Thomas, K (2009) The four intrinsic rewards that drive employee engagement, *Ivey Business Journal* [Online] https://iveybusinessjournal.com/publication/the-four-intrinsic-rewards-that-drive-employee-engagement/ [Last accessed 30 April 2018]

Recognition and appreciation 08

One often overlooked element of performance management is appreciation. Traditional performance management only focuses recognition on those who perform above and beyond what's expected. And, while providing acknowledgement of top performers is a good idea, that means a vast majority of employees – who are performing as expected – are potentially going without any positive reinforcement or appreciation.

In 2004, Gallup founder Don Clifton published, with Tom Rath, the book *How Full Is Your Bucket?* to present some simple tools to address this issue. The findings shared in the book, based on decades of research and millions of employee survey responses, found that nearly 65 per cent of those surveyed felt that they had received no positive recognition during the past year. Zero. While this is a pretty stark data point, it's not all that hard to believe. Feeling valued is always among the highest drivers of employee engagement in the surveys I've conducted throughout my career. It's also an area where most organizations and leaders struggle to be effective at meeting the needs of employees.

We aren't good at appreciation and recognition, particularly most managers and leaders. Again, this isn't too surprising when considered in the context of the 'work as a contract' approach that has dominated the workplace for the past century. Beyond merit-based performance bonuses or incentives for high achievers, there was little consideration given to appreciation in the contractual model. The employee does the job and the employer pays them a salary in recognition for their compliance. Early in my career, I remember a leader saying something that perfectly captured this mindset. As a reaction to the suggestion that maybe we should provide more recognition, he said 'What do you want, a sticker for doing your job? We give you a pay cheque. That's your reward.' Hopefully, you don't hear these words uttered as often today. But this way of thinking about recognition and appreciation is still very much alive and well in the minds of far too many managers who were schooled in traditional management practices.

We have not invested in appreciation and recognition historically because until recently we didn't realize its importance. Despite what our employee surveys would reveal about the importance of ensuring that employees feel valued, we didn't really understand. Thanks to research in the field of positive psychology, we're starting to create an evidence-based argument to support what seems like an obvious conclusion in hindsight: everyone needs to feel appreciated.

Some psychologists even argue that the pursuit of feeling valued by others (social worth) is a primary human motivator in all areas of our life, not just work (Grant and Gino, 2010). This would help explain why receiving recognition and appreciation from others can feel so nourishing and uplifting. And why it's hard to stay motivated when no one seems to notice our effort and contributions.

Increasingly research is revealing that expressions of gratitude and appreciation at work have far-reaching positive impacts on individuals. One study found that work can literally be a 'place of healing' when employees have positive daily experiences at work such as positive feedback and goal achievement along with socialization. These positive experiences were found to reduce stress levels and improve the health of employees (Bono et al. 2013).

Appreciation and gratitude seem to create a virtuous cycle for human beings. A 2010 study by Adam Grant and Francesca Gino revealed that receiving expressions of gratitude promoted prosocial behaviour. Prosocial behaviour is any action deliberately taken that is intended to help another, often without any expectation of reciprocity (Good Therapy, 2018). Being appreciated appears to make people more generous and helpful. Which often results in receiving further gratitude from those helped and so on. It seems to fuel a virtuous cycle.

To really unlock the power of appreciation and recognition in the workplace, organizations have been increasingly turning to programmes aimed at ramping up what most refer to as 'peer-to-peer recognition'. These efforts are aimed at encouraging coworkers to recognize and express appreciation for each other directly. Clifton and Rath were early promoters of this approach in *How Full is Your Bucket*, where they encouraged people to write positive notes to one another on water-drop-shaped note cards. These notes were designed to put a positive 'drop' in another's emotional 'bucket' to help fill them up with positivity. Today, there are a number of software platforms that have been designed to enable and scale the appreciation process within an organization.

While this may seem a little touchy-feely to those still rooted in old-school management thinking, there's a powerful secondary benefit to this approach that extends beyond the positive impact on those who are receiving the recognition. The expression of gratitude has been found to have an equally powerful positive effect on an individual's experience of work. Studies have shown a link between expressions of gratitude and job satisfaction, suggesting that when an employee takes the action to express appreciation for another, they improve their own job satisfaction (Waters, 2012).

This insight is supported by increasing research within the field of neuroscience that reveals that feelings of gratitude are linked to biological responses in our brain that reduce anxiety, depression and stress. In addition, feelings of gratitude have also been shown to trigger the release of dopamine, the chemical in our brain considered the reward neurotransmitter because it makes us feel good. This release of dopamine has the effect of acting as a positive reinforcement of the behaviour that caused it, compelling us to do it again (Korb, 2012).

To summarize, the acts both of receiving and giving appreciation have positive, motivating effects on the individual. Gratitude also has the potential to create a virtuous cycle where the appreciated are more likely to help and appreciate others. And recognition doesn't have to be complicated or formal. It can be very simple. It's about creating positive, affirming moments that help employees feel appreciated and valued.

As I've studied positive workplaces over the past decade, one of the consistent things the best all have in common is that in some way, they've operationalized appreciation and gratitude into how they do work. This can look very different from one organization to another, but the goal is the same: to ensure that employees feel valued. In the rest of this chapter, I will highlight some common and effective practices I've observed.

The shout out

One practice that has become more common is to make 'shout outs' a part of regular meetings and team gatherings. Whether it's at a monthly all-hands meeting or a daily huddle, there is time on the agenda for individuals to express appreciation and thanks to others. These shout outs serve the dual purpose of promoting expressions of gratitude and shining a light on positive behaviours and outcomes.

The Behavioural Insights Team (BIT), a London-based behavioural sciences consultancy, has a novel approach to ongoing recognition with a twist. They call it 'Whoops and Whoopsies'. The team at their headquarters location holds a short meeting on Mondays to kick off the week. Each meeting closes with the opportunity for people to share 'whoops' which are shout outs and expressions of appreciation for their teammates from the previous week. The twist is that they also use this time to share their 'whoopsies'. These are mistakes or failings they personally made the previous week and what they learned as a result. In this way they can turn a failure into a positive learning experience for the team, finding a positive moment in what could otherwise be demotivating.

At Wistia, a growing video hosting technology company, they have a one-hour 'show and tell' meeting every Tuesday. Employees use this meeting to share work they are proud of that they'd like to receive feedback about. By sharing, they invite both acknowledgement of their work and appreciation of what they are creating. But this meeting isn't only about sharing your own work, it's also about recognizing the good work of others. People will create a one-page 'Deet' slide to share at the meeting as a way to show appreciation or recognize another's contributions.

Recognition programmes

Beyond the simple shout outs, other organizations have created more structured programmes to encourage and allow for peer-to-peer recognition and appreciation. At The Motley Fool, employees (who they refer to as Fools) are given points that can be awarded to other employees as recognition of living the core values or doing great work. Internally, they refer to these points as 'Fool's Gold'. Employees who receive gold can, as described in their handbook, 'redeem it for prizes, gift cards, travel, and Foolish experiences'.

CASE STUDY Employee recognition at Baystate Health

Peer recognition programmes like these have become more common over the past decade as technology platforms have arisen to help manage and scale them to larger groups of employees. Baystate Health, a 12,000-employee healthcare system, has been on a journey to unlock the power of recognition that started with a desire to improve patient experience. Jennifer Faulkner, Vice President of Team Member Experience, described a strong linkage between employee engagement and patient engagement: 'In general, the data suggests that happier employees lead to happier patients.'

As they dug into their employee engagement survey data, one thing was clear. Employees weren't feeling recognized. The survey item about recognition was among the lowest and that lack of recognition was having some significant impacts.

It was clear that recognition was important to the employees at Baystate Health, but they wanted to understand more about what kind of recognition was most meaningful. Specifically, they were curious about the perceived value of recognition from three sources: leader, peer, and patient. They conducted research with employees to answer this question. What they found was that while all recognition is valued, peer recognition was highly valued. Employees revealed that they value specific recognition (ie what I did and what impact it had) delivered in a timely way. The closer to when the behaviour happened that the recognition is received, the better. Peers, it turns out, are in the best position to provide this.

One of the interesting findings of their research was that employees wanted to be able to share their recognition with family members. The ability to share received recognition with their loved ones seemed to amplify its value.

As a result of these findings, they decided to deploy a social recognition software platform, created by Globoforce, to the organization. Employees could use this platform to share recognition with other employees. The platform not only enabled direct peer-to-peer recognition, it also amplified that recognition by making it visible to other employees. Each recognition given is connected to a core value of the organization to reinforce and strengthen the culture.

Jennifer and her team saw the power of the platform from the very first recognition shared. It was a recognition of a long-tenured groundskeeper at the hospital, written by a physician. Here's what she wrote.

Steve, I have noticed your extraordinary effort to keep our hospital grounds in top shape day after day for many years. I think you are an unsung hero of Baystate. When our patients, families and employees come to Baystate, they are welcomed by immaculate lawns and flowers and it makes a positive impact on our image. Although I have never met you and had to ask around to find out your name, I have long wanted to give you a shout out for your work ethic and dedication. Thank you!

There had been nothing stopping the physician from sharing that recognition and appreciation in the past, but it just had not happened before. It wasn't until the organization took the step to actively encourage gratitude and introduced a mechanism that made it easy that it finally happened. I can only imagine the positive impact that note must have had on both people.

Employees have embraced this new platform and it's having an impact. One area where the impact has been pretty dramatic has been in employee survey results. That recognition item, which used to be among the lowest-rated on their survey, is now among the highest. Additionally, they found that nurses who had been recognized at least once in the past year were three-and-a-half times more likely to still be with the organization a year later. In the highly competitive healthcare labour market, this kind of positive impact on retention was eye-opening and worthy of investment.

Operationalizing appreciation

What these organizations have in common is that they have made appreciation and recognition part of how work happens within their organization. They recognize that we are not naturally good at it when left to our own devices and they've decided not to leave it to chance. Every organization or team needs to find ways to intentionally create more positive, uplifting moments for employees that build that feeling of appreciation and being valued.

For some organizations, this might mean starting with how to cultivate more simple positive moments. The simple act of saying thank you, giving someone a high five, or even just smiling and saying 'good morning' in the hallway can have a positive impact. Leaders and managers must first start to model this behaviour before they can expect it from others. This can create a ripple effect.

Another place to increase appreciation systematically is to make the solicitation and sharing of appreciative feedback a part of any feedback or coaching process. For example, a manager can include in every one-on-one conversation a short list of things they appreciate about what they have observed of the employee in the last cycle. These don't have to be specifically goal or performance related, but could be simple positive reinforcements like, 'I really appreciate the positive outlook you've been bringing to our team meetings lately'.

When using peer-to-peer feedback processes like 360-degree surveys, ensure there is as much or more emphasis on what others value and appreciate about the individual as there is solicitation of critical feedback (more on this in the next section of the book). These processes tend to be geared towards identifying gaps and opportunities that focus the employee on development needs. While this is important, unless it's balanced with uplifting appreciation it can trigger a defensive response that is counter-productive.

Another approach that I've experienced in several settings involves using a structured debrief at the completion of a project or a specific performance period. When a project is completed or at the end of a performance cycle (ie week, month, etc), the team gathers to formally debrief about what went well and what could have gone better. A part of each debrief is the question, 'To whom do we owe some thanks for their support?' This forces the team to think about those who contributed to the both the team's and their individual success to ensure that these people know that their support was valued and appreciated. In one case, we sent a developer a case of his favorite beer as a thank you for stepping up and helping our team solve a major problem.

Key takeaways

- An often-overlooked element of performance management is appreciation. Traditional performance management only focuses recognition on those who perform above and beyond what's expected. Everyone needs to feel appreciated.

- The acts of both receiving and giving appreciation have positive, motivating effects on the individual. Gratitude also has the potential to create a virtuous cycle where the appreciated are more likely to help and appreciate others.

- Creating formal rituals or processes to encourage 'shout outs' is a common way for organizations to create a positive, appreciative workplace.

- We are not naturally good at expressing appreciation to others. A well designed peer-to-peer recognition programme can be very effective in nudging employees towards expressing more gratitude for and appreciation of one another. This can have very positive impacts on overall employee engagement.

- Every organization or team needs to find ways to intentionally create more positive, uplifting moments for employees that build that feeling of appreciation and being valued.

References

Bono, J E et al. (2013) Building positive resources: effects of positive events and positive reflection on work stress and health, *Academy of Management Journal*, **56** (6), pp. 1601–27 [Online] https://pdfs.semanticscholar.org/4a37/5ce73ac7b9 b78c9fc29c7d9086a74b8cb174.pdf [Last accessed 30 April 2018]

Clifton, D and Rath, T (2005) *How Full is Your Bucket? Positive strategies for work and life*, Gallup Press

Good Therapy (2018) Prosocial behavior [Online] https://www.goodtherapy.org/blog/psychpedia/prosocial-behavior [Last accessed 30 April 2018]

Grant, A and Gino, F (2010) A little thanks goes a long way: explaining why gratitude expressions motivate prosocial behavior, *Journal of Personality and Social Psychology*, **98**, pp. 946–55, doi: 10.1037/a0017935

Korb PhD, A (2012) The grateful brain: the neuroscience of giving thanks, *Psychology Today*, 20 November [Online] https://www.psychologytoday.com/us/blog/prefrontal-nudity/201211/the-grateful-brain [Last accessed 30 April 2018]

Waters, L (2012) Predicting job satisfaction: contributions of individual gratitude *and* institutionalized gratitude, *Psychology*, **3**, pp. 1174–76, doi: 10.4236/psych.2012.312A173

Wellbeing and inclusion

09

Beginning in the 1980s, it became increasingly common for organizations to create worksite wellness initiatives. Their underlying purpose was to support employees in achieving and maintaining better physical health. The programmes grew out of a variety of needs, from helping employees to recover from substance abuse to preventing accidents (Khoury, 2014).

The interest in workplace wellness programmes intensified when some started promoting the idea that if employers could help employees be healthier, they would consume less healthcare, use less sick time and generally be less expensive to employ. In my last executive HR role, we invested heavily in wellness, based on the promise of future cost containment by improving employee health.

After years of investment in these initiatives and programmes, the consensus seems to be that wellness hasn't lived up to its billing. There's increasing evidence that corporate wellness programmes have failed to produce any substantial savings for organizations (Greenfield, 2018). We can debate the reasons for this failure or if it can be rectified, but I think that misses the point.

Most organizations are still overlooking the real value of investing in wellness. The impact of wellness was never in mitigating risks or cost containment but rather as a way to improve performance. And the commonly narrow focus on physical health limited the scale of the impact these programmes could have.

As I reflect back on my career and particularly the times when I wasn't at my best, the issues interfering with my performance at work often had nothing to do with work. In many cases, my failures of performance related to stressors in my personal life. Sometimes, it did involve my physical health. Early in my career, I took socializing pretty seriously so I was often up late with friends consuming far too many adult beverages. The hangovers and cumulative effective of too little sleep took a toll on my capacity to perform at work. My employers during that era of my career certainly did not get my best.

Other times in my career, it was all about my emotional health. I participated in what some call a 'starter marriage' in my early twenties. It was an ill-advised choice to get married as this relationship had always been characterized by enormous and dramatic ups and downs. In the short 20-month tenure of this marriage, it would never have been described as 'stable', and this instability at home meant that I existed in a regular state of being emotionally unsettled. This made it hard to focus on some days and limited the amount of positive emotional energy I had to contribute to my work or my coworkers.

The other major stressor I remember throughout my career is money. While all of my financial issues were self-created, the weight of money issues can be all-consuming. When you aren't sure if your next pay cheque will cover your bills, it's hard to think about much else. And, feeling financially strained makes any conversation about salary or compensation at work seem very high stakes and personal.

In all of these circumstances, even if I was crystal clear about my expectations, had all the resources I needed, and got plenty of support and encouragement at work, I wasn't going to do my best work. Due to these various issues with my personal wellbeing, my ability to perform up to my full potential was limited, if not impossible.

To cultivate peak performance requires embracing the fact that employees are human beings who have lives and circumstances outside of work that impact on what they bring to work. The idea that work and life are somehow separate or don't affect one another is a fallacy. The individual 'wellness' or 'wellbeing' of employees is a performance capacity issue. The more 'well' each employee feels in all dimensions of their life, the more capacity of their full potential they can offer up to the organization each day.

Many models of wellbeing have emerged to help organizations and leaders think about how they can more actively support each employee both at work and beyond in a journey to be more well and whole as a person. One of the most popular models of wellbeing is called the 'Gallup-Sharecare Well-Being Index' (Gallup and Sharecare, 2018). This model defines and measures individual wellbeing on five categories:

Gallup-Sharecare Well-Being Index

1 Purpose

2 Social

3 Financial

4 Community

5 Physical

The full model is explained in depth in the book, *Well-Being: The five essential elements* (Rath and Harter, 2010). My purpose in sharing this isn't to advocate for this as the only or best model of wellbeing (it's not even my favourite), but rather to illustrate how this approach is a departure from traditional thinking about what is 'work-related'. It also helps prompt our thinking about the ways in which we can support each employee on their own individual wellness journey.

My own experience illustrates how the stress and disruption of each circumstance I describe could have likely been minimized or prevented through better choices. Had I been more knowledgeable or equipped to make these choices or at least to manage the impact of what was happening to me, my wellbeing may have improved. If my employers at that time had provided the resources or support to navigate a rocky marriage or shaky finances, perhaps I could have leveraged those to improve my life outside of work and, as a result, improve my performance at work.

Wellness is another concept that makes no sense in the context of traditional management thinking where work is a contract. The notion that an employer or manager should actively support an employee in these ways goes far beyond the scope of the contract. Should my employer have to help me learn how to have a better marriage at home or teach me how to handle conflict more positively? We can debate that if you would like, but it's the wrong question to ask.

Embracing wellbeing leads to a couple of different questions. How might helping our employees have better relationships at home improve their capacity to perform at work? And what's the lost opportunity of not doing so? Organizations who excel at cultivating performance view their wellbeing commitment as a way to succeed by helping employees to be more healthy and whole in every facet of their lives. By so doing, they unlock a

CASE STUDY Farm Credit Services of America

Farm Credit Services of America (FCSAmerica) has been recognized many times as a best place to work and is generally thought of as one of the employers of choice in the communities where they employ people. Lynette Campbell, who serves as Vice President of Organization Development and Learning, attributes this in part to a belief espoused by their long-time and recently retired CEO. He would commonly say that the organization wanted to help each team member to become a better person in whatever ways mattered most to them (as a spouse, parent, leader, etc). He believed that when the organization could help a team member in this way, the team member would pay it forward by giving customers a great experience. And it appears to have worked if growth and expansion are any indication.

One way that FCSAmerica delivers on this ideal is through ongoing development and educational opportunities made available to employees. They offer classes covering topics including personal finance, being a better listener, and how to manage stress. They've even offered classes titled 'Change Anything' to help empower employees to shape any important aspect of their life. As Lynette shared with me, it's not uncommon for employees to approach her and her team to share stories of how these and other programmes offered at FCSAmerica have changed their lives for the better.

Another way that FCSAmerica has invested in wellbeing is through the physical work environment. As they built and remodelled workspaces, they designed these spaces to promote collaboration and comfort for the people who occupy them. The workplace is designed to feel open and every employee is exposed to natural light in their workspace. They also incorporate living plants and take care to ensure the environment is clean and functional at all times. When things break, they get fixed immediately. Their goal is to create a workplace that feels enriching and promotes teamwork.

greater share of the individual's potential to perform and create value at work.

Employee benefits consultancy, SIG, has also fostered an award-winning culture in part by investing in wellbeing. These efforts at SIG are supported by a volunteer employee committee which guides and plans many of the activities and programmes. They have even branded their wellbeing efforts internally, calling it the 'Spark' programme. As Rachel Druckenmiller, SIG's Director of Wellbeing, explained, they liked the metaphor of a spark to describe their efforts because a small spark has the potential to light a big fire. And by lighting a fire, they mean helping the employee to 'come alive more fully'. SIG has evolved from a traditional wellness focus on only physical health to a broader, more holistic view of wellbeing. 'We're not necessarily trying to make them healthy, we're trying to help them feel more alive and connected.'

For a smaller organization, SIG offers a wide range of programmes aimed at throwing those 'sparks' of wellbeing, ranging from mini-meditation session and cake-decorating classes to self-defence courses and breakfast potlucks. They have even offered a 'make-and-take' aromatherapy class during the most stressful time of the year in the business as a nudge to remind people to take a break and connect with each other. The Wellbeing committee hosts an annual employee scavenger hunt followed by a happy hour in the city. It also collaborates with the Social and Community Service committees to plan other events throughout the year in order to build community.

What is perhaps most interesting and powerful about SIG's approach to wellbeing is an underlying intention revealed by Rachel in our interview. Regardless of the activity or programme planned, they are always think-ing about how to foster relationship building and helping employees feel a deeper sense of connection to one another and the organization.

Investing in the wellbeing of your employees is beneficial on several levels. As I highlighted above, wellbeing is a performance capacity issue. The more whole and well employees feel when they show up each day, the more they are able to bring their full potential and gifts to bear through their work that day. Beyond that, it's also an investment in the relationship with the employee. Our healthiest relationships are with those who look out for and advocate for our wellbeing. And, as FCSAmerica has shown, the reciprocal nature of relationships means that when we invest in the wellbeing of our employees, they are more likely to look out for the wellbeing of the custom-ers, which in turn leads to the success of the organization.

The importance of inclusion

If I asked you to describe your best friend and why you enjoy spending time with them, you'd probably list a number of things. On the list is likely to be something along the lines of, 'I can be myself around them'. Our best friends tend to be people who have seen us at our best, our worst and everything in between. And they embrace it all. They don't judge us. Nor do they try to change us. They simply love us for who we are and support us in the best way they know how.

This suggests that to promote the kind of employee experience that feels like a great relationship, we must find a way to create this sense of belonging and acceptance at work. In the context of a best friend, this is a pretty easy task. Your best friend is probably a lot like you. You probably share a lot in common and have common interests. It's easy to accept someone who you like and share commonality with.

The task is not so simple at work where employees can be very different and have widely varying interests, experiences and backgrounds. The challenge is to create a work experience, like our closest relationships, that embraces and accepts all of that diversity openly without judgment and without trying to change it. Many refer to a work experience like this as being inclusive.

Inclusion is critical to cultivation of performance. Each employee possesses a unique set of perspectives, experiences and talents unlike any other person alive. This unique perspective is among the most valuable contributions the individual has to offer. They can view their work and the organization through a lens that only they possess, revealing perspectives that only they can see.

Traditionally, organizations have been far more invested in assimilation than inclusion. Onboarding programmes try to help people learn how to 'fit in' at the organization more quickly, not realizing that the side effect is that employees hear that it's not valued to 'stand out'. Organizational dress codes encourage people to dress alike, often requiring individuals to change or cover up things important to their sense of identity like special clothing, jewellery or tattoos. In meetings, the person with the biggest title or longest tenure speaks the most while new people just listen and wait for the time when they have been assimilated enough to have an appropriate opinion.

While this may sound a bit cynical, I recognize that these things are rarely done with ill intentions. It's another manifestation of our management heritage of maximizing output in the easiest and fastest ways possible with little or no thought given to the employee's experience. In that model, it's far easier to manage a group of people who have been assimilated to act, dress and talk similarly than it is a group who act and behave differently. Diversity is messy and harder to manage.

Investing in creating an inclusive work experience has benefits on several levels. On the relationship level, feeling accepted and embraced for your uniqueness is vital to building a lasting bond. Your best friends have probably been in your life for a long time. When you find a relationship like that, you don't want to let it go.

Inclusion also fuels both performance and innovation by inviting employees to make their broadest possible contributions. When the environment makes it safe and invites employees to share what makes them different, these unique perspectives unlock opportunities that would have been invisible in a more assimilated environment.

Creating a truly inclusive work experience is hard work. It's something that requires intentional commitment and dedicated action over time by leaders and employees. It requires putting processes and mechanisms in place to actively draw out and include diversity. Because assimilated, homogeneous groups are easier to manage, it can become our unintended default mode of operation. When we allow assimilation to be the norm, the relationship (and performance) will suffer.

Entire books have been written on how to create inclusive cultures, so I won't attempt to provide a comprehensive list of recommendations here. I encourage you to seek out additional resources and learn more. One way to move towards greater inclusion is to take actions to actively draw out diversity and celebrate what makes people unique. By actively demonstrating appreciation for uniqueness, you make it safer to be unique at work. While it's become increasingly common to find 'diversity and inclusion' as a part of a company's values, that commitment must be backed by action.

At Wistia, for example, they want their workplace to feel like an authentic, creative place. As part of that, they actively encourage people to show off a weirder side of themselves. One of the ways they do this is by encouraging people to share their hobbies. Whether it's playing a musical instrument or showing off culinary skills on a new office grill, they encourage people to put their interests and talents on display. By doing so, they have also encouraged people to put more of themselves into their work. In one case, a particularly creative employee with a love of the big Hollywood award shows decided to create an award programme for customers. As a video-hosting platform company, the 'Febbies' became an instant hit.

Interestingly, despite Farm Credit Services of America being in a very different industry (banking and finance) with a very different culture, they have employed a similar approach to drawing out employee hobbies and interests as a way to embrace uniqueness and foster inclusion. During a series of brown bag lunches throughout the year, they encourage employees to share and teach their hobbies and interests to others. The events not only invite sharing of uniqueness, but they create an opportunity for real connection. People create a shared experience to bond them together. It's not likely you will forget the co-worker who taught you the konmari method to organize your home or how to make your own bows and wrap beautiful gifts.

Inviting employees to bring their hobbies and interests to work may not seem like an obvious way to impact performance. It is a simple, low-stakes way to take action to embrace your employees as whole people. It also celebrates employees for being a little vulnerable in sharing more of themselves at work. When we are rewarded for showing a bit more of ourselves, it's likely we'll do more of it the future.

At the Arbor Day Foundation, they have found another novel way to foster an inclusive environment while also promoting learning and growth. They call it 'Food for Thought'. Employees are invited to sign up to have lunch with colleagues at one of several different restaurants. At lunch, they discuss some predetermined questions as a way to both foster learning and get to know one another better. What makes the process so powerful is that when employees sign up for lunch, they don't know who they are signing up to have lunch with. The sign-up process is blind, which leads to unexpected lunchmates who might not otherwise find themselves in regular conversations together.

This approach is similar to Randomized Coffee Trials (RCT), an idea made popular in 2013 by Nesta, an innovation foundation based in the UK. It is an incredibly simple idea where employees who volunteer to be involved receive a random pairing each week with another employee who they are to then have coffee with (Soto, 2013). RCT and 'Food for Thought'

Here are some other simple ways to help your team to become more inclusive:

- Open team meetings with a round of sharing. Give each team member an opportunity to share something interesting about themselves that most people at work don't know. Alternatively, ask each person to answer the same question (ie 'What is your favorite movie of all time?'). Each meeting invites a little more sharing and an opportunity to find commonality with others in the room.

- When meeting as a team to review a plan or make a decision, ensure that all voices are heard. At one or two times during the discussion, do a check-in with the group going around the room to ask what people are thinking or what question is at the top of their mind at the moment. The goal is to ensure everyone feels valued and heard, regardless of their title or tenure.

- Assign a devil's advocate for each meeting whose purpose is to ask hard questions and take contrary opinions to challenge thinking. A different person should be assigned this role each meeting so everyone has a turn. Over time, the group will learn both how to ask and respond to hard questions. They will also realize that having a contrary or unique opinion is valued and important to the team's performance.

Key takeaways

- Most organizations are still overlooking the real value of investing in wellness. Rather than being a tool to contain costs, the real value in wellness is to unlock greater performance capacity within each employee.

- Organizations who excel at cultivating performance view their wellbeing commitment as a way to succeed by helping employees to be more healthy and whole in every facet of their lives. They provide training, resources, and an environment that equips employees to improve their lives outside of work.

- Beyond increasing performance capacity, investing in your employees' wellbeing is also an investment in your relationship with them. We are motivated to take care of and look out for those who do the same for us.

- To create an employee experience that feels like our closest relationships, it must embrace and accept diversity openly without judgment or a desire to change it. We call this an inclusion.

- Investing in creating an inclusive work experience has benefits on several levels. On the relationship level, feeling accepted and embraced for your uniqueness is vital to building a lasting bond. Inclusion also fuels both performance and innovation by inviting employees to make their broadest possible contributions.

- One powerful way to move towards greater inclusion is to take actions to actively draw out diversity and celebrate what makes people unique.

both actively encourage relationship building and the sharing of unique perspectives by bringing together people who would otherwise be less likely to connect.

References

Gallup and Sharecare (2018) About the well-being index, *Sharecare* [Online] https://wellbeingindex.sharecare.com/about/ [Last accessed 30 April 2018]

Greenfield, R (2018) Workplace wellness programs really don't work: they aren't saving money or making employees healthier, a new study finds, *Bloomberg*, 26 January [Online] https://www.bloomberg.com/news/articles/2018-01-26/workplace-wellness-programs-really-don-t-work?utm_campaign=ED_HCM_HR%20News%20Brief_Q1%202018&utm_source=hs_email&utm_medium=email&utm_content=60328148&_hsenc=p2ANqtz–DuCo8VOppAkh-MIw1ypGn1AfgDDCpj9Z7XH5nkFRiuXoUsNKwmjEBRrftFkKz_rjsX8Ie5-My8BCAjdgdrSPN3Jf7Mg&_hsmi=60327829 [Last accessed 30 April 2018]

Khoury, Dr A (2014) The evolution of worksite wellness, *Corporate Wellness Magazine,* 29 October [Online] http://www.corporatewellnessmagazine.com/worksite-wellness/the-evolution-of/ [Last accessed 30 April 2018]

Rath, T and Harter, G (2010) *Well-Being: The five essential elements*, Gallup Press

Soto, M (2013) Institutionalising serendipity via productive coffee breaks, *Nesta*, 21 January [Online] https://www.nesta.org.uk/blog/institutionalising-serendipity-productive-coffee-breaks [Last accessed 30 April 2018]

Removing obstacles

10

In farming, if you don't work to combat and remove invasive weeds and insects, the damage to crops can be catastrophic. Even if all other conditions are favourable, these invasive organisms can thwart any hopes for a productive harvest. This makes their removal particularly vital.

In cultivating performance at work, obstacles can be just as disruptive and important to remove. For example, I recently conducted a series of employee focus groups for a client where employee turnover was increasing and morale seemed to be an issue. Employee focus groups always uncover a variety of issues that need to be addressed, ranging from communication breakdowns to a lack of appreciation. This was no exception.

In this case, what was striking about these focus groups was the consistency with which they identified a common obstacle that they felt was hindering performance and leading to burnout. The issue they described is what I often refer to as 'death by meetings'. These employees were spending so much time in meetings during the day that they lacked time to complete their work. They described a culture where scheduling a meeting was the default action. The result of this meeting culture was long hours for employees, poor work – life balance, and decreased performance due to rushed work.

Employees were, as you'd expect, feeling frustrated and exasperated, which explained the increased morale issues and increase in turnover. Many were nearing their breaking point. They desperately needed relief but most of them felt powerless to change the situation. In most cases, they didn't have the power to either cancel or opt out of these meetings, even when they didn't seem valuable. Meetings had become a pretty significant obstacle. As you'd predict, I recommended a number of interventions to the leaders of this organization aimed at reducing the number of meetings they were holding. I also recommended improving the effectiveness and shortening the length of those they kept.

As with the farming analogy, obstacles can be particularly disruptive to the employee experience and performance overall. An obstacle is something that interferes with your progress. It stops you in your tracks until you either remove it or find a way around it. This is what makes obstacles so dangerous. Even when you are cultivating performance through effective motivation and appreciation, an obstacle like 'death by meetings' can thwart performance and kill employee engagement.

Type of obstacles

Obstacles can take many forms. They can be systemic like the meetings example shared above. But, they can also be very individual and specific. An example might be discovering that you lack the right tool or resource to complete a task. If you've ever attempted a home-improvement project only to find that you lacked an essential tool, you know how disrupting this can be to making progress.

Obstacles can also be interpersonal. Being in conflict with a colleague whose cooperation you require is an example. In my years as an HR leader, this was an obstacle I had to confront frequently, both in my own interactions and between peers. In order to solve many of our stickiest HR problems, it was necessary to make changes to management processes and sometimes in how managers were expected to behave. Not every manager appreciated being asked to do things differently, so they would resist and even undermine the changes – sometimes overtly and other times covertly. In either case, if we couldn't influence those managers to embrace the changes, there could be no progress. Our performance was dependent upon resolving this conflict to gain their cooperation. This was a significant obstacle to our performance that, if not addressed, could have substantial consequences.

Mindset can also be an obstacle. Over the years, one of the most common examples I've encountered is what psychologist Martin Seligman describes as 'learned helplessness' (Seligman, 2011). Based on past experiences where they've tried something and failed, individuals will come to believe and accept that if they attempt the same thing in the future, they will always fail. So they stop trying. This mindset can reveal itself in a variety of ways. For example, one person never speaks up in meetings or shares ideas because they've been silenced or ignored in the past. Another common example is someone who won't try something new because the last few times they did so, it didn't work out or blew up on them. So they stopped taking risks like that. They've learned to accept a feeling of helplessness in these circumstances. This type of obstacle is particularly dangerous to performance if not addressed. The only way through a mindset obstacle is with coaching and support. To do that, you have to first identify that the obstacle exists.

Removing obstacles

The key to identifying and removing obstacles is continuous and ongoing communication about the work experience. Obstacles can arise at any moment. The simplest and most common way to ensure obstacles aren't missed is to make it part of regular one-on-one meetings or check-ins. By making the question, 'What challenges are you facing right now?' a part of your regular agenda in these meetings, it's likely that any substantial obstacles will be revealed. In addition to this question, simply listening closely in one-on-one conversations for anything that sounds like an obstacle is important. When discussing work, it's only natural that frustrations and challenges will come up. If they do, ask questions to understand what's causing them. This is often where potential obstacles will reveal themselves.

Stand-up meeting

Another way organizations are proactively addressing obstacles is by making it easier to ask for help. At Menlo Innovations, they have a daily meeting called the 'Stand Up'. This is a common practice in teams that use the Agile methodology for software development. At Menlo, this is literally a stand-up meeting that lasts about 15 minutes and is attended by all employees. The meeting happens at a brisk pace and covers a lot of ground quickly. One of the things that happens in this meeting is that anyone can raise up an issue or challenge they are having to request help in resolving it. By making their challenge visible to the organization, they invite help in resolving it. They have found that there's likely to be someone in the room who has the skill, experience or know-how to assist with almost any problem.

Employee survey

One of the most efficient ways to identify potential systemic obstacles is through an employee survey. Thanks to advances in technology, it has become relatively easy to field a survey to employees as a way to collect valuable feedback. Employee surveys often reveal where common obstacles exist and where resources are lacking. These surveys can be simple and short. To get the most valuable insights, use creative, open-ended questions.

Below are examples of questions that help reveal perceived obstacles and challenges to be addressed.

- If you were the CEO for a day and could change one thing about the organization, what would it be?
- What is the biggest obstacle you face each day in your work?
- What is the most challenging part of your job?

The goal with a survey isn't to try to uncover and fix every single complaint, but rather to get a sense of broadly felt issues that might be affecting many employees. This allows you to give the removal of these obstacles priority. If you use a survey in this way, as with any request for feedback, it is important to validate the employee's input by confirming that it was heard. This can happen in a variety of ways, but at a minimum, leaders and managers should share and discuss the findings of the survey with their teams.

Survey follow-up

When there are systemic issues or obstacles raised in the results, the process of sharing and discussing the findings with the team can help bring greater clarity to the issue. For example, if employees shared that too many meetings were getting in the way of completing work assignments, a discussion could reveal which meetings are viewed as the biggest offenders and which are viewed as beneficial. This can bring focus to what action needs to be taken.

To ensure that your survey is viewed by employees as effective, it's important that you not only share results, but that you also take action based on the feedback you receive. This doesn't mean trying to address every issue raised in the survey, but it does mean finding at least one obstacle or opportunity where you can take specific action. Continuing with the meetings example, a good next step might be to facilitate a conversation with the team to identify how to minimize the negative impact of meetings. You might discuss the following questions:

- What makes a meeting valuable?
- How could we make our meetings more effective?
- What guidelines could we put in place to shorten meetings?
- Which meetings should be eliminated?

By engaging the team in problem solving and exploring how to most effectively remove an obstacle, each member of the team gains a sense of ownership and motivation to make it better.

While a survey is one way to find and address obstacles, you don't need a survey to make progress. Conducting a 'focus group'-type discussion with your team about their work experience can be equally effective, particularly with smaller teams. When common challenges or issues are identified through that conversation, you can use the same action planning approach described above for survey feedback to further diagnose the issue and invite the entire team to participate in its solution.

Key takeaways

- In cultivating performance at work, obstacles are incredibly disruptive and important to remove. Even when you are cultivating performance through effective motivation and appreciation, an obstacle can thwart performance and kill employee engagement.

- Obstacles can take many forms including lack of tools, interpersonal conflict and mindset.

- In order to remove an obstacle, you must first identify that it exists. One of the most effective ways to do so is through regular one-on-one meetings and check-ins.

- Employee surveys can also be effective ways to identify systemic obstacles. When using a survey, it is critical to follow up and validate to employees that you heard their feedback and then take visible action in response to what you heard.

Reference

Seligman, M E P (2011) Building resilience, *Harvard Business Review* [Online] https://hbr.org/2011/04/building-resilience [Last accessed 1 May 2018]

SECTION 4
Performance accountability

Accountability is one of those words that has developed a pretty bad reputation. When someone uses the word accountable, it's usually meant to suggest that someone needs to be punished for some kind of failure. It sounds something like this:

'Someone should be held accountable for this!'

Or even, 'You need to take accountability for your actions. You are the one who made this mess.'

As a result, people seem to spend as much time trying to avoid accountability as embracing it. It has become something to be dreaded. It shouldn't be surprising that we have come to have this relationship with the word and concept.

Accountability has some deep roots in both legal and business proceedings. In law, you'll find words like liable, answerable, or culpable used in defining accountability (US Legal, 2016). All of which point towards the ability to punish in circumstances when you've either done wrong or not done what you should have.

In business, the term is often used to represent obligations (accountability). Particularly for top leadership, accountability is meant to reflect the responsibility taken on by individual leaders to ensure proper governance of the organization. Since this is often a legally defined responsibility, the intention and meaning of the word echoes the legal definition. Take care of the business in the right way or there will be severe consequences. In other words, if you abuse your power, you will be held accountable and punished accordingly.

Even in psychology, some definitions frame accountability in a way that feels a bit punitive, describing it as having to justify one's actions to others (accountability definition). As a result, most applications of accountability at work tend to reflect the same thing. When work is viewed as a contract, it only stands to reason that employees should be held to account for upholding their end of the contract. Performance appraisals and performance improvement plans were designed with this 'perform or else' mindset.

If work were a contract, then it might seem reasonable to manage work in this way. But since work is a relationship for employees, we must re-examine what accountability means in that context.

Accountability in relationships

Accountability is an important ingredient in creating healthy relationships. When you think about the strongest relationships in your life, they are usually built on a foundation of mutual commitment and reciprocity. You keep secrets and promises with one another. You show up when you are needed. You will invest of yourself in making sure the relationship stays healthy and positive.

By contrast to what it means in law and business, in healthy relationships accountability is about feeling a responsibility and desire to meet the needs and expectations of others. It's about being accountable *to others* instead of being held to account *by others*. It's not something done to you but rather something you willingly embrace as part of your commitment to the other person. To create a work experience that builds healthy relationships and unlocks performance, we must shift from the contractual model of holding others to account and instead inspire others to be accountable for their actions and behaviours.

To illustrate the difference more clearly, let's compare how accountability works in my relationship with my children versus with my wife. I love each of them immeasurably and am fully committed to their growth, happiness and success. But as you would expect, my relationship with my children operates very differently than my relationship with my wife.

As I write this, my youngest children are eight and ten years old. As their parent, my role is to love them, protect them, encourage their growth, and teach them. I willingly embrace this role and have committed myself to being the very best father I can be. I am choosing to be accountable to my children in that way. But this is not a mutual commitment. My children love me (at least they tell me they do) but they didn't choose to be in this relationship. They were born into it, and they are stuck living with me for the first 18 years of their lives. As a result, they aren't committed to the relationship in the way that I am. They are dependent upon the relationship and they reap some benefits from it regardless of their individual choices or behaviour.

My kids are not motivated at this stage in their life to have any feeling of accountability to the relationship. Instead, they look to us as parents to provide the guidelines and rules for what it means to be a member of the family. And it's our role to hold them accountable to these rules. Because of the lack of mutual commitment and their dependency upon my wife and I for their survival, this relationship functions very much in a contractual way. This type of accountability happens when there is a significant power imbalance in the relationship.

My relationship with my wife is very different. She, thankfully, chose to be in this relationship with me and I with her. In adult relationships, we choose to commit to one another and this commitment is what ultimately forms the bond that either preserves or corrodes the relationship over time. In healthy relationships, the commitment is what drives an inherent desire to strengthen the relationship and avoid doing anything that would harm it. When both parties to the relationship feel this sense of accountability to one another, the relationship can flourish.

Learning what it meant to be accountable within a relationship wasn't a lesson I learned quickly. What I discovered over time was that it meant making small (and sometimes big) choices on a daily basis that weren't necessarily required, but that were important to my wife and thus represented a small investment in our relationship. It means picking something up off the floor and putting it away instead of walking past it. It means doing the dishes when I don't want to. It means spending time talking and listening, even when there are a million other things I want to do in that moment.

Each one of these small actions is one I could avoid, but in so doing I may slowly kill the relationship. And it will be my fault if that happens. Accepting full ownership of my own behaviour and its intended or unintended effects is what accountability means in our relationship. I adopted the 'happy wife, happy life' mantra early on as a husband. If she's unhappy, then I will do everything in my power to help her find more happiness.

As our relationship went on, I learned to pay greater attention to what she seemed to value most and to ask questions to gauge how I was doing in the relationship. I'd ask questions like, 'How can I help?' and 'How could I be a better husband?' At first, these conversations revealed pretty basic things that I could do to have an immediate impact on the relationship. Over the years, these conversations have gone deeper to focus on how we can support each other in achieving our dreams and more fully realizing our purpose in life.

My relationship with my wife is built on a mutual commitment that drives a sense of individual ownership of our own behaviour within the relationship. Because there's no power imbalance, the relationship works on a currency of reciprocity and trust. Either of us could opt out of the relationship at any time, but we choose to remain in it and to invest in it. We choose to be accountable to each other.

As we support this shared accountability with communication and a curiosity about how to make it work better, the relationship strengthens. As that happened, we needed less time and energy to make the daily relationship work and instead we could invest in each other's growth. In the end, we've both become better spouses, parents and ultimately people.

Accountability in performance management

The challenge in unlocking performance potential is to reframe what accountability means in performance management. Instead of a punitive, fear-based system of holding people to account in fulfilling the obligations of their contract, we need to foster an approach based on mutual commitment and shared ownership supported by ongoing, open communication and feedback.

So much of what we find packaged today as performance management resembles the relationship I described with my children. Even good employers, who really care about and feel a sense of accountability to their people, approach the creation of employee experience as if employees have no power or choice in the situation. They create rules, policies and expectations to govern employee behaviour in the same way I create rules for my children. No discussion is needed because the parent knows best. And when you don't view yourself as being in a mutual committed relationship with balanced power, the natural default is to a model of holding those employees to account for compliance.

Breaking this cycle requires a change in mindset about the balance of power at work. Each employee is engaged in their own, individual relationship with work. We must meet them in the middle as organizations and managers, matching commitment with commitment. We must take on the responsibility of doing whatever we can to make sure the relationship is healthy for each employee.

Accountability in relationships, both personal and work, should feel natural and productive. It should be something that we both expect and crave. When we have mutually clear expectations and we are motivated to meet one another's needs in a relationship, it's almost natural to feel a sense of commitment and a desire for information that helps you ensure you are adequately contributing to keeping the relationship healthy. This should also be true of the work relationship for employees.

Accountability in healthy relationships is achieved in the following ways:

1   mutual commitment to the other's happiness;

2   transparency of impact through ongoing communication;

3   taking ownership for failures and learning from them;

4   resolving issues quickly with care and respect.

Designing accountability into our performance management system means creating processes to achieve each of these four things on an ongoing basis.

A well-designed performance management system should foster mutual commitment. The organization demonstrates commitment by thoughtfully designing and deploying great processes that support each employee's success. The first two performance processes we unpacked in the previous sections, planning and cultivation, will create commitment with employees. When performance planning is working, employees are clear about what is expected of them and how their performance is measured. And performance cultivation will ensure that each individual is motivated and supported in meeting their goals and objectives.

The impact of accountability

Performance accountability processes, then, should be focused on creating transparency of impact, encouraging ownership of failure to learn from experience, and resolution of issues quickly to protect the relationship. In the following pages we'll explore processes and examples for how organizations can successfully create accountability in a way that feels natural and supportive to the relationship.

Of the three performance processes, accountability is the one that seems to create the most anxiety. Planning and cultivation can be challenging and require diligent effort, but there's nothing unpleasant or uncomfortable about the work of creating clarity or motivating employees.

Accountability, on the other hand, is the part of the process where we have to face reality and ask the hard questions. Are we living up to our commitments? Are we meeting expectations? When the answer to these questions is no, the resulting conversation can be pretty uncomfortable.

This is also the part of the process where we face the consequences of our actions, both positive and negative. When we excel, this is where we find rewards and promotional opportunities. And when we struggle, it's where we might face tough choices connected to confronting our own behaviour and commitment.

When expectations are clear and understood, the next key ingredient in performance is to know how you're doing at meeting those expectations. It's one thing for me to say 'happy wife, happy life', but it's another thing to ensure that my wife is indeed happy. To be accountable to ensuring a happy wife, I need ongoing information about her level of happiness and how I'm either contributing to or diminishing it. This requires ongoing communication and feedback.

It's no different in the work relationship. If one of my expectations is to be great teammate to others, the only way I can gauge my progress is with feedback. Without information from my colleagues about the perceived impact of my behaviour on them, the expectations wouldn't do much to change my behaviour. Without that input, I might think I've become a much better teammate, when in fact my team hasn't noticed any change. My belief about my performance drives my behaviours; without information to shape my belief, there will be minimal behaviour change.

We need this ongoing awareness of progress to inform our beliefs about our performance. In addition, we also need ongoing input about what's working and where changes are needed with regard to our expectations. To become a better teammate, it's imperative that I understand what a good teammate does, where my behaviour aligns with that, and where I can make changes to improve. Accountability depends upon achieving this transparency of impact. This is the most challenging aspect of the process because it depends on the F-word of performance: *feedback*.

In the following chapters we'll dive into the processes of performance accountability. This starts with feedback, the thorniest practice of performance management. The next two chapters are dedicated to breaking us free from our dysfunctional relationship with feedback. We'll first address why we hate and avoid it (totally natural, by the way) and then explore how to fix it.

We'll then explore the role of measurement in performance management, including a discussion of the infamous performance rating. Chapter 14 explores the importance and power of individual and team reflection and how organizations are using it successfully. Finally, while a well-designed performance management system should dramatically minimize performance issues, we'll tackle how to confront and address these issues when they do arise without permanently damaging the relationship with the employee.

References

Accountability, *BusinessDictionary.com* [Online] http://www.businessdictionary.com/definition/accountability.html [Last accessed 2 May 2018]

Accountability Definition, *Psychology*, [Online] http://psychology.iresearchnet.com/social-psychology/social-cognition/accountability/ [Last accessed 2 May 2018]

US Legal (2016) Accountability law and legal definition, *US Legal* [Online] https://definitions.uslegal.com/a/accountability/ [Last accessed 2 May 2018]

Fixing feedback 11

The moments in my career that I think of most fondly are all connected to moments of achievement:

- solving a complex problem;
- finishing a big project;
- landing a new client.

That aligns with how I'm motivated. Your list might be similar or perhaps yours is about helping others or major moments of acknowledgement from others.

The worst moments in my career are all tied to one thing: critical feedback. It's very possible that I'm overly sensitive, but I can point to several days in my career when in the course of one hour, I went from feeling valued and engaged in my job to demoralized, defeated, and even angry. I don't think I'm alone in this experience. Most people I know cringe at the mere suggestion of feedback because they've had past experiences like mine.

I'll just say it. We suck at feedback – both giving and receiving it. We are particularly bad at giving feedback in a way that doesn't damage relationships.

It's strange that we have not got better at this skill given its relative importance to both performance and growth. Based on my experience, I don't think we are much better at feedback in our personal lives than we are at work. Mostly, we just try to avoid it. Where I grew up, it was even a part of our culture. I was taught at a very young age, 'If you don't have something nice to say, don't say anything at all.'

Even when we understand and embrace the importance of feedback to our growth and development as individuals, the process of receiving feedback often triggers emotional responses and defensiveness. It's common when receiving feedback to argue, get defensive, or rationalize away our own behaviour. We can be downright combative at times. This reaction explains why a manager or colleague might choose to avoid providing well-meaning and potentially helpful feedback. It's exhausting to provide feedback to someone who reacts this way. This ultimately makes the whole effort of sharing feedback feel like a waste of time and energy. It's a vicious cycle.

Why we hate feedback

When trying to understand why feedback is so challenging, It's helpful to again turn to the fields of psychology and neuroscience. For starters, remember that our brain is hardwired to protect us. When we perceive a threat, our brain triggers a defensive response. We are all familiar with our 'fight or flight' response to perceived danger. Recent neuroscience research suggests that our brain reacts to 'social' threats similarly to physical threats. Perceptions of negative social comparison or being treated unfairly have been shown to trigger a brain response similar to physical pain (Lieberman et al., 2009). This would help explain why we tend to react defensively to critical feedback – particularly when we think it may be unjust or threatening to our social status at work. It's a natural, biological response to avoid pain.

To compound this issue, there's an increasing body of research in psychology that shows how people, particularly in Western nations, tend to overestimate their competence while overlooking their weaknesses. There are a lot of factors that contribute to this phenomenon. For one, we tend to place more importance on the things that we are good at while downplaying others. This has been reinforced by the strengths-based management philosophy promoted by Gallup and others over the past two decades. By extension, because we are good at these few important things, we tend to think we are good overall (DeAngelis, 2003)

Researchers also suggest that a lack of quality and balanced feedback may also be contributing to this issue. Because of our tendency to avoid critical feedback and the relative ease of providing positive feedback, it's likely that our overestimation of our competence is reinforced by our environment and those around us. You are likely to get positive feedback on the things you do well and fail to get critical feedback on other areas where you might need to make improvements (DeAngelis, 2003). It's easy to see how this cycle could, over time, lead us to have a falsely inflated sense of our own abilities and some significant blind spots related to weaknesses that might be holding us back.

A cognitive bias known as the Dunning-Kruger Effect further enforces both the importance and complexity of feedback. It is an effect first identified in studies by social psychologists David Dunning and Justin Kruger. They found that ignorance plays a significant role in over-inflation of our own abilities. In their initial studies, university students were asked to complete simple tests and then, upon completion, estimate how well they had done. Those who performed most poorly greatly overestimated their performance compared to others who did well (Kruger and Dunning, 1999).

Is it any wonder we struggle with feedback? Most of us are operating on a belief that we're better than we actually are and we're blind to at least some of our weaknesses. These beliefs have been reinforced over the years by a lack of quality feedback. So, when that critical feedback comes, it makes us feel threatened. This can naturally trigger a defensive, fight or flight-type response. When that happens, the value of the feedback can be diminished or lost.

So, what are we to do?

In my opinion, much of what we've got wrong about feedback can be attributed to two things: relationship and approach. In the upcoming sections, we'll address how we can create a more effective approach to feedback using this foundational understanding of human psychology. And we'll explore practices from some companies who have done just that.

Making feedback work

The conventional wisdom about how to make feedback more palatable was to use what many refer to as the 'sandwich' approach. If you've been in management for any length of time, it's likely that someone taught or suggested this to you. The general idea is that critical feedback should be 'sandwiched' between positive feedback or praise. The underlying idea was to provide some positive reinforcement as a way to offset the negative response to criticism.

This approach was taught for years in management training classes but there's a problem. It doesn't work. At best, it makes the person delivering the feedback feel better, but it does little to help the receiver of the feedback. In many cases, the positive feedback offered feels inauthentic or contrived, which actually undermines the credibility of the critical feedback.

Sandwiching critical feedback does nothing to offset our natural reactions to the criticism. Taking something distasteful and putting it in a sandwich doesn't make it more appetizing. As we learned earlier, what makes us react to feedback defensively is that it feels like a threat. Our brain perceives it as danger and triggers a response designed to protect us. To increase the effectiveness of feedback, we have to find ways to make it feel less threatening.

In Chapter 3, I introduced you to the relationship test as a simple tool to help explore ways to make the work experience feel more like a healthy relationship. When exploring how to create a safer, less threatening experience of feedback, using this exercise can be helpful. When you decide that it's important enough that you must share some critical feedback with your best friend or spouse, how do you approach it?

Approach

Like most people, I don't enjoy giving critical feedback to anyone I'm close with. But there are occasions when it's warranted. In most cases, the feedback is needed to either help them achieve something that's important to them or to protect them from harm. In all cases, I am very thoughtful and intentional about what I am sharing and why, and I try to think about how to make the feedback feel as safe as possible. Thinking about how we approach these conversations with loved ones can provide some insight into how we might better approach feedback at work. By treating everyone at work with this same care with which we treat those who mean the most to us, we might find lessons for how to make feedback more human-friendly.

There are three approaches that I've found to be particularly effective for providing critical feedback in both personal and professional relationships.

Ask permission first

Critical feedback often feels threatening. Unexpected critical feedback always feels threatening. It's vital to take the surprise element out of feedback. When we request feedback from someone else, it decreases the likelihood of a defensive response because we are prepared for the feedback and we've given the other person permission to provide it. When the feedback hasn't been requested of us, the next best thing we can do is ask permission to share it. While the simple statement, 'Can I give you some feedback?' is a request for permission, it's likely to elicit a defensive response based on our past experience.

I recommend a more empathetic approach. For example: 'Jason, I noticed a few things about your presentation that might be helpful to you the next time you present. Would you be interested in hearing my thoughts?' In this request for permission are both context and an expressed desire to help.

In some cases, if I know the feedback might be hard to hear, I'll share that in my request for permission: 'Jason, I know how hard you're working to put yourself in a good spot to be promoted this year. I want to help you get there. There are some things I've noticed recently about your interactions that I'd like to share with you. The feedback might not be easy to hear. Are you open to me sharing with you what I've noticed?'

In this request, there again is an expression of intent and the context of why it's important. But there's also a foreshadowing of the fact that the feedback might be challenging to hear. When the person gives you permission to share the feedback, which nearly everyone will, your request gives them the chance to prepare themselves to hear and receive the feedback. It also allows them to shape the terms for when and how they receive the feedback. They might ask to do it later or that you share it with them in writing. Either way, it helps create a feeling of control for the person receiving the feedback to hopefully reduce their threat response.

Share a story

The second approach that I've found to be effective is to share a personal story of when you were on the receiving end of feedback and how you turned it into something positive. Any time I'm faced with sharing critical feedback with someone else, I always reflect on my own experience to identify times where I was in a similar position to the person I'm about to share feedback with. This not only helps me understand what their reaction to the feedback might feel like, but it gives me something I can share with this person to help them see how they can process the feedback.

Thankfully, I've been on the receiving end of a lot of feedback throughout my life. Some of it was pretty brutal and I didn't respond well. Sharing our own experiences is a great way to teach and to highlight the choices that one can make when given the gift of feedback. Knowing that others have been through a similar experience and emerged successfully can make it feel less threatening.

Give feedback like a gift

When we give someone a gift, we are often very thoughtful about what the gift should be. We might spend significant time and resources selecting or creating the gift. Then we give the gift, hoping the receiver will love it and do with it what we intended. But once we give the gift, it's no longer in our control. My kids have taught me this lesson well over the years. Regardless of how great I think a particular gift is or how much energy I put into finding and selecting it, there's no guarantee that they are going to like it or use it. Sometimes, they love it. Other times, they open it and won't play with it immediately, only to rediscover it a year later and fall in love with it then. Once in a while, the gift is a total failure on my part and they never use it. When giving gifts, you hope that all of the thoughtfulness will pay off, but that's not always the case. Forcing my kids to play with a toy that they aren't interested in only makes them dislike it more. The best gifts are given freely and without expectation.

It is powerful to treat feedback this same way. Treating feedback like a gift implies that while a lot of energy and effort might go into its creation and delivery, it is freely given without expectation. This is harder in practice than it sounds, particularly when the person you're providing feedback to is someone you supervise or manage. Critical feedback is typically shared as a means to effect behavioural change. It's helpful to remember the purpose of feedback is to create awareness of the impact of our actions. The individual has to internalize and process this new awareness to arrive at a new belief. This belief then leads to choices about changing their behaviour.

Trying to force an individual to take action on feedback is about as effective as forcing a child to play with a toy they aren't interested in. They will resist. We don't like being told what to do, as children or adults. When feedback is given freely without expectation, the choice of what to do with it lies with the individual. They might decide to act on it immediately. They might put it on the shelf for a while and come back to it later. Or, they might never use it. The choice is theirs.

Making it clear that your feedback is given as a gift without expectation reduces the threat level of the feedback and makes it much easier and safer to hear – even if the feedback itself is a bit harsh. Here's an example of how this might sound: 'Jason, the feedback I'm about to give you might be hard to hear. My motivation in sharing this is to help you be as successful as possible. That said, these are only my observations. You'll have to process through it and decide what actions you want to take, if any. I have no specific expectations of what you'll do with this feedback once I share it. That's up to you. I'm here to help should you need me.'

Relationship

If we use the relationship test to understand feedback from our own perspective, we can also gain some valuable insight. Why is it easier to receive feedback from those with whom you have a strong relationship? For the past decade and a half, my wife has been giving me ongoing feedback in our marriage. For the most part, the feedback was pretty easy for me to process and take action on. When she gives me feedback, it often sounds like this: 'Honey, I love you, but if you don't stop slurping your coffee, I might lose my mind.'

While her approach may strike you as a bit backhanded, it's meant with humour and it works for us. That's her style and I get the intended message ('please don't slurp your coffee'). The most important thing is what she said first: 'I love you'. Our commitment to each other is strong and I trust her completely. Because we have invested in creating a strong relationship, any feedback she shares doesn't feel much like a threat. That doesn't mean that I don't get a tiny bit defensive when she tells me that a new shirt I bought doesn't look good on me, but I am able to move past it pretty quickly. I absolutely trust her intentions. I never worry that our relationship is in danger.

What the relationship test reveals in this case is something that you've likely found true throughout your life. When a relationship is healthy and built on a solid foundation of trust and mutual commitment, feedback doesn't feel nearly as threatening. Instead of trying gimmicks like the sandwich method, it's far more important to first invest in building a better relationship so when the time comes for feedback, it is more likely to be received well.

CASE STUDY Feedback lunches at Menlo Innovations

At software development firm, Menlo Innovations, feedback is built into how they do their work on a day-to-day basis. One of the formal processes they use is called the 'Feedback Lunch'. They use it to ensure that all employees in their team-based work environment are getting the feedback they need for ongoing growth and development. It is one of the most relational approaches to feedback that have I encountered in my research. It's a one-hour, in-person feedback session with five peers. Here's how it works.

The employee initiates the process and requests that a Feedback Lunch be scheduled. The next step is to identify a few teammates (as many as five) who they would like involved in the process. These are people they have worked with closely on recent projects and who would have a good perspective into their contributions and performance. Once this group is identified, a date for the actual lunch is set, several weeks in the future.

Next, the individual requesting the feedback will write up a summary of what projects they've worked on and any specific questions they would like the group to think about. When the day of the lunch arrives, the group gathers in a conference room together. Over the next hour, they share and discuss feedback for the individual who requested the meeting. They offer up both positive and critical feedback along with coaching and suggestions for how to improve. The individual receiving the feedback can participate and ask questions throughout.

To close the lunch, the individual who requested the meeting is often asked to answer the question, 'How can the team better support you?' This provides the opportunity for the employee to request support or help where it's needed. It reinforces the mutual nature of the relationships and the process. The meeting then ends and everyone returns to their day-to-day work.

When first hearing about this process, it's natural to react with a bit of scepticism. For most of us, the idea of inviting your colleagues to sit down around a table and provide face-to-face feedback sounds simultaneously terrifying and pointless. For all of the reasons we outlined earlier, this process sounds like a train wreck. People aren't likely to be comfortable sharing any sort of critical feedback in this forum and even if they did, we'd probably not receive it well. I spoke with organizations who had tried this approach and then abandoned it because that was their experience. It just wasn't effective.

So why does it work for Menlo? Their employees embrace the process, and find it to be extremely valuable and mostly free of defensiveness and tension. The answer boils down to relationships. Menlo's culture is built on a core idea that each employee's role is to make their teammate successful. They succeed and fail on the strength of their commitment to one another. This is built into the DNA of the organization. Their elaborate, group interviewing process includes a clear instruction to those eager would-be new hires: 'Your objective in this process is to get the person next to you hired.' And they mean it. Getting hired at Menlo means you are a consummate team player who takes as much or more joy in helping others succeed as you do in individual achievement.

Everything about how Menlo works reinforces this idea. This has led to a workplace culture rich in trust where employees feel deeply committed to one another's success. It is this strength of relationship with one another that makes the Feedback Lunch work. The people sitting around the table trust one another's intentions. They are all there to help and everything shared is done so in the interest of the person who requested the feedback. The experience feels safe. The feedback isn't threatening, so it can be received openly and embraced as an investment in their growth.

The Feedback Lunch is an effective and simple process at Menlo. But what is extraordinary about this example isn't the process, but the strong foundation of commitment and relationship that exists between colleagues. Without the relationships, the process would likely fail like it has elsewhere.

As we continue to explore different ways to handle and structure feedback processes, it's critical to remember that the relationship comes first. Investing time and resources to build and strengthen relationships will enhance the effectiveness of any feedback process you use. The stronger foundation of healthy relationships, the more effective your feedback processes will become at motivating behaviour change and growth.

Key takeaways

- Feedback is challenging in large part because of how our brains process it. Perceived threats to social status or a lack of fairness cause a reaction in the brain similar to physical pain – something to be avoided. This is troublesome because we tend to overestimate our competence and ignore our weaknesses, making most critical feedback feel socially threatening or unfair.

- We suck at feedback. We are particularly bad at giving feedback in a way that doesn't damage relationships.

- Making feedback more effective starts with using a different approach. Three effective approaches include asking permission first, sharing a story, and giving feedback like a gift.

- The other key to effective feedback is to establish healthy trusting relationships. The stronger the relationship, the more likely the feedback will be received positively and not feel threatening.

References

DeAngelis, T (2003) Why we overestimate our competence: social psychologists are examining people's pattern of overlooking their own weaknesses, *American Psychological Association* [Online] http://www.apa.org/monitor/feb03/overestimate.aspx [Last accessed 2 May 2018]

Kruger, J and Dunning, D (1999) Unskilled and unaware of it: how difficulties in recognizing one's own incompetence lead to inflated self-assessments, *Journal of Personality and Social Psychology*, 77 (6), pp. 1121–34

Lieberman, M D et al. (2009) Pains and pleasures of social life, *Science*, 13 February, **323** (5916), pp. 890–91 [Online] doi: 10.1126/science.1170008

A new approach 12
to feedback

Another reason that we tend to cringe at the mention of feedback is that by its definition, it's information about the past. Critical feedback is essentially shining a light on a circumstance in our past where we failed to perform up to others' expectation of us. And since it's in the past, there's nothing that can be done to change it. Receiving this kind of feedback is demoralizing because it reminds us that we failed without being given an opportunity to change it.

'You handled the question from that customer very poorly. You came across as defensive and unprepared.'

This is an example of the type of feedback we prefer to avoid. It ensures that you know you've done something wrong without providing clarity about how to fix it. This kind of feedback only leads to uncertainty and frustration. If positive behaviour change happens as a result of this kind of feedback, it is more about luck than it is about the feedback.

Feedforward

Early in my HR career, I had the opportunity to hear the esteemed executive coach and author Marshall Goldsmith speak at a conference. Among the things he talked about that day was an approach he teaches to his clients call 'Feedforward'. The idea was incredibly simple. When asked for feedback, instead of critiquing the situation, offer up some potential solutions that might help. The rationale for this approach is that no one likes to be criticized, but most people are open to recommendations and suggestions that might help solve their problem or help them achieve their objectives. This is further reinforcement that being presented with improvement ideas is empowering because it reinforces the potential for progress and leaves the choice in the hands of the individual receiving the recommendations. That's the magic of feedforward.

For example, if I were struggling with finishing my work on time, feedback would focus on what I'm either not doing or doing wrong and where my results are insufficient. Feedforward instead focuses on providing some ideas that could help me complete my work in a more timely fashion in the future. This might include ideas like using a planning tool to organize my work or setting deadlines in my calendar for one day in advance of when it's actually due. While these might not be the ideal solutions for me or my style of working, it prompts me to think about how I can change my results instead of simply feeling bad about them. It reinforces my belief that I can make the change.

When I first heard the concept, I thought it was novel, but didn't really appreciate the power of it. It wasn't until nearly a decade later at another conference where I heard author Marcus Buckingham talk about a slightly different approach to feedforward that its genius finally hit me. The difference between feedback and feedforward can seem slight at first glance, but it can produce very different reactions from the person on the receiving end.

The fundamental difference between feedback and feedforward is in the directional orientation of the person providing the information or insights. Critical feedback is oriented towards the past, focusing on what went wrong and how things could have gone better. Feedforward is oriented towards the future, providing suggestions and recommendations for consideration that are informed by observed performance. The difference in the approach won't feel dramatic for the person on the delivering end but will feel dramatically different on the receiving end.

Let's examine the contrast in approaches in the following example. An employee on your team shows up to your weekly team meeting late and clearly unprepared for the second time in a row. This disrupts the meeting and decreases its value for the others who are in attendance. It is clear that this is frustrating to the other members of the team.

Providing feedback to the employee based on this situation might sound like this: 'Jason, it's important that you arrive on time and come prepared for our meetings. You've been late for the past two meetings and it's clear by your lack of participation and rambling updates that you were not prepared. This negatively impacts our meeting and everyone attending. Don't let it happen again.'

The feedback is pretty clear and the expectation is reinforced. If you received this feedback, you would know that your behaviour needs to change. But what if you thought you were prepared for the meeting? Or what if you had every intention of getting there on time, but despite your best efforts, you just seemed to lose time somewhere? In other words, what if you are trying but it's just not working? If that were the case, the feedback would feel pretty demoralizing, and it wouldn't leave you with any idea of what you should do differently in the future.

Now, let's try applying feedforward to the situation. Same circumstance, but instead of highlighting what went wrong, we focus on providing suggestions for the future. One way to approach this might sound like this: 'Jason, it's important that you arrive on time and are prepared for the meeting. Could I offer a couple of suggestions that might be helpful for the next meeting? In terms of being on time, I've found it useful to block out my calendar for 30 minutes before the meeting to make sure I have an opportunity to review my notes and plenty of time to get there. Maybe that would work for you too. In terms of preparation, it might be good to schedule 15 or 20 minutes the day before to collect your thoughts and make some notes. One way to help organize your thoughts might be to have a question or two to prompt your thinking, like "What are my two biggest priorities this week?" and "What would the team want to know about what I/we are doing this week?" This team depends on you to be on time and to contribute fully in these meetings. I hope these ideas are helpful.'

The underlying message being delivered in both cases is the same: be on time and come prepared. But the experience of the person on the receiving end of the message is markedly different. One of the powerful things about the feedforward approach is that it is built on a positive assumption that every individual wants to perform well. When performance doesn't align with that assumed intention, the reaction is to help, not criticize.

Feedforward is a coaching mindset. In sports, coaches use this type of approach with players, particularly during games when the stakes for performing are the highest. Criticizing a player for a mistake or failing in some way doesn't help them perform better. A demoralized athlete is rarely a high-performing athlete. Instead, the coach teaches and provides guidance for how to execute better on the next play or in the next period. They equip the athlete with the information they need to change and improve their performance moving forward.

Making peer-to-peer feedback work

The feedforward approach can be used to make group feedback processes more effective as well. Let's consider the 360-degree assessment, a common feedback process, particularly for those in management and leadership roles. The idea underlying the 360 is to use feedback to paint a full picture of the individual's performance from the perspectives of those with whom they work most closely (ie co-worker, boss, subordinate, etc). The concept of gathering a broad perspective of an individual's performance from those who are best positioned to observe it is a great one. However, the problem with the 360 lies in the design and execution of the process.

I've had the displeasure of being on the receiving end of a 360-degree assessment a number of times throughout my career. While the specific 360 instrument varied from one time to the next, the process was generally the same. Those with whom I worked most closely were sent a confidential assessment (ie I wouldn't know who said what) to complete about me and my performance. Typically, they were asked to rate my skills and behaviours based on their observations using a numeric rating of some kind.

As part of the 360 process, I was also given the opportunity to complete the same assessment on myself, ostensibly for the purpose of highlighting gaps in my self-awareness. As with most feedback instruments, these assessments focused on a critique of my past performance, not on my future potential. Most of the results came back in the form of numeric ratings or as part of some visual charting of responses. To make matters worse, the data is collected confidentially so there's no opportunity to put feedback in context of who provided it or to ask clarifying questions.

I honestly don't remember much from the results from any of these assessments. Due to the process, the feedback itself was sort of lost on me. I do, however, remember how terrible and angst-ridden the process felt. Nothing about the 360 process feels safe. Knowing that your peers are providing confidential feedback about you feels threatening. The expectation of receiving critical feedback often triggers a negative response. That effect is amplified by the 360 because the feedback is coming from the people with whom you work most closely. The only people who seem to really enjoy the 360 process are those who administer it; it's an uncomfortable process for the people both giving and receiving feedback.

In fairness, I think some of the 360 assessments I took part in may have asked some questions about how I could improve. But by the time we got to that part of the process, I was typically feeling pretty threatened and defensive, so I'm not sure I was able to reap the benefits of those suggestions. The process definitely caused more angst for me than it motivated growth or behaviour change. The traditional 360 assessment is a flawed process. In the context of creating a work experience that feels like a healthy relationship for employees, it might be one of the most harmful practices within our organizations today. Nothing about it builds relationships.

That doesn't mean that all peer-based group feedback is bad or that you should abandon the practice entirely. But it does mean that we need to approach it very differently from how we have in the past.

The Menlo Innovations Feedback Lunch described in the last chapter accomplishes a similar objective as the 360, but with a very different approach. In large part, their process works because it's mindful of relationships. The process is supported by a strong culture of mutual commitment and trust that makes giving and receiving feedback safer. The process also honours the relationship by having the feedback delivered in person so the individual can put it in context and ask questions. While I'm sure there may still be some anxiety heading into a feedback lunch, particularly the first few times, I'm sure it's minimal in comparison to the experience of a traditional 360.

While your culture might not be ready to embrace the feedback lunch approach yet, there are some ways to design group feedback processes to feel safer and more relationship friendly.

1. Ask open-ended, feedforward questions

It was common in my research to find organizations that have begun using a simplified peer-to-peer group feedback process in place of the 360 but with the same objective: to give people well-rounded and supportive feedback to encourage their growth. In several cases, the assessment used consisted of only two open-ended questions, one focusing on what the individual is doing well, and the other on providing suggestions for how to improve in the future.

For example:

- What does Jason do best?
- How can Jason have a bigger impact in the future?

These questions are designed to positively reinforce what's working and solicit suggestions to improve future performance. Using a feedforward approach like this makes the process less threatening and more actionable. It's built on the assumption that the employee wants to succeed, provides acknowledgement of their current impact, and empowers them with ideas for ways to find greater success in the future. This approach is far less likely to do harm to relationships, particularly when the feedback is attributed (you know who provided it).

2. *Abandon confidentiality and anonymity*

The traditional 360 assessment fails the relationship test on multiple levels. Most pointedly, any type of feedback given anonymously or without attribution will never build relationships and will almost always do harm. You can't build a relationship with a faceless, unknown individual.

Providing feedback anonymously to someone you care about also violates our expectations of trust, respect and reciprocity. We'd never use anonymity to provide a family member or spouse with feedback if we cared at all about preserving the relationship. Anonymous feedback breeds suspicion, defensiveness and distrust; not the sort of emotions you want to cause in any important relationship.

Organizations that are truly committed to creating a more human-friendly work experience have removed anonymity and confidentiality from the exchange of feedback between humans. Not to do so is to intentionally damage the employee's relationship with work.

When these organizations discover that employees can't or won't provide each other with feedback directly, they recognize that they have a trust or ability problem (or both), not a feedback problem. When the relationship is healthy and a positive feedforward approach is used, there is no reason employees can't provide each other feedback directly and with their name attached to it.

3. *Give control to the employee*

For most of the history of management, feedback processes like the 360 and performance appraisal were done to employees, not with or for employees. These processes were imposed, in most cases without much input and limited participation from the employee. The lack of influence or control on these experiences is another reason they don't feel great.

In healthy relationships, commitment and participation are mutual. While I may have to force some process or rule on my children for their development or protection, I would never presume to do so with my wife. Just the act of trying to force some rule or process on her without discussion and mutual agreement would severely harm our relationship. We make decisions like this together.

We must keep this in mind when we design feedback processes. To make peer-to-peer feedback less threatening, put the process in the hands of the employee so they have more of a feeling of control. When employees feel a sense of ownership of the process, they are less likely to feel threatened by it.

Here are two simple ways to give employees a feeling of ownership and control in a structured peer-to-peer feedback process:

- Let them choose and invite the people who will share feedback with them. No one is better positioned than the person receiving feedback to identify who has the best vantage point to provide it. In addition to offering some control of this process, inviting others to provide feedback helps the employee to be more receptive to what they receive.

- Give them the ability to add to or shape what questions are asked. If an employee is specifically interested in feedback on a particular aspect of their performance, why not allow them to request that feedback specifically? If allowing employees to add a question to the process isn't possible or is too cumbersome, invite them to add some context to the invitation for feedback they send. For example, they could share that they are actively trying to improve their communication skills and that any feedback or suggestions in that area would be particularly helpful. Again, this type of ownership of the process not only makes it less threatening, but makes it more likely that the feedback with be embraced when received.

CASE STUDY   Vistaprint

At Vistaprint, they have discovered the value of empowering employees to own their own feedback process. Vistaprint, a Cimpress company, offers customized printed and produced marketing materials and employs roughly 7,000 people globally. A few years ago, as the organization was in the midst of a transition to using the Agile methodology for software development, the technology teams began to notice that the traditional performance management processes weren't effective in this new environment. As more and more autonomous teams were being established around outcomes, managers were losing line of sight to each employee's performance. The structures of these teams were calling for more of the feedback, and even overall team management, to happen more directly and within the team. This was a problem for their old, manager-centric approach to performance.

The HR team, led by Colleen Fuller, who supported the technology and admin groups, took this as a cue to take a critical look at their performance management processes. They began a discovery process of collecting input from employees about what was working and what needed to change. The resounding message from employees was that they wanted to be managed, developed, and rewarded differently than in the past.

Vistaprint's traditional performance management process involved a 360-degree assessment which provided input into an annual formal performance review with rating. The first step taken as a result of employee feedback was to remove the formality and rigidity of the process itself. This included making the formal 360 process optional. Managers were simply told that they needed to have a meaningful conversation with their employees. They could still collect feedback to prepare for this and create a simple (bullet-style) summary, but they could do it in a way that resonated with them and they were no longer required to use the cumbersome tool and accompanying forms. As a result, better and more meaningful conversations began to take place and use of the traditional 360 process decreased to almost zero.

Next, they eliminated the requirement for managers to complete the formal review including ratings and all the forms involved. Instead, they simply asked managers to engage with employees at least once a year in some way to discuss and share feedback about performance. They found through employee survey data that removing any formal requirement of managers to provide a review did not reduce the number of employees receiving feedback from managers. The old process only seemed to make the experience less pleasant.

The final stage involved shifting the responsibility of who owns feedback from managers to the individual employees and teams. In this new way of working, giving and receiving feedback is an expectation of every employee. Employees are expected to request and collect feedback from those who would have the best exposure to it. In addition to this self-request, the expectation is that they are also receiving feedback regularly from the team within which they work. The responsibility is then on the individual to take received feedback and process it independently before sharing it with their manager.

According to Fuller, this approach has made the feedback process feel safer for employees. By hearing it directly, employees can better understand the context, seek additional clarity, and have more opportunity to ask for help. They also hear from team members what they are doing well. This approach has also positioned the manager as more of a coach than an evaluator. When the employee shares the feedback with their manager, they spend their time processing what it means and what to do as a result. The entire process is designed to focus on learning rather than compliance with expectations. At the one-year mark of the new process, employee performance is steady and sentiment about the process is that it's a definite improvement. In particular, employees like the feeling of being in control of the process.

Building skills for receiving feedback

While we've reviewed many ways to make feedback less threatening and more constructive, it's impossible to guarantee that everyone who shares feedback with someone else in your organization will do it in a positive way. Some people will be blunt or critical because that's their style. Your passive-aggressive employees will unload a series of stored-up grievances any time they are invited to share feedback. There's no way to eliminate bad feedback experiences.

So, while it's incredibly important to teach effective approaches to giving feedback and design processes to help others share feedback more effectively, that's not enough. It's also important to equip people with the tools and mindset for how to receive feedback, particularly critical feedback that can often be delivered in less than optimal ways.

This is a lesson I learned the hard way many years ago when I was leading a corporate talent management team. We'd spent months designing a new competency-driven process for developing talent within the organization. The process started with a manager assessment and employee self-assessment which they discussed and compared. The manager would then meet with their management peers to have a calibration meeting where they presented each of their direct reports to compare how their assessment and perception of each individual they managed aligned with that of the group. After the calibration meeting, the manager was to take the feedback from that discussion and share it with the employee to supplement the assessment discussions they'd already had. All of this feedback was then to be used for creating a career path and development plan for the individual.

Since this was a new process and was viewed as strategically important to the organization, we decided that those at the top of the organization should be first to go through it. This meant that if you reported to a member of the executive team, you were first up. This included me. I was to be subject to my own process and I was pretty excited about it.

The initial steps of the process involving the manager and self-assessment went relatively smoothly. Then the executives met for their calibration meeting. Following the calibration meeting, the executives began sharing the resulting feedback with their direct reports. By coincidence, I was among the first to go through this step in the process. In our design of the process, we had made the assumption that executives and directors at this level were tenured enough to have the skills to handle the process of giving, receiving and processing feedback. We were terribly wrong.

I still vividly remember the day I received my feedback from the calibration meeting. I don't remember much of the actual feedback, but I remember exactly how I felt during and after it. I walked into the meeting that day with really positive expectations and optimism. I'd been performing well against my expectations and believed that I was likely viewed as a future executive at the company. In the prior conversation where we compared our self-assessments, my boss and I were relatively well aligned. No major surprises had come from that conversation.

My optimism and positivity were quickly dismissed. My boss had a sheet of notes in front of her on the table. On it were maybe ten specific notes of feedback she had captured to share with me. Without any particular context about the discussion, she started in on the list. It was clear that she was uncomfortable. The feedback was pointedly critical, calling out things I needed to fix or do better. Each new item felt like a dagger stuck into me. About halfway through the list, I stopped her and asked her if there was anything positive on the list. She said that there was not and then continued. By the time she was finished, I was an emotional mess. I was confused. I was angry. And I was completely defensive.

I left the meeting and went home for the day. By the next morning, my emotional state hadn't changed, so I called in sick. I knew that if I were to go to the office, I might say something that I'd regret, so I gave myself a mental health day to recover. I needed time to process and come to terms with what I now affectionately refer to as my 'You Suck' list.

In hindsight, I'm not proud of how I reacted. I wish I hadn't been so defensive. I wish my emotions hadn't got the best of me. But I'd never had an experience like that, and I wasn't the only one. Many of my colleagues were experiencing similarly painful feedback meetings with varying types of responses. None of them particularly positive.

Once my head was back in the game, we recognized that we had a major gap in our process design. The success of this process was completely dependent upon individuals receiving quality feedback to inform their development plans for the future. As it stood, we had a good process for collecting feedback, but it broke down when it came to turning that feedback into learning and motivation. My own experience was incredibly informative as we considered how to improve the process.

First, we knew we'd need to train and coach managers and leaders on how to more effectively deliver feedback. In my case, my boss had neglected to share with me in our meeting that when she presented her assessment of me in my current role, there was agreement. It was only when they began talking about me as a potential successor to her as an executive that they began to offer up the developmental feedback. This context completely changed the feedback for me. It turns out I didn't suck, I just had a lot of work to do in order to be ready for the next step in my career. It was my boss's first time delivering feedback like this and she admittedly handled it poorly. She would have benefitted from guidance about how to make the meeting more effective. I learned to never assume anyone is skilled at feedback (or management skills in general) regardless of their tenure or level within the organization.

I also handled the situation very poorly. I was caught off-guard and had no idea how to deal with the situation. I'd had critical feedback in the past, but nothing like this. I didn't have any strategies to fall back on for how to handle the situation or my resulting emotions. Had I been equipped with the right tools and mindset for how to handle any type of feedback, it would have mattered less how the feedback was delivered.

Going forward, we did invest time in teaching managers better skills for delivering feedback. But the more important advancement we made was to offering training to all employees on how to receive feedback. Our belief was that if we could create a workforce of people who were skilled at receiving and extracting the learning from feedback, regardless of how it was delivered, then we could accelerate development. Once we took this step, the process began to work more as it was intended, creating motivation and focus for development rather than resentment and defensiveness.

Key takeaways

To help others learn to receive feedback more effectively, there are some key lessons to share:

1 *It's natural to dislike feedback.* We don't enjoy feedback. Even when we say we like it, we aren't really talking about the experience of being critiqued but rather the resulting opportunity to improve and grow. For the many reasons we have outlined in this section of the book, feedback often triggers emotions that don't feel great. That's natural and we should expect it. When we know the reaction is coming, we shouldn't be surprised by it. We can learn to embrace these emotions as part of the process.

2 *Receive feedback as a gift.* How would you respond if a friend gave you a gift for which you had no use or interest? You might be confused at first, but you'd probably still say 'thank you'. If you wanted to keep

the friend, you'd probably avoid an argument over why it was not a good gift. You'd simply receive it and give your friend credit for their thoughtfulness in making time to even consider getting you a gift. Then you might stash it away in a closet where you would never think about it again. When we view feedback as a gift, it helps both parties to process the experience. As suggested earlier, the giver should spend time thoughtfully selecting and preparing their gift. The receiver should graciously receive it. If it happens to be a great gift that the receiver loves and can use, that's terrific. But that's not always going to be the case. The receiver of the gift is in control of what happens once it's given. When presented with feedback, no matter how well or poorly it was shared, the best thing to say is 'thank you'. Remember that was likely as awkward for the person giving it as it was for you to hear it.

3 *Seek first to understand.* After saying thank you, our first reaction to feedback should be to ask clarifying questions. As in my example, context is important to feedback but is easy to overlook. When presented with some critical feedback, the first objective is not to react or internalize but to understand the gift that is being presented. Having some questions at the ready can be helpful to combat any emotional response that you might experience. For example:

- Can you share with me an example or two of when you've observed this?
- How often would you say this occurs?
- How long has this been happening?
- What kind of an impact is this having?
- What ideas do you have for how I could improve?

4 *Take time to process.* Emotional responses to feedback might be intense at first, particularly when the feedback is unexpected or feels unfair. It's important to allow time for the emotions to calm before deciding what to do with the gift of feedback. If the feedback at first feels unfair or wrong, before discarding it, ask yourself this question: 'What if this were true? What would be the implications?' What we discovered in our talent management process was that part of what made the feedback discussions so intense was that much of the feedback was

in the individual's blind spot. Because there had been no process in the past, some of us were getting feedback about things that had probably been issues for us for a long time but which we were totally unaware of due to lack of feedback in the past. Once I took time to process my feedback, I realized that, regardless of whether I agreed with the feedback or not, it was very real in the minds of those who needed to be on board with my future career path. These were real obstacles, fair or not, that stood in the way of my growth and needed to be addressed.

5 *Decide what action to take (if any).* Having spent time processing and understanding the feedback, it's time to decide what to do about it. In most cases, if someone has taken the time and made the effort of providing you with feedback, it's a good assumption that it is important. Taking action on feedback is a good practice but deciding what action to take can sometimes be challenging. When you are unsure what to do about some particular feedback, a helpful step can actually be to seek out more feedback and advice from others. Share with them what you've heard and ask for their thoughts or suggestions. For example: 'I've been given some feedback that I don't listen very well at times. Have you experienced that from me? And what suggestions do you have for how I might become a better listener?'

Taking action on feedback is a good idea, but not a requirement. Just because someone gave you feedback doesn't mean you have to do anything with it. Sometimes the best thing to do with critical feedback is to ignore it. Every time I give a keynote, there is always at least one person in the audience who has some criticism of me that they will happily share in the evaluation. If I made changes based on every one of those comments, I'd lose my mind and my confidence. I typically accept their gift of feedback gratefully and choose to ignore it. Remembering that you have a choice is important to having a healthy mindset about receiving feedback. You are in control. There will be consequences from your decision, positive or negative, regardless of what you decide. But the decision of what to do next is yours.

The most reliable way to ensure that feedback becomes a healthy part of your performance management system is to equip every employee with the right tools and mindsets to receive and process this gift when it's given.

Key takeaways

- Adopting and training a feedforward approach to providing feedback can help make the exchange less threatening and more positive. Simply put, feedforward shifts the focus from criticism of past performance to suggestions for how to improve in the future.

- The traditional 360 assessment is a flawed process. In the context of creating a work experience that feels like a healthy relationship for employees, it might be one of the most harmful practices within our organizations today.

- To make peer-to-peer feedback processes more effective, use open-ended, feedforward questions, abandon anonymity, and give employees control of the process.

- Despite your best efforts, some feedback will always be delivered poorly. To unleash the full potential of feedback for growth and development, train all employees on how to effectively receive and process feedback – regardless of the skill with which it is provided.

Measurement and ratings   13

One thing I've found fascinating throughout my career is the difficulty we seem to have with measuring employee performance effectively. There's no doubt that we understand the importance of measurement. Leaders repeat the old saying 'what gets measured, gets done' as if it were a universal truth of management. And the idea of measuring performance is intuitively obvious. We are naturally motivated by a feeling of progress and that's impossible without measurement of how much we've accomplished or how far we've come.

Accepting accountability for my performance requires that I understand and have visibility into how it is measured. To take ownership of my results, I must understand what counts, how it is counted, and how much constitutes success. And I need visibility into my progress relative to my goals on a frequent basis. I'm amazed how often these simple and seemingly obvious components of performance management are overlooked.

When you talk to employees about why the performance review process is so nerve-racking and unpopular, two of the common complaints revolve around measurement. In some cases, they were unclear on how their performance was going to be measured. They also complained that they had no concept of how well they had performed until they received their review. Their performance evaluation would be a surprise because they had no visibility into their progress along the way. This is unacceptable when you consider the role that performance evaluations often have in employee compensation decisions. We don't like surprises when they have an impact on our pay cheque.

Measurement of performance is another way we can create clarity and reduce uncertainty for employees. If I'm clear on what's expected of me and I know where my results stand relative to meeting those expectations at any given time, then I have a feeling of control over my performance. Accountability for achieving success is in my hands.

Why ratings failed

For decades, the primary 'measurement' of an employee's performance at work was the dreaded performance rating. This annual ritual of reducing a year's worth of effort to a single number is one of the most obvious examples of treating work like a contract to be enforced on the employee. Considered through the relationship test, ratings fail every time as a way to build rather than harm relationships.

What would happen if you said this to one of your close friends: 'You've done an okay job as a friend this year. I'm giving you a 3 out of 5.' You'd probably end up with one less friend to rate next year.

Or how about this use of ratings in a personal relationship? 'Thanks for inviting us over for dinner. I'd give the experience a 2.5. It was a little below what we've come to expect from you.'

We don't use ratings to convey feedback to those we really care about. If we did, it would most certainly harm those relationships. Reducing human behaviour to a number doesn't feel right. It minimizes the complexity and nuance involved. But that's not the only reason they are a bad idea.

Maybe, most critically, ratings are one person's subjective evaluation of another. And we just aren't good at assessing other people with any accuracy. One major research study revealed that when analysing the accuracy of a subjective rating of one person by another in the workplace, more than half of the variance (up to 62 per cent) had nothing to do with *the person being rated*. Rather, the rating variance had everything to do with *the person doing the rating*. They described this as 'idiosyncratic rater effects', which means for performance ratings, your rating has more to do with who's rating you than it does with your actual performance (Skullen, 2000).

In addition, trying to reduce something as complex as employee performance down to a single number is a questionable practice. In professional sports, a player's performance is evaluated using many different variables. In basketball, for example, using only a player's shooting performance paints a very limited view of their overall impact on the game. One player with a high shooting percentage might turn the ball over frequently and allow a lot of points on defence. Only looking at shooting percentage would miss the fact that this player actually does more damage than good when they are in the game.

In medicine, health is never measured using a single number. A simple blood test typically measures six or more different factors to provide a broad assessment of health (NHS, 2016). Even in school, teachers use a variety of measures to gauge overall student performance. The last report card we received from our children's school had over 20 different grades for each child.

Reducing something as complex as employee performance to a single number is bad practice. A broader, more intentional application of measurement is required to have impact. Not only are ratings bad data in most cases, the rating itself cannot begin to capture the nuance and context of human performance over any period of time.

Ratings should have no place in performance management. But measurement, as we've highlighted, is critically important. To create performance accountability requires effective processes for measuring performance. Effective performance measurement is accomplished through three steps: define, assess, and share.

The three steps of performance measurement

Define

Figure 6

The first step of measurement is definition. For employee performance, this should happen in the planning process. Clear expectations make it explicit how performance will be measured. It's the answer to the question, 'How will I know that I've been successful?' This can be easy if your work is easily quantifiable (ie average number of customers served per hour).

But it can also be challenging when the expectation is harder to count. For example, what if your goal had to do with having a more positive attitude at work? There may not be an obvious and easily countable output to rely on. In these cases, we have to ask a few more questions to determine the best definition of success.

First, what specific instances or interactions led to the creation of this goal? Perhaps it was making negative comments in meetings. Or maybe it was because the employee was instantly critical and dismissive of any new idea shared with him. One possible measurement would be the absence of these behaviours. Success could mean the absence of negative contributions in meetings or never being immediately critical of new ideas. But this isn't a very compelling way to measure success. While stopping a bad behaviour can be progress, a better goal is to replace it with something more constructive.

To identify a more constructive way to measure progress, ask yourself what kind of behaviours would signal an improvement? In this example, it could be as simple as making some positive or affirming comments in meetings. Another example might be replacing a critical response to new ideas with something more constructive like 'That's interesting' or 'Tell me more about that.'

These are just a few simple examples. The important point to remember is that measurement starts with definition. You cannot measure what you have not first defined. Regardless of how challenging it might be, the effort is always worth it.

Assess

Figure 7

Equipped with clear definitions, you can proceed with the core of measurement, which is to actually assess, count, or evaluate progress. When outcomes are easy to isolate and quantify, this part of the process is pretty straightforward. It's not hard to collect and analyse data that is counted as part of doing business (ie revenue dollars, customers served, etc). What is more challenging is when the outcomes are harder to quantify, like the attitude example above.

Much of employee performance is behavioural and falls into this category we'd consider difficult to quantify. Since so much of the impact of our behaviour is tied to how it affects others (co-workers, customers, and others), to assess it requires gathering feedback from those very people. By clearly defining what success looks like for performance expectations, you inform the kind of feedback you might ask for.

In the case where the goal is to help an employee have a more positive attitude, specifically in meetings and in responding to new ideas, soliciting peer feedback could be incredibly valuable. Applying the feedforward approach, here are some specific questions you might ask the peers who interact with the employee most frequently:

- 'Could you please describe a recent time when Jason showed a positive attitude in a meeting?'
- 'What ideas do you have for how Jason could contribute more positivity to meetings?'

The feedback request could be made through an online system or directly via e-mail. In some cases, a face-to-face meeting might be the right way to request the feedback. These requests would reveal both how frequently Jason is demonstrating a positive attitude and surface some ideas for how he could continue to improve. If the behaviour is not happening, that will also surface. It's impossible to cite an example of something that hasn't been observed. By requesting this feedback periodically throughout the performance period, a measurement of progress could be observed.

CASE STUDY K&N Management game films

There are other creative ways to assess performance against designed standards that go beyond peer-to-peer feedback. At Austin, Texas-based restaurant management company K&N Management, they use a process called 'game films' to assess customer service. K&N takes service very seriously. In fact, one of their eight key business drivers at the organization is what they call 'Texas Hospitality'. This service level standard is defined very specifically and clearly down to the behavioural level for cashiers, who they know are vital to the customer experience.

Game films are video recordings captured secretly in real time by professionals posing as customers. These 'mystery shoppers' will visit the restaurants periodically to capture recordings of their interactions within the restaurant. Sometimes they will even make a complaint to a cashier to see how they respond to the situation. The cashiers are well aware that the company uses mystery shoppers and game films, but they don't know when or if they might be participating.

The goal of the game film process is to help employees see the service experience through the eyes of the customer. It's applied with a very feedforward approach. According to Gini Quiroz, Director of Team Member Engagement, the goal of the process is to catch employees doing something good and provide them with information for how to do even better in the future. The company is so committed to this process of service assessment that they hired an internal replay analyst whose job is to assess the game films against the defined expectations to 'score' the film and provide store management with notes for coaching. Top-scoring cashiers are individually recognized for their performance. Cashiers also like to know their score when they see their films to have a sense of how they are doing in comparison to the expectation.

This game film process is a great example of how clear definition enables assessment of behaviour and the application of skills that are traditionally considered hard to quantify. K&N recognized that their approach to service was critical to their success, so they've operationalized it in a way that helps them maintain and sustain a high level of service across all of their locations and brands.

Share

Figure 8

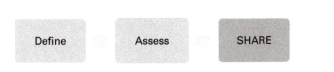

The final step of measurement that creates accountability is to openly share the results of assessment with the employee. When work is a contract, measurement is something the employer does to ensure the employee is complying with requirements. It's done to the employee, not with the employee. And the assessment results aren't always made visible to the employee.

In a relationship, measurement is about creating an open and transparent view of progress that fosters a sense of both individual and shared accountability for achieving success. If we have collaborated to create clarity with regard to how we define successful performance, then it's natural to assume that any measurement of progress towards these goals would be openly shared.

The K&N game films process is a great example of sharing. Once the films are scored by the Replay Analyst, they are sent to the manager of the restaurant so that they can be viewed and discussed together with the employee who was filmed. The film score makes it clear what went well and what can be done better in the future. The manager also receives a coaching sheet that guides them through providing the employee with positive coaching in upcoming shifts. The entire process is known to the employees and they have full visibility into their performance.

Define, assess, and share is the path to effective performance measurement; this approach will help you foster accountability and improved performance.

Key takeaways

- To accept accountability for performance requires an understanding of and visibility into how it is measured.

- Subjective ratings have no place in performance measurement. Subjective ratings are bad for employee engagement because reducing human behaviour to a number is damaging to relationships. They are also unreliable at best. Humans are bad at evaluating other humans and any attempt to do so tends to reflect more about the person doing the evaluating than the person being evaluated.

- The steps of performance measurement for accountability are define, assess, and share. Definition requires creating clarity about how progress will be measured. Assessment is the consistent tracking or evaluation of progress towards goals. Sharing is the act of creating transparency of progress for the employee.

References

NHS (2016) Blood tests [Online] https://www.nhs.uk/conditions/blood-tests/types/ [Last accessed 2 May 2018]

Skullen, S (2000) Understanding the latent structure of job performance ratings, *NCBI* [Online] https://www.ncbi.nlm.nih.gov/pubmed/11125659 [Last accessed 2 May 2018]

The role of reflection 14

A little over a decade ago I started a blog. At the time, I was working in corporate HR and my blog represented an outlet for me. I often described it as a place to get out my crazy ideas so that I wouldn't wear out my team at work with them. In the early days, I didn't really worry if anyone was reading the blog. While it was nice if someone read a post and reacted to it, the writing was primarily a way for me to express myself.

If you had asked me then why I wrote the blog, I would have told you it was to share ideas with others to help them do better work in HR. What I realized much later was that the writing served a much more important purpose for me individually. It was a structured way for me to process and extract the learning from my experiences at work and in my life. In most posts, I'd write about some situation or challenge I'd faced in my work. As I wrote about it, I worked out what was important and what could be learned from it. Usually, I tried to translate those insights for the reader into some recommendations or rules of thumb that could be applied to their own work.

In learning and development, taking time to process our experience for the purpose of finding the insights and lessons is often referred to as reflection. Writing my blog was more about reflection than it was about anything else. Reflection is important in human development. It's a process that helps us discover an answer on our own rather than being told. Many of the things I wrote about on my blog had probably been written about elsewhere, so the lessons weren't necessarily new or unique. But they were new to me. And because I had found my way to those lessons by reflecting on my own experience, they had more meaning and staying power.

Recent research has revealed the real value of reflection not only in learning but to performance. One of the primary focuses of this research, published by Harvard Business School, was to understand the relative importance of reflection in comparison to additional experience when building skills and competence (Di Stefano et al, 2016). For example, let's imagine you are learning to complete a new complex task like writing a computer program or performing a medical procedure. Your first 10 attempts are supervised by a trainer or expert to ensure you do it correctly. Once you have this base level of experience, what is the most effective next step to ensure that you master this skill and can perform it best? Would it be best to simply get more repetition by doing this new task 10 more times on your own? Or should you do the task fewer times but with structured reflection in between each effort?

Conventional wisdom suggests that the more we do something, the better we become at it. This would lead us to believe that doing the task 10 more times would be the fastest way to become competent. But, as is often the case, conventional wisdom would mislead us. The research revealed that individuals who were given time to reflect on a task improved their performance significantly more than those who were given the same amount of time to accumulate more experience with the task. Reflection significantly impacted both the individual's understanding of the task and their confidence to complete the task successfully.

Given this power of reflection to improve performance, you'd expect to find it as a common part of performance management processes. But that's not the case. While technology has enabled us to be more efficient and effective in many ways, it's been accompanied by a blanket expectation to produce more and do it faster. As a result, we've come to over-value efficiency in performance management. 'Doing' is favoured over all else.

Reflection requires that employees are given guidance and some time away from 'doing' to process what they are experiencing. It won't look efficient in the short run because time spent reflecting isn't producing output in that moment. But the research supports that investing time in reflection improves individual competence, leading to higher performance over the long run.

Self-review versus reflection

Before we look at a few examples from organizations that are successfully using reflection in performance management, let's take a moment to clarify the difference between reflection and the self-review process that many organizations use as part of their performance evaluation. They might sound similar but in most cases they are designed for very different purposes.

The purpose of reflection is learning and growth to unlock future performance potential. Reflection is developmental and for the benefit of the individual. Here are examples of questions used in reflection:

- What worked well? Why did it work?
- Where and why did I struggle?
- What could I have done differently to get a better outcome?
- How would I approach the same situation differently next time?

Each question leads towards a potential lesson or insight that could benefit future performance. Reflection questions also lead the individual towards reviewing and making sense of feedback or performance measurement data they've received.

Self-reviews on the other hand are often used as a means to make the performance review more comprehensive and complete. Even the best managers don't have visibility into everything that an employee does in their job. Self-review questions tend to look more like these:

- What were your major accomplishments this year?
- What accomplishments are you most proud of this year?
- What challenges did you face?

The self-review tends to be an exercise in which the employee is given the opportunity to ensure that their manager (and others who matter) realizes how much work they are doing. It also allows the employee to remind the manager of their accomplishments throughout the entire performance cycle. In the best circumstances, this self-review simply supplements and adds depth to the manager's review. In other cases, it's a crutch for managers who have done a poor job of monitoring performance throughout the year. Sadly, my experience has found this second use to be a far more common application of this process. The employee is asked to compensate for poor management.

Self-reviews are an exercise in documentation, compliance, and self-promotion that exist primarily due to the 'work as a contract' model. When good performance accountability practices around feedback and measurement are in place, self-reviews aren't needed. It's the sense-making process of reflection that should be applied instead.

Building reflection into performance management

Despite its importance to performance and growth, it's clear that reflection is not likely to happen without some formal structure and support. The organizations that understand the value of reflection are designing it both directly and indirectly into their performance management processes. This can be accomplished in a variety of ways at both individual and group levels.

Earlier, I shared the story of how Vistaprint have replaced their traditional 360 assessment and performance review process with a less formal process driven by the employee. As a reminder, in their new process the employee initiates a request for feedback from the peers they feel are best positioned to provide it. Upon receiving the feedback, the employee is empowered to review and process the feedback before sharing it with their manager. They don't call it reflection time, but that's exactly what it is. This reflection step has been effective for increasing both the employee's ownership of their feedback and their openness to coaching from managers about how to take action on what they have learned.

One large, global organization I interviewed, which is early in its journey to reinvent performance management, has also made reflection a key part of its new process. When employee survey results revealed that their traditional approach to performance management was broken, they decided to start from scratch.

After considering the employees' feedback and studying both best and next practices related to performance management, they designed a new totally new approach. Their goal was to create a process that was simple, nimble, and focused on empowering employees to improve future performance, abandoning entirely the compliance-driven approaches of the past.

Their new approach consists of four processes that are connected and mutually reinforcing. They have developed a technology platform internally that supports and enables each step of the process.

1 *Priorities*. This process is about identifying the most important goals and expectations for what's coming next. This might be for the next month, quarter or year. While each employee is expected to create and document priorities, what they are and how they are created is left up to the manager and employee to determine together: they set them collaboratively. They also have the flexibility to adapt and change them should changes warrant it.

2 *Touchpoints*. These are frequent and ongoing conversations between an employee and their manager. These touchpoints can range from simple check-ins to longer, more traditional one-on-one reviews. The expectation is that meaningful conversations about performance are happening throughout the year.

3 *Feedback*. Through the new technology platform, it is much easier for feedback to be shared. Employees are expected to request and provide feedback frequently. In the new process, they've adopted a very feedforward approach. When providing feedback, you first select whether it's 'Continue' (a positive behaviour to reinforce) or 'Consider' (a recommendation for how to improve in the future). Then you write the feedback out in a text box, with no numbers or ratings involved.

4 *Summarize*. This is where their process really connects together and harnesses the power of reflection. When an employee accomplishes or closes a priority (or a set of priorities), they are prompted to complete a performance summary. The summary formally prompts the employee to reflect and document learning from their experience working towards these specific priorities. The online form prompts them to assess how well they demonstrated accountability, built their capabilities, and enabled the success of others. The employee is then asked to summarize the 'continue' and 'consider' feedback they received from others about their work on this priority. Finally, they can add a narrative summary that shares their overall thoughts and learning. As the employee works on their summary, their manager is prompted to complete a summary for the employee simultaneously, a trigger to prompt the manager to reflect on the employee's performance as well.

This is a good example of how process and technology can be used to unleash the power of reflection in a performance management system. To support the new process, this organization also produced and shared training resources with employees, managers and leaders to help them understand the new process and the 'why' behind it. The positive reaction to and adoption of the new process has exceeded their expectations.

Group reflection

Some organizations have also found that a group reflection process can be an effective way to support learning from experience, particularly when work is done through teams. As with individual reflection, it's not something that naturally happens without being made a part of how work gets done.

CASE STUDY NVIDIA post-mortems

At technology company NVIDIA, to survive and thrive in the ultra-competitive industry they occupy requires ongoing and relentless innovation. This means that they have to move very fast and learn quickly from experiences. Beau Davidson, Vice President of HR, describes the challenge as 'building the airplane while flying'. Learning from experience, particularly from mistakes and failures, is high stakes at NVIDIA.

The majority of the work at NVIDIA is organized into projects. Employees often work on several project teams throughout the year; sometimes they belong to a few of these teams at the same time. With many teams moving at a fast pace, it would be easy to miss what is being learned along the way through each experience. To prevent the potential loss of learning and opportunities for improvement, at the end of each project they use a process they call the 'post-mortem'.

When a project is completed, the team spends time together reflecting on the experience of the project. They ask questions like these to prompt discussion:

- What worked?
- What didn't work so well?
- How can we get better?

By taking this time to reflect, the team identifies and learns from what positively impacted the project and how they could do it better next time. Each team member has the opportunity to learn from this conversation and then take those lessons forward into their next project.

Hubspot, the marketing automation company, has a novel way of using reflection to stimulate group learning. In the Hubspot Culture Code, which we visited in Chapter 3, you will find this statement: 'Better to try and sometimes fail than to sit tight... and fail for sure.' They recognize the importance of helping employees to become more comfortable with risk and failure as a required ingredient in innovation. But they also know that failing without learning is unproductive, so, they created their 'Failure Forum' (Burke, 2017).

The Failure Forum is an event hosted a couple of time per year at Hubspot's headquarters and broadcast live to all global employees. The forum exists for one purpose: for employees to share stories of failure and what they learned from the experience. Employees volunteer to speak at the event. Their presentation is required to answer three questions about their failure:

1 What didn't work?

2 When did you know it wasn't working?

3 What did you learn from the experience?

An event like the Failure Forum should accomplish a few things. First, the very existence of the forum sends a strong message to the organization that failure isn't fatal and should be treated as a learning experience. Also, the open call for employees to share stories is a great way to provoke reflection. It leads everyone to consider the question, 'What have I learned from failing lately?' Even though most employees won't ever present at the forum, many of them will at least spend a few more minutes in reflection than they would have if it didn't exist.

The other big advantage of this process is that it amplifies the benefits of reflection for broad learning across the organization. You can be certain that those who present their fail stories have spent time reflecting in order to share the most meaningful learning. Everyone who attends or watches the broadcast benefits from that effort.

Reflection can be thought of as the secret weapon of performance accountability. Without the step of reflection, the true value of feedback and measurement may be lost. As you consider how to foster accountability in your performance management system, make sure you design the process to allow time and guidance for reflection.

Key takeaways

- Research reveals that individuals who are given time to reflect on a task improve their performance significantly more than those who are given the same amount of time to accumulate more experience with the task.

- Self-review processes and reflection tend to be very different. Self-reviews are an exercise in documentation, compliance, and self-promotion that exist primarily due to the 'work as a contract' model. Reflection is focused on growth and development to unlock increased performance potential.

- Reflection does not naturally occur within our efficiency-obsessed organizations unless supported by structured processes. To reap the benefits of reflection, it must be built into individual and team performance management with practices like the 'performance summary' or 'post-mortem'.

References

Burke, K (2017) Does your company need a failure forum? The one mistake a company can't afford is becoming complacent, *Inc*, 31 March [Online] https://www.inc.com/katie-burke/hubspot-scaling-failure.html [Last accessed 2 May 2018]

Di Stefano, G et al. (2016) Making experience count: the role of reflection in individual learning, *Harvard Business School* [Online] http://www.hbs.edu/faculty/Publication%20Files/14-093_defe8327-eeb6-40c3-aafe-26194181cfd2.pdf [Last accessed 2 May 2018]

Confronting performance issues 15

One of the things that managers seem to stress about the most is how to deal with employee performance issues. When an employee is underperforming in some way, it can become all-consuming to a manager. As a manager, you worry about what to do, what to say and how this reflects on you. Sometimes, this can leave us feeling sort of paralyzed, doing nothing while the issue continues or becomes worse.

As a result, human resources departments have created entire functions and procedures in reaction to this management angst regarding confronting performance issues with employees. The 'Employee Relations' function in most mid- to large-sized organizations exists largely to help managers deal with performance and other behavioural issues. And the 'performance improvement plan' or PIP is the 'work as a contract' process designed to deal with this problem. It creates the 'improve your performance or else' documentation needed to help managers fire people with a clear conscience and HR's blessing.

No one likes being involved in these performance improvement processes or conversations when there's a problem. It's painful for the employee and awkward at best for the manager. So I'm never surprised when I get questions about how to handle performance issues more effectively. The best way to handle these issues is to prevent them in the first place.

Most performance issues are of our own creation. They are failures of management in one way or another. The primary reason to implement a well-designed approach to performance management is to prevent performance issues before they happen. When employees are clear on what is expected, given the resources they need, properly motivated and supported, and have visibility into their progress, performance is a natural outcome. The system itself helps to identify and eliminate issues. When expectations are clear, there can be no complaint or argument related to 'not knowing what I was supposed to be doing'. When progress is visible, the employee can take action at any time to change or get help if they are falling behind.

Most performance issues are a failure in the performance management process. The first step is to identify where the process failed. When an employee is failing to meet expectations, there are five main reasons.

1. 'I am not clear on what's expected of me'

This is one of the most common and easily corrected issues I've encountered in my career. In most cases, when an employee was not performing or behaving as I expected, it could almost always be tracked back to a failure on my part to ensure clarity of expectations. Often, it was my own assumptions that got in the way. As managers, we tend to assume that people know and understand things when they don't.

For example, I have always had an expectation as a manager that involves never showing up to a meeting without some way to take notes, on paper or electronically. While you may not always use it, you need to have a means to capture information and follow up commitments. Having it also signals to others that you have come prepared and are focused on making the meeting valuable.

I used to assume that by the time someone made it to a professional workplace, it was common knowledge that you would come prepared in this way to any meeting, regardless of your role in it. I've was surprised by how many times this was not the case, even in circumstances where the employee should have anticipated a need to capture notes for future reference. It used to frustrate me. I eventually realized that it was my assumption that was the issue. Once I started sharing feedback about this with those employees, I learned that no one had ever set that expectation with them before. One quick conversation, and it was fixed. They were more prepared and I was less frustrated.

To address this cause of poor performance, return to the fundamentals of performance planning discussed at length earlier in the book – clarify and document expectations. Never assume that something is clear. If it's important, it should be discussed and written down. When the employee tells you it's clear, it's clear.

2. 'I was not aware that I wasn't meeting expectations'

This is the second most common cause of performance issues. When measurement and feedback isn't a regular process, employees can operate for months (sometimes longer) without any idea of how well they are performing. As mentioned before, one failure of the annual performance review process is that it easily becomes the only time each year that employees receive feedback on their performance from their manager. Finding out at the end of the year that you have failed in some way without being given the opportunity to fix it is demoralizing.

When employees aren't aware that they are falling short of expectations, it's a failure of feedback and measurement. As a manager, it is easy to assume that the employee can see what you see when they are underperforming, but this is frequently not the case. If no one has told me I'm underperforming, it is easy to think I'm doing okay. It's like the old saying goes, 'No news is good news'. This is another example of where manager assumptions can derail performance.

Addressing this cause of poor performance requires focusing on the performance accountability processes we've outlined in this section of the book. Review the employee's expectations with them and discuss how you can create more visibility into progress over the next cycle. Solutions might include increasing the frequency of one-on-one meetings or adding new agenda items to the existing meeting. Maybe the employee should request peer feedback at fixed intervals throughout the year. The objective should be to ensure the employee has transparency into their progress towards goals and expectations so they are empowered to take ownership of their results going forward.

3. 'I don't know how to perform as expected'

Being clear on expectations is critical, but if I lack the skill or ability to deliver on those expectations, failure is inevitable. In some cases, when we hire new employees or put employees in new roles with different expectations, we discover that regardless of how much effort they apply to their work, they fall short. This can represent a gap in the performance-planning process. We may have failed to provide the training and coaching needed to equip the employee to achieve these expectations.

To diagnose this issue requires observation and feedback. In particular, requesting feedforward recommendations from those who work most closely with the employee can reveal insights into what training or coaching might be most helpful. Once you identify the learning needs, create a short-term development plan with goals for the employee. The emphasis of this plan should be achieving competence in the areas identified as needs. Once the employee closes their 'know-how' gap, the performance issue will likely disappear.

4. 'I'm unable to meet expectations'

There will be cases occasionally where the performance issues aren't a matter of a lack of know-how, but a lack of ability or suitability in the role. This isn't common, but it usually occurs when an individual takes on a new position or responsibility and then it becomes clear that the demands of the role aren't a match. The most common circumstance in which I've seen this is when employees are promoted into their first people management role. Frequently, a high-performing individual with great technical skills is promoted to manage the team because it was time for a promotion and this was the only career path available. Suddenly, this individual finds that they are in a role in which they are ill-suited and disinterested. They may not even like people, but now they are responsible for managing them.

In these circumstances, the default solution is to apply a healthy dose of management training. We tell ourselves that 'everyone has the potential to be a manager'. But if this new manager doesn't like talking to people, much less having difficult conversations, and would prefer to just do the actual work, all the training in the world isn't likely to change that.

When you discover that you have an employee who is in a situation like this, engage them in an honest conversation about it. Ask some questions about what they really love doing and what parts of their job they really dislike or drain their energy. Then find a way to get them into a role that's better suited to their talents. The organization put them into a role that isn't a fit for them and that should be rectified. The alternative is to leave them in a role where they are likely to be miserable and destined to fail.

5. 'I choose not to meet expectations'

When your performance management system is doing a good job of planning, cultivation and accountability, most issues will disappear. People want to do a good job and when the system works, they have every opportunity to do so. On rare occasions, you will encounter this last type of poor performance issue, where an employee is choosing for some reason not to perform. These circumstances are rare and the causes are varied. It can be the result of a perceived injustice by the employee, such as being passed over for a promotion. It can also be a result of issues happening outside of work that have negatively affected the individual's attitude or concern about work.

While these situations can seem on the surface like the most awkward to deal with, they are actually pretty straightforward. In most other types of performance issues, the problem is mostly one of our own making. In this case, the employee is making the choice not to perform or behave as expected. Navigating this issue is mainly about helping the employee recognize the consequences of the choice they are making while inviting them to make a different choice.

In circumstances like this, we tend to default to the 'work as a contract' model of compliance by turning to policy and documentation over human conversation. When we understand that work is a relationship, we hold off on the PIP and engage with the person directly as a first step. Start with empathy by trying to understand what's going on with the employee and what might be causing them to behave in this way. In these conversations, be open, caring, and direct. A conversation might start off sounding something like this.

> 'Jason, I want to chat with you about what's been going on lately because I'm concerned about you. Your performance is suffering and what concerns me the most is that I don't get the feeling that you are worried about it. I'd like to help you turn this around before it's too late. What's been going on?'

If you can draw them into a conversation to learn about what the underlying issue is and how to address it, you can potentially make some pretty quick progress. But not everyone will take the opportunity to step into the conversation with you. If they respond by being aloof, resistant or belligerent, then the next step is to stress the consequences of the choices they are making and put the decision of what happens next in their hands.

The mistake that many managers make at this point is to allow the individual to stay in willful underperformance for far too long. Once you recognize that it's happening, you force the employee to make a decision to move in one direction or another – fix performance or find somewhere else to work that might better meet your needs. The status quo is not an option.

This conversation is pretty straightforward. Here's an example for how it might sound.

'Jason, your performance and behaviour lately can't continue. So, you have a decision to make. Option 1 is that you step up and fix the issues we have right now. If you choose this path, I will need you to outline in writing a list of what you will commit to do differently in the next 30 days to get back on track. Option 2 is that you don't work here anymore. If you can't bring yourself to do the work anymore, then this might be the right path for you. There is no option 3. I truly want you to be happy and successful in your job and neither of those things seem to be true right now. Something has to change. I'll schedule another meeting for us in two days so you can share your decision with me.'

Through the lens of the relationship test, this conversation wouldn't look a lot different if you had to confront your best friend about repeatedly breaking commitments with you. It's respectful, candid and empowers the individual to reflect and make a (hopefully) thoughtful decision.

When we assume the best in people and put a comprehensive system in place that addresses planning, cultivation and accountability in performance, addressing performance issues will become a small part of the job of manager. When issues do arise, diagnose where the process failed and correct the failure. In those cases where the employee is choosing not to perform, use the relationship test to remind you to approach them like an adult who you truly care for and handle it in a way that respects and preserves the relationship without enabling poor performance and behaviour.

Key takeaways

- Most performance issues are of our own creation. They are failure of management in some way.

- To confront and fix performance issues, you must first diagnose what is causing them. There are five main causes for poor employee performance:

  - *'I am not clear on what's expected of me.'*
  - *'I was not aware that I wasn't meeting expectations.'*
  - *'I don't know how to perform as expected.'*

- - *'I'm unable to meet expectations.'*
  - *'I choose not to meet expectations.'*

- When we assume the best in people and put a comprehensive performance management system in place to address planning, cultivation and accountability in performance, confronting poor performance will become a small part of the job of manager. Most issues will be prevented before they even happen.

SECTION 5
Building a sustainable and effective performance management system

Hopefully, there are a lot of ideas swirling in your head. Maybe you've got a mental list of all the ways your current practices are designed more for compliance than relationship. Or you've been considering some ways to start on making feedback less painful for your employees. The goal of this book is to equip you with inspiration and a variety of possible solutions. Just like there's no right way to be in a relationship with someone else, there is no single right way to manage performance. There are some foundational elements that are needed in all cases, but how those look depends on your culture and the people involved.

It's natural at this point to feel a little overwhelmed, particularly if you've come to the conclusion that your organization needs to make some serious changes to how you approach performance management. When it feels like there's a lot of opportunity to seize, knowing where to start can be challenging.

Throughout the book, we've been talking about the idea that an organization needs a performance management system to create and sustain the intended experience for our employees. Designing a performance management system for your organization is the most reliable path to truly unlocking employee performance in the long term. Doing that effectively will take time, patience and a smart process. In the next few chapters, we'll break down how to approach designing a system for your organization.

Maybe you don't have the time or appetite to design a system for your organization. That doesn't mean you can't make some great progress. Short of a system redesign, there are some powerful ways to use the insights of this book to make some immediate impact. You may have already seized on some of them by taking action on a particular tactic or insight. In this chapter, we'll review some steps to take in the direction of fostering a better relationship with your employees that are relatively simple to implement in the near team.

Let's recap

Before we get to specifics, let's take a moment to recap the big ideas we've covered in the book to bring them back to top of mind:

- Most of our current approaches to performance management (and management in general) are based on a model of work as a contract with the employee. This model was born out of necessity over a century ago as organizations were first taking shape in an era of industrialization.

- The nature of work has dramatically shifted over the past century, even if the way we manage it has not. Research reveals that as work has evolved, the employee's experience and expectations of work have also changed. Rather than as a contractual obligation, employees experience work as a relationship. The things that engage and motivate employees at work is very similar to what makes for a healthy relationship between two people.

- This disconnect between the employer's view of work as a contract and the employee's experience of work as a relationship is a major contributor to why employee engagement has remained stagnant for decades. To improve engagement and unlock each employee's performance potential requires that employers and managers adopt a different perspective on work. Instead of treating it as a contract to be enforced, it must be approached as a relationship to be fostered.

- You can use the 'relationship test' as a tool to improve both processes and interactions. Consider, 'How would this approach work if someone

I really care about outside of work were on the other end of it?' If it preserves or strengthens the relationship, proceed. If not, consider a different approach that will.

- Performance management should no longer be focused on compliance and contract enforcement as it has been in the past. That approach has failed. To unlock higher performance, we must design and implement performance management practices that create an employee experience that feels like a healthy relationship rich in elements like trust, appreciation, acceptance and mutual commitment.

- Performance management consists of three distinct and overlapping processes: planning, cultivation, and accountability. In order to optimize performance, you must have processes in place for each that create the conditions for optimal performance in a way that fosters the relationship with the employee.

The remainder of this book is dedicated to taking the insights and practices provided and putting those to work in your organization. The next chapter is for those who are impatient for results and want to make some changes now. In this brief chapter, you'll learn how you can use the tactics of stopping and hacking to have an impact now.

The remaining chapters will illustrate how to use the design process to first gain a deeper understanding of your organization and employees and then use that knowledge to define the kind of employee experience you need to create. Then, we'll explore how this foundation helps you determine which practices and processes from each (planning, cultivation, and accountability) are the best fit for inclusion into your performance management system.

Finally, we'll review how to test, improve and deploy your new system. By the end, you will be equipped with what you need to lead your organization through the design of a new system to unlock the performance potential of all employees in a way that feels healthy and affirming for all involved.

Making immediate improvements

Before we explore in the next chapters how to lead your organization through the process of designing a performance management system, there are two tactics you might consider for making an immediate impact.

Stopping the process

I'm not sure who first said it, but it's been repeated many times since: 'Insanity is doing the same thing over and over while expecting a different result.' By this definition, we've been trapped in a cycle of insanity with performance management for decades. Hopefully, this book will help us break that cycle.

One of the quickest ways to start breaking the cycle is to simply stop. When I joined the corporate ranks, one of my immediate frustrations was the amount of busy work that I felt burdened with. The number of weekly reports and updates my team produced seemed incredibly wasteful when you considered the time and resources we spent creating them compared to actually doing productive work. To amplify my frustration, I wasn't sure anyone was even looking at all of these reports and updates we were creating.

Thankfully, a mentor shared some advice with me. She advised me to start with the reports I suspected were least valued and stop sending them. She told me to make no announcement about stopping and not to ask permission. Just stop. If people were using the report and it was valued, we'd hear from them pretty quickly. They would come looking for it. If that happened, we would apologize and start sending it again.

That didn't happen very often. In a majority of the cases, no one even noticed that we'd stopped. When they did notice and asked for the report, we asked questions about how they used the report and what information was most valuable so we could improve it and make the process of creating it more efficient. The idea underlying this approach is that if something valuable goes missing, we look for it. So, if you aren't sure if a process or approach is adding value as part of your management processes, try stopping. Just as it was with our reports, this can be a great test to see if anyone comes looking for it. And, if they do, start a conversation about what they missed and why.

Other times, stopping isn't needed as a test. It's just the right thing to do. I shared earlier in the book some analysis we did on the effectiveness of our performance appraisal process. We couldn't find any evidence that the performance appraisal was impacting performance positively in any significant way. Given that fact, when you consider the hours of time, energy and emotional toil the process put on managers and employees, there is little question that the process was actually doing more harm to performance than good. The best thing we could have done was stop immediately.

If your organization is in a similar situation, stopping your annual performance appraisal should actually improve performance. Not only will hours of productive time be reclaimed for doing other (hopefully) higher-value work, but people's general happiness should improve by removing the anxiety and angst connected with this process. It would be logical to make this move. But you may find as I did, that despite the logic of the move, we've become addicted to our faulty practices. Even when it made sense to simply let go, it was difficult to convince leadership to make that call. They had become so accustomed to the annual cycle that they couldn't simply let it go. The fear of change outweighed the pain of the current process.

When you encounter or feel resistance to stopping, there's another approach that might be more palatable and accomplish similar results. *Make the process optional.* As you might remember from Chapter 12, this is the tactic that Vistaprint used in the early phases of their performance management reinvention. They had received feedback that the 360 assessment wasn't liked by employees or seen as adding value to the review process, so they decided to make it optional. It was still available, but they removed the requirement to complete it as part of the annual review process. They communicated this change to the organization and in response, everyone stopped using it. Employees didn't request it. And the managers who had to complete the reviews didn't miss it either. Plus, it didn't seem to affect either the quality of the reviews or individual performance overall. It was an artefact of a different era of management that was no longer serving a purpose.

Are there things in your current process that you can stop? If you spend significant time and energy trying to get people to complete a mandatory process, that may be a sign that it's either not valued or is in need of a redesign. Another signal to monitor is the general sentiment about a process or approach. If you hear a lot of grumblings or complaints, that's worth noting. Using the relationship test, if you knew something you were doing in your relationship caused your partner or friend anxiety or discomfort, you'd stop as soon as you knew. If it was something important, you'd find a different way to approach it that minimized or eliminated the pain. We should do the same for our employees.

Hacking your current processes

The other way to make some near-term progress is to consider where small changes to existing approaches might have impact. I like to think of this as hacking your system. By scanning your process using the relationship test and what you've learned in this book, you may notice some places where instead of stopping, a change to 'how' something is done could have an impact. A hack can also mean adding a step or interaction to your process.

There are some common areas I've observed in organizations where a hack can be helpful. While you consider how to create a better system overall, these areas might be where you could make some improvements right away.

One-on-one meetings

If managers aren't spending at least a little dedicated time in conversation with their employees, they aren't building relationships. When an organization has no formal expectation of managers to hold regular one-on-one meetings with the people for whom they are responsible, that's the first thing I recommend they do. In Chapter 2, we learned how a Merck manufacturing facility dramatically improved employee engagement by adding a requirement that managers hold regular meetings with each employee.

If your organization is new to one-on-one meetings or hasn't put much emphasis on them in the past, providing some simple guidelines and questions can improve their effectiveness significantly.

Simple guidelines for effective one-on-one meetings could include:

- minimum of 30 minutes in length;
- regularly scheduled at least monthly (ie the first Wednesday of every month at 9 am);
- no technology use during the meeting;
- let the employee drive the conversation;
- manager should spend as much time listening and asking questions as talking.

It's also helpful to provide a few questions for employees and managers to discuss in these meetings as a sort of simple agenda. When just starting out, these are examples of effective questions to use:

- Where do you feel you made progress last week/month?
- What were you able to accomplish?
- What are you going to be focused on next week/month?
- What challenges are you facing in getting things done?
- Where can I be of more help to you?

The primary goal of the one-on-one is to create time for the employee and manager to be together to have a conversation. At first, the nature of the conversation isn't critical. The fact that the manager is making time for the conversation conveys that the employee is important and valued. The quality of the conversation can be improved over time.

Written expectations

When in doubt, start at the beginning. Do employees have clarity about what is expected of them? Uncertainty about expectations is highly disruptive to performance, so even a bit of added clarity can go a long way. If you lack a formal process for goal and expectation setting, that can be addressed right away and doesn't require a complicated solution.

Ask managers to work with employees to document their goals for the upcoming year or performance period. The method used is less important than the act of committing them to writing. The simple process of documenting expectations does two things. First, it forces the creation of tangible goals or expectations if they don't already exist. Then, it prompts that they be shared and discussed with the employee.

Documentation of goals and expectations will not eliminate all uncertainty, but it will move the organization in the direction of clarity. And clarity is great for relationships.

Make feedback less painful

We've discussed at length in the book why feedback can be so problematic. And yet, feedback is the rocket fuel needed to propel growth and unlock performance potential. Changing the organization's relationship with feedback won't happen overnight because most of the people working in your organization have built up resistance and coping mechanisms for feedback throughout an entire career. Getting to a place where feedback is both valued and desired could take years.

To effect some change more immediately, focus on what you can do to mitigate some of the pain caused (or perceived) in feedback. One way to accomplish this is to train managers and employees in the feedforward method. Equipping employees with the mindset and simple tools to shift from criticizing past performance to suggesting ideas for the future can take hold and have a positive effect right away.

Another hack might be to offer training broadly for how to receive and process feedback individually. Without changing anything about your current feedback processes, their effectiveness can be improved by helping employees to be more effective at finding the gift in feedback, regardless of how it's delivered.

These are just a few ways that you might hack your current processes while you consider a long-term systemic solution. Wherever you find a process that has the potential to harm the feeling of a healthy relationship with the employee, hack it. Make some small changes and track the impact. Try the easy, most obvious fix first. If it helps, keep it and go to the next thing. If it doesn't, try something else.

Key takeaways

- A well-designed performance management system is the best way to unlock your organization's performance potential, but it is not a quick fix. It takes time. However, there are ways to make immediate impact as well.

- One tactic for improving your current performance management practices is stopping. When a process or practice is disliked or the value is questionable, consider stopping the practice to see if anyone misses it or complains. Short of stopping it all together, consider making a once mandatory process optional to see what effect this has on its utilization and overall performance outcomes.

- Use the relationship test to evaluate and hack your current processes. When you suspect that one may be harming the relationship, consider what simple changes you might make to improve it.

- For immediate impact, consider using the tactics outlined in the book to improve one of these three high-impact processes: one-on-one meetings, written expectations, and feedback.

Getting buy-in for change and recruiting a design team   17

If you are a business owner or executive, you may have picked up this book because you know that you need to improve organizational performance but weren't sure what exactly to do. Or you lead the human resources or organizational development function for your organization, and you may have picked this book because you knew your current performance management and employee engagement practices were not working and you were searching for answers. In either case, you came looking for system-level improvements that could dramatically improve the results in your organization. Hacking a few processes is nice, but that's not enough.

The remainder of this book is for you.

The transformative impact of the content in this book comes not when you unlock the performance potential of a few employees here and there, but when you can build a system that through its design and execution will unlock the performance potential of all employees. That's the elusive holy grail of performance management that we've been pursuing for decades. Throughout the book, I've referred to this work as creating a 'performance management system'. The system is a series of interconnected processes that create an employee experience that unlocks performance at the individual and group level.

To this point in the book, we've been building a deeper understanding of performance within the organization. As we embark next on the work of building a system, our attention turns away from the practice of performance management and instead to design process and change management. Design as a process is about creating things with intention. We'll use a simple four-step design process as a guide to first clarify your intentions, as we initially discussed in Chapter 3, and then to identify, test and ultimately determine the series of processes that will create a performance management system that is uniquely suited to your organization's needs and aspirations.

Then comes the hardest part. Even if you design the perfect system for your organization, there's another complicating factor that we need to address. People hate change, even when it's in their best interest. So, we will also explore some key steps that will help mitigate the effects of change resistance. This will include some suggestions about how to engage others in the process as a way to improve the likelihood of rapid adoption.

What follows are suggestions and ideas based on my experience for how to approach and structure an organizational effort to accomplish this work. It is not comprehensive and is not intended to represent the only way to successfully navigate it. As with everything else in this book, I leave it to you to decide what fits for you and how to adapt the ideas here to fit your specific situation. If you read for the underlying purpose of each step rather than the specific approach, you'll be able to easily adapt it to fit your circumstances.

Making the case for change

It was one of my great frustrations during my tenure in corporate HR how often we found ourselves spending significant time and energy building justifications and business cases to gain permission to solve a problem everyone already agreed should be addressed. Regardless of how valid or necessary it is, creating a justification for any change project is a ritual within most organizations, particularly large ones. If you are lucky enough to either be the boss who can authorize things to happen or you have already been given the green light to proceed with this work, please feel free to skip ahead to the next section. If you aren't so fortunate, keep reading.

To gain the support and participation needed for a change effort like this, you will need to clearly define what you are trying to accomplish and why it matters. At this point, the goal isn't to propose a solution but rather to make the case for change by highlighting what isn't working and the cost of not fixing it.

Even if it seems most people share your opinion that change is needed with regard to performance management, to get the support and resources needed to make a substantial change requires more than positive sentiment. It's important to provide evidence that the current approach isn't working and that not taking action to address it isn't an option.

There are a variety of places to look for evidence of the ineffectiveness of your performance process.

- *Ratings distribution.* If your organization uses performance ratings, chart the distribution of ratings to understand if they reflect accurate evaluation and distribution of talent. Often, a majority of ratings will reflect 'meets' or 'exceeds' expectations when actual performance reveals something different. If the ratings show everyone at the same level or in a narrow band, then the process isn't differentiating between good, average and bad performance.

- *Employee survey data.* Most employee engagement surveys ask questions to assess performance management effectiveness. Questions focusing on clarity of expectations, management support, and frequency of feedback can provide powerful data in support of change.

- *Quality of documentation.* An audit of performance review documentation for content and quality can be a revealing look at the effectiveness of your current process and the skill of your management at evaluating performance. When doing this, we found evidence of cut-and-paste content by more than one manager who submitted the exact same appraisal content for an employee several years in a row.

- *Timeliness of appraisals.* If it's an annual battle to get managers to complete the performance review process, that's important feedback in and of itself. When managers actively avoid a process that is supposed to help them do their job successfully, it's a good sign the process needs to be improved.

- *Executive participation.* One interesting data point to consider is the participation of executive leaders in the current process. If they aren't using it or don't use it as designed, this reality can be helpful in starting a conversation about change. If they don't see enough value in the process to use it, why force it upon everyone else?

- *Resource utilization.* By collecting some simple data from managers and employees about time spent in the current process, you can extrapolate using the averages to get an idea of how much time is being invested in your current processes. For example, you might discover that employees report spending an average of two hours in the performance appraisal process between preparing information, answering the manager's questions, and discussing the actual appraisal. On top of that, you could find that managers report spending at least four hours per employee in the process. That's six hours per employee that may not be adding any value. Multiplying that number by total employees adds up quickly. If you have a 360 component to your appraisal, the numbers get even bigger.

Once you've gathered evidence in support of the need for change, you need to bring it all together to paint a picture of both the current situation and what's possible in the future. To do this, it's valuable to create a short summary document that can be used as a conversation starter and communication piece. In the startup world, they'd call this their 'pitch deck'.

This summary should be a formatted, one-page document or a few simple PowerPoint slides that include the following information:

- *Project name.* What will you call this project (eg Performance Management 2.0) to make it easy to talk about and reference?

- *Description.* A short overview of what you are trying to accomplish or the problem you are trying to solve. This should include a short summary of what you are asking them to support. For example, 'In response to the overwhelming feedback that our current performance management practices are ineffective and disliked, we will form a cross-functional task force to review current state and design a more effective set of processes for managing employee performance.'

- *Evidence.* Summary of the evidence and data that reveal the scope of the problem and the need for change.

- *Potential impact.* How will the organization, management and employees benefit as a result of solving this problem?

Start by creating a draft document of this information. Then, share it with trusted colleagues to get feedback and make improvements. Encourage them to poke holes in your arguments and ask tough questions. This will force you to make it better. The goal is to create a document that can be shown to the decision makers within the organization to gain their support.

How formally you package this document will depend on your organization. At a minimum, ensure it's well written and easy to understand. This document and the clarity you gain through its creation will equip you to recruit supporters and create momentum. At the very least, this exercise will help you find and create greater clarity about the scope of lost opportunity you are experiencing at your organization. In addition, by taking the time to build an evidence-based argument for change and presenting it in a polished and professional way, your odds of gaining support and interest increase dramatically. This level of investment and effort signals a high level of importance to those charged with evaluating whether to offer support or approval.

Your goal should be to make it easy for those who must say yes to give you their support. Since the performance review process is so universally hated, this should be an easier sell than other projects. One reason I've included so many case studies throughout the book is to offer up inspiring stories that can be used as proof that there is a better way. Share those stories in your pitch to help leaders envision what success will look and feel like once you've successfully designed and deployed your new system.

Recruiting your design team

Once you've got the approval and resources to proceed, you'll need a cross-functional team to participate in your design efforts. One reason many HR processes meet resistance is that they are viewed as 'HR processes' instead of helpful tools to facilitate work and drive performance. The perception is that HR procedures are forced upon the organization as opposed to meeting a need or enabling an outcome. And as we've shown, that reputation is largely earned. Many HR processes were designed with contract compliance in mind and were not created to be useful to the manager or employee.

In order for a new performance approach to be widely embraced, it must be viewed as emerging from the organization for the good of the organization. To accomplish this, you must enlist leaders and managers to join the effort.

In my experience, the best way to accomplish this is to form a 'task force' to participate in the process. The role of the task force is to serve as both a design team and an advocacy group. The task force will play a vital role in ensuring that the system designed is based on input and knowledge of how work actually happens throughout the organization. They will provide input, opinions, and feedback throughout the process. The task force will also play an important role as advocates of change. They will help share the story of the project and build support for what comes next.

An effective task force needs to be small enough to be agile but big enough to represent a broad section of the organization. I've found a good task force size to be 10 to 12 committed members.

The key to a great task force is to identify the right people for the job. A successful task force member should have these qualities:

- a strong desire to improve performance management processes (ie they have a strong dislike of current processes);

- diverse perspective and experience to contribute;

- representative of a key area of the organization (ie different divisions, locations, etc);

- respected and trusted influencer within the organization (people look to this person for guidance and leadership).

As you construct your task force, ensure it is diverse and representative of a broad range of experiences and perspectives. This should include diversity of gender, race/ethnicity, tenure, management level, etc. The more diverse the committee and the more fully it represents the different parts of the organization, the higher the likelihood that the end result will both be effective and embraced broadly.

To successfully enlist members, be prepared to discuss with them the expectations of serving on this task force. Be prepared to discuss how long the project will take to complete and how much time is expected of each member. This will require that you have created a project plan or outline. The next chapter should help you in creating this plan. Your task force will want to know not only how long the project will last but also how much time is expected of them on a weekly or monthly basis. The best task force members will be in high demand because what makes them valuable to you makes them valuable to everyone else too. You will need to be mindful of that. Be intentional in where and how you ask them for time. And make sure any time you ask of them has clear purpose for the project.

It is critical to set the expectation early that task force members are expected to represent and think broadly about the organization, not simply to express their own opinions. Another expectation to share is that, as a task force member, they will occasionally be asked to share the work of the task force with colleagues to solicit feedback and build support.

Creating a task force may seem like a cumbersome way to approach the process. It is true that the more people involved in any process, the slower it goes and the harder it is to reach consensus on any decisions. It would be much faster to simply take some ideas from this book and design a system. Doing so would allow you to have a new system created in the next month and it would probably be an improvement on your current process. This shortcut of creating processes and forcing them on the organization is part of the reason we've found ourselves in this mess in the first place. Remember the relationship test. If you were contemplating major changes in your family, surely you'd involve others in that decision-making process rather than simply making a call and hoping for the best.

To be clear, the approach of using a task force is not meant to optimize speed or efficiency. The goal is to design a culturally calibrated system that is not only highly effective for those who use it, but is also quickly and widely adopted to have the broadest possible impact on improving performance. Remember, people will resist any change, often even that which benefits them. And they will doubly resist change that they don't understand. A good task force using a solid design process will produce a much better system that will feel as though it was built by the business, not forced upon it.

Key takeaways

- A performance management system is a series of interconnected processes that creates an employee experience that unlocks the full performance potential at the individual and group level.

- Since the performance review process is so universally disliked, finding approval to design a replacement will hopefully not be terribly challenging. However, when constructing the business case, use evidence and case study stories from the book to make it easy for the decision makers to say yes.

- For a new performance management system to be widely embraced, it should be viewed as emerging from the organization for the good of the organization. To accomplish this, you must enlist a task force of the right leaders and managers to join the effort.

- Using a task force for this process does not improve the speed or efficiency of the process. The goal is to engage broad perspectives, to design a culturally calibrated system that will be highly effective and quickly embraced upon deployment.

The design process and avoiding the best practice trap

18

Design, most simply defined, is creating something with clear intention. Applying design to people processes starts with articulating the impact you wish your work to have on others. If you've ever planned a birthday party for your child or a surprise party for a loved one, you may have already experienced informally what it's like to design people process and experience.

Even before you began planning, you probably had a good idea of how you wanted the party to make them feel. For your child, you may have wanted them to feel like it was the best birthday party *ever*. For your loved one, the goal could have been to make them feel overwhelmed with love and joy.

The first steps of design include knowing who you are designing for and declaring how you want to make them feel. This is true whether you are designing a birthday party or a process at work. While this may seem obvious, the frenzied pace of our work and lives often means that we skip over these steps. We crave the quick fix. So, instead of spending the time to do the work and design with intention, we instead look around to see what everyone else is doing, hoping to find a shortcut. What kind of birthday party did the neighbour have for their kid? How do the other organizations in our industry handle these processes?

Let's imagine that you've been charged with the task of improving the skill level of the managers within your organization. If you used design process, as you will learn in a moment, you would start by doing some research and investigation to understand the current state of management skill more deeply and why improvement is being mandated. Through this discovery work, you would develop a clearer understanding of the problem you are trying to solve. But who has time for that? Certainly, your organization isn't the first to have this problem. A quick search of the internet reveals thousands of management training solutions and case studies. Some are even labelled 'best practices' based on the success other organizations have found in using them. If it worked for them, surely it will work for you. You found your quick fix.

Best practices have become the shortcut of choice in corporate America over the past several decades. We love best practices because they appear to be low risk. Nobody gets fired for implementing a 'best' practice. Plus, it's much faster to apply a best practice to your problem than it is to do the work to create your own solution from scratch. This perpetuation of best practice is one of the key factors that set us so far behind in the practice of performance management.

Best practices can be dangerous. 'What is the best practice for this?' This question is asked daily in offices and boardrooms everywhere. It seems like the right question to ask. Why not look to other organizations who have faced a similar problem and then do the same thing they did to solve it?

First, the very notion of a best practice is flawed. Organizations are complex and unique. Even when two companies are in the same business, they are made up of different people and a resulting corporate culture that makes their own environment one of a kind. Due to this complexity, it is often difficult or impossible to isolate exactly why a particular practice or process works in a particular organization. The context in which any practice was applied is critical and often overlooked when trying to understand its effectiveness. Sometimes, timing and luck can have as much to do with why a practice succeeded as the practice itself.

There are no universal 'best' practices. There are only 'right' practices given your specific context and objectives. Best practices are too often assumed to be best for everyone and are applied as if they cannot fail or do harm. The annual performance appraisal is a great example. It was probably a reasonably effective practice when first deployed in unionized work environments where work really was a contract. But it was then perpetuated for decades as 'best practice' in very different organizational contexts where work was very different than it had been in the past. In hindsight, it's obvious that performance appraisals haven't been 'good' practice for more than a half century, considering the changing nature of work. But they persisted nonetheless because everyone treated them as best practice. Sometimes, the shortcuts you take may feel faster but end up leading you in the wrong direction.

The other issue with best practices is that they are, by necessity, old practices. A best practice earns its label over time. It's created in one organization and used with some success. That practice is then shared with or carried to another organization by an employee. This new organization then applies the practice and finds some positive results. This cycle continues until enough people have heard about this approach that it gets labelled a 'best practice'. This takes time, often years and sometimes decades. In a global economy that is volatile and dynamic, relying on practices designed years or decades ago to solve new problems is irrational and bound to fail.

I'm not suggesting that all best practices are bad. It's labelling them as 'best' that's dangerous. They are simply practices that worked for others given the context of their organization at the time. When we fail to apply design to the creation of new processes and systems, it's easy to get seduced by the promise of best practice. By applying some basic design principles, we are forced to clarify our intentions and ground them in who we are designing for. When we do that, we can evaluate practices or solutions through the lens of our specific context to explore if they are right for us. Design helps us avoid the best practice trap.

There are a variety of ways to approach and articulate a design process. Among the most simple and easy to apply is a four-step process created by the UK Design Council. This 'double diamond' process describes design as having four steps: discover, define, develop and deliver (Design Council UK, 2018).

Figure 9 Design Council's Double Diamond, created in 2004

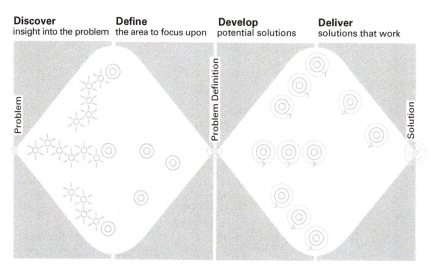

Discover
insight into the problem

Define
the area to focus upon

Develop
potential solutions

Deliver
solutions that work

Problem

Problem Definition

Solution

4D Design Process

1 *Discover*. The first step is research. The designer(s) works to gain a deep understanding of the problem and situation including who will be impacted and their needs and motivations. They collect information and scan the environment trying to see the challenge in new and different ways.

2 *Define*. The next phase is to distil and make sense of what was learned in the discovery phase. As the label implies, it's about defining more clearly what is being designed and the intentions that will drive decisions about it. This step of the process involves wrestling with questions like 'What is most important?' and 'What should be addressed first?' The goal of the define phase is clarity of the design challenge.

3 *Develop*. It is during this phase that potential solutions and practices are created or identified. These are then evaluated, tested, and iterated. This process can include creating solutions from scratch or applying ideas from elsewhere that appear to be potentially valuable. It is in this process that you seek feedback and use pilots to validate that a solution is the right one for your organization or team.

4 *Deliver*. Upon validating the right solution or processes, this is where it gets operationalized and launched to the organization. It is here that the work is done to support and scale the implementation of the designed final product, process, or experience.

There's nothing magical about this process beyond the fact that it reminds us to work with both intention and information in creating solutions. It also emphasizes the importance of using cycles of creativity, or divergence, to identify many possible solutions which can then be narrowed down and the best one selected using feedback and testing (convergence).

Once you've formed your task force (aka Design Team) to power the design process for your new performance management system, the 4D framework is a great way to structure the work to be done for the project.

Discover and define

The arduous work of any design project is in the first two steps. It takes time and effort to understand the current situation, identify needs, and clarify intentions. All of this needs to then be articulated clearly in a way that can act as a guide for the creation and selection of processes that will ultimately make up your performance management system. In Chapter 3, we reviewed the Hubspot Culture Code and the Motley Fool handbook as examples of this type of clarity.

The output of the first two design steps should define the employee experience you intend to create. This will become the foundation for everything else you do. You will also identify where the biggest gaps and opportunities lie between the current situation and the desired future state.

The first discovery effort should focus on what your organization is currently communicating about employee experience. Scan the environment for documentation of anything that could be construed as impacting employee experience. Corporate values and policy manuals are examples that most organizations usually have in place. Employer branding, culture documents, and leadership competencies all give clues as to the intended (and unintended) employee experience that your organization is trying to create. Current performance management and other HR processes are also important in this review. Anything that either shapes the current employee experience or hints at the organization's aspirations is valuable to consider.

The process of discovery may also require some interviews and conversations with key leaders to draw out more clarity about the type of experience the organization wishes to create. How do you want employees to feel about work?

You may also want to conduct focus groups with employees to gain a better understanding of the current experience. If your organization conducts employee surveys, the results can also be a great source of insight into the current state.

Key questions to explore about employee experience:

- What kind of experience does it appear we are creating today?
- What seem to be our intentions about employee experience based on what is being communicated today?
- How does our desired culture impact the experience we want to create?
- How do we want employees to feel about work?
- How can we more clearly articulate our intended employee experience?

Once you've done your discovery research there comes the hard part: distilling it down into a clear and understandable articulation of your intentions. When we see a definition like this, it's inspiring and compelling. The Hubspot Culture Code is fun to read and paints a clear picture of their expected and aspirational culture. Arriving at an articulation that is clear and compelling requires diligent effort. You'll need help.

In my experience, soliciting help at this point in the process can be life-saving. Sometimes, it can come in the form of your internal marketing and communications teams who have the expertise in refining and articulating clear messages. Other times, it requires hiring an external consulting team to help. I've found that bringing in an external partner who has expertise in helping companies define and capture their culture or employer brand is invaluable. One reason is that by not being internal, they can usually see and articulate things more clearly. They also have expertise in doing this work, which means not only better outcomes, but also faster outcomes.

Regardless of where (or if) you find help, the part of the define process that is most important is the feedback loops. When you feel that you've captured the desired employee experience or culture, take that back to leaders and employees for feedback. Ask them how it feels. Ask them what's missing. Ask them what's not quite working yet and why. Take the feedback and iterate. Improve your articulation and then go back for more feedback. Keep doing this until the feedback validates what you are trying to capture. Depending on the size and scope of your organization, this can take some time. But it will be worth it in the end.

When you arrive at the end of the 'Define' step for your employee experience, you should have a clear definition of the experience you are trying to create. The specific way you articulate and document this should fit with your organizational norms and culture. What's important is that it's clear and can be used to inform decisions about how processes will change and evolve. And it should be specific enough that you can measure it in the future through employee feedback.

The example from Farm Credit Services of America in Chapter 5 demonstrates how this might look. As a reminder, they have defined their culture through a set of 'We are' statements. These statements taken together speak to both the employee and customer experiences they intend to create. Each is then further illustrated by specific behavioural expectations to make it easier for employees and leaders to align themselves and their actions The example shared was '*We are servants*'. One of the behavioural expectations in support of this is '*Continually searches for ways to improve customer and teammate experience (including the removal of barriers and providing solutions).*' It's easy to see how this expectation lends itself to measurement, coaching, and feedback.

In designing a new performance management system, it is also important to do some discovery research with regard to your current performance management practices. This is a great place to engage your task force and ask them to help with some data gathering. The goal of this process is to both gather feedback from employees and managers about the current situation and to understand their needs and desires relative to how it could be improved.

This research is an important step in the process. Rather than assuming how employees and managers feel about the process, go ask them. If you ask the right questions, you'll learn what is both liked and disliked about the process. And you may validate some of what you feel is missing. In addition to providing great feedback and input in the process, this research step serves some other purposes. For one, it is an active way to demonstrate to employees and managers that their input is important to shaping any decisions made about the new process. This is helpful in creating buy-in for the change when it comes.

By asking the task force to participate in collecting this information, it creates a deeper engagement for them in the process. When they hear the stories and experiences of people directly, it often furthers their commitment and energy for the project. It also builds their understanding of the dynamics of performance management.

In my experience, it is valuable to give the task force a specific assignment. Ask each member to interview 10 people at different levels and in different roles within the organization. The goal to is gather some broad feedback from a variety of perspectives. Provide them with a short list of questions to use in their conversations.

The interview guide should include questions like:

- How do you feel about the current performance management/appraisal process?
- What do you like about it?
- What do you hate about it?
- What would you change about that process?
- What is missing from the process?

Each member of the task force should present the findings of their conversations at the next meeting. Once each member has shared their findings, work together to summarize the collective findings and identify common answers to each of the interview questions.

To bring this information together into a definition of what you need to design into your performance management system, lead your task force through an analysis of the current state through the lens of your desired employee experience and the three key processes of a performance management system explained in this book: planning, cultivation, and accountability. It might be helpful to ask your task force to read Sections 2, 3, and 4 of this book to provide a foundation and framework for this conversation.

The three questions below can provide a framework for that conversation:

- **What's already working?** Start by identifying what in your current process and approach is effectively working. What processes or practices support the employee experience you intend? Which practices are effectively building a sense of relationship? For example, you may already have objective measures of performance in place that would be a part of any improved process in the future. Or maybe your managers currently do weekly check-ins with employees. Identifying what's working helps avoid making unnecessary changes and ensures you can leverage existing strengths.

- **What's not working yet?** This will be a list of things from your current process that aren't aligned with the intended employee experience, and are harming relationships or failing to deliver the needed impact. For example, some managers may be having one-on-one meetings with their staff but the meetings happen infrequently with little or no structure so they aren't viewed as having a positive impact on performance. You'd add manager one-on-ones to this list because while being a good practice, they aren't working in their current form. Items that show up on this list are things that will likely be part of a new process, but in a new and improved form. As you create this list, it's also important to capture why these items are placed on the list and how you believe they could or should be better.

- **What's missing?** It is in this discussion that you identify where the gaps in your current process exist. An example might be that your current process focuses exclusively on extrinsic motivators for employees (merit increases, annual bonuses, etc) with no focus on intrinsic motivators. Based on what we know about performance, this would be a major gap to be addressed in your new process.

At the end of the discover and define half of the design process, you should have clarity about what kind of employee experience you are trying to create and why. You should also have a sense of where you are already doing things right and where the biggest gaps or issues exist. It's now time to move to the Develop phase to explore how to address those gaps and design a system to ensure that you are creating an experience for employees that will unlock their potential.

Key takeaways

- Design, most simply defined, is creating something with clear intention. Applying design to people processes starts with articulating the impact you wish your work to have on others.

- Best practices can be dangerous. There is no such thing as a best practice, only a 'right practice' for your organization. The effectiveness of a practice is always context specific. Design is the opposite of best-practice thinking.

- Discovery is the first step of design and involves doing research and investigation to understand the current and desired state for both employee experience and performance management.

- Definition is the second step of design where the work of discovery is used to create a clear articulation of your intended employee experience. Successful definition often requires help and several rounds of feedback. Achieving clarity is challenging but worth it.

Reference

Design Council UK (2018) Design process: What is the Double Diamond? [Online] https://www.designcouncil.org.uk/news-opinion/design-process-what-double-diamond [Last accessed 3 May 2018]

Developing and testing your performance management system

19

When most people think of design, this is the part of the process they envision. Creating new products or processes to solve a problem. This is the fun part of design for most people because it's an opportunity to be creative and innovate. It's where brainstorming and big ideas come into play. It's where questions that start with 'what if we…' and 'how could we…' are not only welcome but encouraged.

The hard work done in the Discover and Define steps of design should provide a clear understanding of the experience you are trying to create, the effectiveness of your current approaches and the opportunities that need to be seized. The Develop step in the design process is a divergence process where the goal is to envision and consider many possible solutions as a way to find the right one. This is where Sections 2 through 4 of this book can serve as a guide and inspiration for your work. If you recall, I referred to this section as a 'cookbook' full of recipes to consider, try, and adapt to your needs. That is how I encourage you to use them.

If we stick with the metaphor of cooking for a moment, the performance management system is the meal and you (and your team) are the chef preparing it. For this meal to be great, it must have the right balance of complementary courses. In this case, those courses are called planning, cultivation, and accountability. To decide what goes into each course, you must first know your audience and what kind of meal you are creating. This is the work you've already done in the Discover and Define steps. Only then should you start looking for recipes and other inspiration for what you might prepare.

If cooking isn't your thing, let's put it more plainly. Your performance management system must include processes for planning, cultivation and accountability to be effective. Determining what processes or approaches will be right for your organization is the goal of this phase. To find the right approach, it is helpful to review a variety of different examples for inspiration. Sometimes the right approach can be found by looking at what another organization has done and adapting it to your context. I once heard someone describe R&D as 'rip-off and duplicate'. Contrary to best-practice thinking, this isn't about looking for that best practice that can't fail but rather evaluating practices that might be 'right practices' for you once they are adapted and tested.

You may decide that you need to create something from scratch if none of what you see elsewhere looks anything like what you need. For example, most feedback approaches used in organizations today aren't designed with a good understanding of relationships, human psychology, or brain science. So, finding inspiration for a better feedback process in other organizations might be challenging. There are a few good examples shared earlier in the book like the Menlo Innovation Feedback Lunch, but there are many other ways to approach feedback positively. Instead of applying someone else's approach, you might decide to focus on what you can learn about how humans process feedback and brainstorm some new approaches for feedback that could be tested and evolved specifically for your organizational context.

As you begin to develop your system, take on the development of solutions for each of the performance processes individually at first to make sure the overall process doesn't feel overwhelming. By using the earlier chapters in this book, you can guide your task force through the process to identify and consider potential solutions for each process: planning, cultivation, and accountability.

For example, when developing possible approaches to performance planning, use these questions to guide your exploration:

- How will we ensure everyone has clear expectations at both individual and team levels?

- How could we make cultural expectations related to behaviour and values crystal clear?

- How might we make goal and priority setting more meaningful?

- What approach could we use to ensure that employees have the support and resources they need to succeed?

There will be many possible answers to each of these questions. The case studies shared throughout the book are intended to demonstrate that there are many effective ways to approach any one of these processes. By considering a broad array of options, you are more likely to find the one that fits the best for your culture and people.

As your task force identifies processes or approaches that they feel could be a possible fit for the organization, use the following questions as a framework for outlining the process. These questions will prompt them to think broadly about the impact of the process while also defining enough specifics to ensure there is clarity about how the process would work.

Process design questions:

1 Name/descriptor: What are we going to call this?

2 Details: How will the overall process work?

3 Rationale: Why is this approach right for us?

4 Employee role: What is the employee's responsibility? What will they do?

5 Manager role: What is the manager's responsibility? What will they do?

6 Other roles: Who else is involved? What will they do?

7 Frequency: How often will it happen?

8 Technology: How might technology enhance or enable this process?

9 Dependencies: What other performance processes will this impact?

10 Outputs: What are the measures of success for the process?

After putting a variety of solutions on the table for consideration, use these questions to create conversation to ensure alignment with your intentions. This will help you to begin narrowing the list to those that might be best suited for your organization:

1 Does this approach pass the relationship test? How does it build relationship?

2 How does this approach create our intended employee experience?

3 Why do we believe this solution is best for our employees?

As you work through defining approaches for each of the three processes, it's likely that you'll find some that address or impact several needs when you outline them in greater detail. For example, a regular one-on-one meeting between the manager and employee could be intentionally designed to have impact across all three processes: planning, cultivation and accountability. Other processes, like goal setting, might be narrower in focus.

Deliver

Once your task force has worked through the divergent process of imagining and developing potential solutions, it's time to enter the fourth phase of design, Deliver. This phase has two parts. You start with testing and feedback to identify which of the possible solutions you have identified comprise the right set of processes for your system. This is an exercise in testing, iterating, and validating which solutions are in fact the right practices for your organization.

The second part is to deploy and implement the new system. A new system isn't of much use unless the organization knows about it and uses it. This work is usually referred to as change management and adoption. There are entire books written on these topics, so we aren't going to go too deep in either area because there would be no way to do them justice in a few pages. What we will review are some general recommendations and tips that I've found to be effective through both my research and my own experience.

Testing and feedback

The Deliver step of the design process prompts us to think like an entrepreneur. As an entrepreneur, you can't have any success if your potential customers don't like or consume your product. Before bringing a new product to market, a smart entrepreneur solicits feedback and tests variations of the product with customers to improve their likelihood of success. The same should be true as we develop a new performance management 'product' for managers and employees. Prior to rolling anything out broadly, it's a good idea to go collect some feedback and do some testing with those who will actually have to use it.

There are several ways to collect feedback. Your task force is your first focus group, certainly, but because they participated in the design and selection of processes, it can be hard for them to maintain the objectivity needed to truly evaluate the impact of a new process. The two most common ways to validate and test a new process are focus groups and pilots.

Focus group review

One way to quickly get feedback on new performance processes is through focus groups. By sharing your process design with a group of employees or managers, you can at a minimum gauge initial reactions to the design. Since one of the objectives of this project is to create a system that supports an employee experience that feels like a healthy relationship, this kind of feedback is crucial. If an employee or manager reacts negatively to one of your new designs when simply hearing about it, that's probably a signal that the design isn't quite right.

Lee Burbage at The Motley Fool summarized how they approach designing processes in this way: 'We go for compelling over mandatory.' By that, he meant that processes should be designed in a way that makes managers and employees want to use them. Another way to view this idea would be that if you have to require an employee or manager to use your process, it's probably not designed very well. Resistance and reluctance by participants are feedback on the process itself. Treat it as a signal that you may need to make some changes.

When conducting focus groups to gather feedback on a new process or processes, a good result isn't necessarily universal approval and no criticism. There will always be some criticism based on different individual preferences and experiences. Particularly due to the nature of these performance processes, some of the criticism and scepticism might simply be due to past experience that has little to do with what you've designed. As an individual, if you've always had bad experiences when given feedback, it might be hard to accept that feedback isn't inherently unpleasant. If someone has that as an internalized belief, any mention of feedback is likely to trigger a negative response. That person will likely never give you an enthusiastic thumbs up on any new feedback system. Listen carefully to their responses, however, because you will need to evolve their belief over time. By understanding their fears, you might be able to alleviate some of their concerns through communication and training.

Focus groups can provide some robust insights into how the new processes might be received by employees and managers. Some of this feedback can be useful in improving the process itself and some can help in shaping how the communication and change management may need to look.

Pilot programmes

The best way to validate a new process or system is to actually test it out in the work environment, to let managers and employees try it out. These tests are often called 'pilots'. The goal of a pilot is to test the concept and design of a process in an early phase to ensure it is effective. This is a good way to ensure that prior to sinking substantial investment into building a solution for the entire organization, you can validate that it is likely to have the desired impact

In a pilot, a leader typically volunteers to deploy the system or new process in their group for a fixed period of time to see how it works and measure the impact. The purpose of a pilot is to validate that the design of the process works as intended both in terms of performance impact and employee experience. The pilot generates feedback on the participants' experience of the process and provides evidence of how well it works in producing intended outcomes.

When creating a pilot, the question of technology and training often arises. If you were deploying a solution broadly, you'd probably look for a technology platform to automate and make the process work as smoothly as possible for those involved. You'd also prepare some formal training and support resources to help ensure people are best equipped to use the system. This kind of investment of resources and time is often not practical for a pilot programme.

When developing the pilot, you aren't looking to test the optimal solution, but rather the simplest way to validate that the process will work. For example, let's assume you are looking to test a new process for planning that involved the creation of quarterly goals between manager and employee with shared updates on progress every two weeks. To have an effective pilot, you'd need to ensure that managers and employees have the skills to set and update these goals. You'd also need a way for goals to be captured, shared and updated collaboratively throughout the quarter.

If you were preparing the process for broad roll-out, you might create formal training materials or videos on goal setting and measurement to make available on demand. To facilitate the process, you might buy access to a goal or performance management technology. But, for a pilot, we'd take a faster and more lightweight approach to the process. Instead of creating formal training materials, you might schedule some less formal training classes or webinars for the employees and managers involved in the pilot to give them what they need to get started. As for technology, a simple spreadsheet form could be built to help provide structure for the process. The training and technology approach to the pilot may not be scalable or ideal for a full roll-out, but as long as the fundamentals of the process work and can be tested, then it works.

One further note on technology to consider. Over the past few years, the availability of good tools for the various processes of performance management has exploded. Most of these tools are available as online platforms that are affordable and easy to use, particularly for deployment to smaller teams. When setting up a pilot, it might be worth exploring if you can find a tool to use that is simple and easy to implement. While this isn't critical, having a good tool to automate a pilot can make a positive impact on the user experience and give you better information about how it might work when fully deployed to the organization.

CASE STUDY The Behavioural Insights Team

Mia Samaha at The Behavioural Insights Team in London has been using pilots to evolve the performance management processes in her organization. After two different directors in separate areas of the organizational inquired about improving the feedback processes within their groups, she organized a pilot programme for their two groups. They collectively designed a process, found a flexible technology tool from technology company Small Improvements to support it, and then deployed it for use.

As the employees and managers in these pilot groups have been using this new feedback process, they have also been regularly surveying the participants for thoughts about their experience with the new process. By collecting user pros and cons regularly, they have been able to use that information to make continuous improvements to the process.

One of the reasons Mia is excited by the pilot programmes is that they are not only helping her test and improve this new process, they are also amassing proof that it works. This evidence of effectiveness is particularly important in her organization since it's an organization of highly educated (and naturally sceptical) scientists. Conducting experiments to validate the process is culturally important at The Behavioural Insights Team. It's what they do for clients.

Pilot programmes can be extremely valuable when done well. The length and scope of the pilot can vary based on what you are testing. In general, the pilot group(s) should be large and diverse enough to get a good sampling of how the process will work in a few diverse settings. And it should be long enough to allow the process to have some effect, usually as least three months. If you have more than one approach that your task force thinks might be worth testing, it can be really powerful to run two separate pilots simultaneously with different groups within the company. Then you can let the results of the pilots determine which is the right one.

One key to a successful pilot is measurement. Before launching the pilot, clearly document how you plan to measure success and what success looks like. The feedback gathered from the pilot can help you address and fix any issues with the process before you deploy it broadly. And, even if your organization isn't full of scientists, having evidence from within the organization that the process works and employees like it is pretty valuable when it comes to rolling it out to everyone.

Since we need to create a system that builds relationship with employees, soliciting feedback from the employees and managers about the process is critical. This can be done through surveys as illustrated in the study, through focus groups, or even in one-on-one conversations. When soliciting feedback on the pilot, it's critical not only to ask questions about how they liked or disliked it, but also to understand how the experience felt. Did it leave them feeling valued, focused, confused, etc? This is important when evaluating the pilot outcomes in context of the employee experience you are trying to create.

At the end of any pilot, it's important to conduct a structured debrief to capture and document what was learned. In this case, as you validate a process or group of processes, you'll want to keep an eye towards what will be needed to roll the system out to everyone.

Questions to consider in your pilot programme debrief:

- What worked as expected?
- What did people love about it?
- What didn't work as expected?
- Where was there a lack of adoption or use of a process or practice?
- Where was there confusion about the process?
- Where did people struggle with the process?
- What information could we have provided up front that would have made adoption of the process easier and faster?
- Where did we discover skill gaps where training may be needed?
- What changes to process are needed before rolling out to new groups?

As you debrief the feedback and pilot results you've collected, you will be faced with making determinations about the processes you've been evaluating. Did we validate that they are ready for full roll-out? Are some changes needed? Do we need to more testing?

There will be times when you need to run a second or third pilot programme to validate the effectiveness of changes or iterations you made to the initial process. This process can take a little time. But when you consider that for decades we've been using ineffective, painful performance processes, spending an extra three or six months to get it right seems like a small investment of time.

Once you've identified what processes will comprise your performance management system, the last step prior to implementation is to create a simple process map of your new performance management system over a one-year cycle. On the left-hand side, list the names of the processes you designed for planning, cultivation and accountability. Across the top, list the months. Then, map out when each process will happen throughout the year. Figure 10 is a sample of what a map might look like. This is simplified example scaled down to fit here.

Figure 10   Performance management system map – 6-month sample

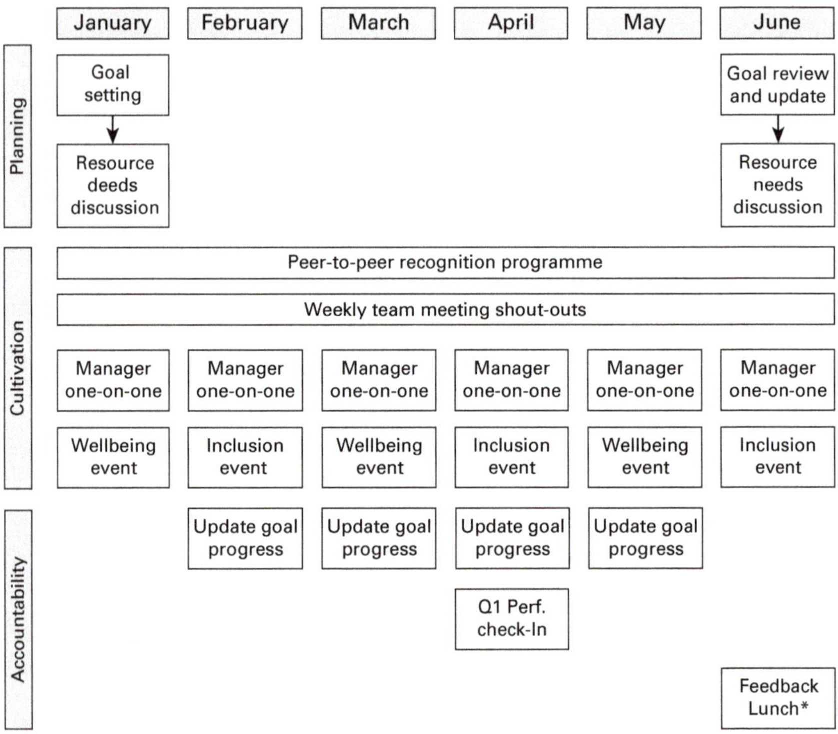

*Feedback Lunches can be scheduled between May 1 and June 30.

This exercise of mapping out the process helps to ensure that dependent processes are slated in the right order and that you haven't overloaded particular months with heavy process work for either employee or manager. Having a visual of the process also helps create clarity for managers and leaders in terms of their expectations and how everything fits together. Additionally, this map will be valuable in identifying technology tools and in planning your change management activities.

You are now ready to implement your new system.

Key takeaways

- The Develop step in the design process is a divergence process where the goal is to envision and consider many possible solutions as a way to find the right one.

- The fourth and final step in design is Deliver. It has two parts. You start with testing the possible solutions to identify those that are the right set of processes for your system. Once tested and validated, you move to full implementation.

- Effective methods for testing and collecting feedback on proposed processes include focus groups reviews and pilot programmes.

- Once your performance management processes are identified, the last step prior to implementation is to create a simple process map of your new performance management system over a one-year cycle.

Implementing your new performance management system

20

Having done the hard work of creating the plan for a well-designed performance management system for your organization, there's one big step left: implementation. At this point, you should have a map of your system and details for each of the processes involved. Now it's time to consider how to best automate, support, and deploy this system to speed its adoption and maximize impact. This means developing a strategy for the technology, training, and communication needed to successfully implement the system.

Technology

When it comes to management and HR processes, technology can either amplify the process or become an obstacle. When I was a young recruiter, I still remember being forced to use what I can only loosely refer to as 'recruiting' technology. This was so long ago that the tool was a simple database program run on a server powering what we used to refer to as 'green screen' terminals – essentially a black and green monitor screen with a keyboard attached. I remember being forced to spend hours using that system, entering in resume and client data, for what appeared to be absolutely no purpose. In my opinion, it didn't help me do my job any better and it pulled me away from where I actually made things happen, talking on the phone. This is an extreme example, but I've encountered corporate HR systems over the years that seemed to make everything more cumbersome and complicated.

On the other hand, there have been some major advancements in technology in the past few years and I've worked with tools that have made management processes much easier. One of the most notable was a tool I used to automate one-on-one meetings with the people I supervised. I had developed over the years a process and structure for these conversations that I found to be very effective and that people tended to really like. It didn't require a technology system to be effective. But then I found a tool that actually helped me make the process more effective by prompting myself and the employee to prepare notes and share those for review and comment prior to the actual meeting. This allowed us to cover a lot of ground before we met which meant that our time together could be spent discussing whatever was most important. The process also captured a narration of our one-on-one conversations over time, including any notes we'd add after our meeting to remind us of commitments or decisions we'd made. This technology tool amplified what was already an effective process.

As you begin to consider what role technology should play in your new system and how you can most effectively use it, here are a few things to remember.

Technology is a tool, not a solution

Good technology is a tool to help you find or create value. We've arrived at a time where we are awash in technology options, particularly in the space of what we consider to be Human Resources technology. Too many of these new technologies are positioned as the cure for whatever ails you. But tools alone don't build or solve anything. Much like building a house, unless you have a blueprint, the right building materials, and skilled builders, having the best tools in the world won't be of much use.

Select technology to fit your solution, not the other way around

This is why we're talking about technology in the last chapter of the book. When you start shopping for technology too early, it's easy to get distracted by features and functionality that look impressive, but don't actually align to or support your processes and the experience you are creating for your employees. Design your process first, then find technology that can automate and amplify your solutions. By ensuring clarity of intention about the experience and system you are creating first, then designing your processes before doing any shopping for technology, you'll be far less likely to get distracted by features that may not matter. And, if you do have to modify your process a bit to fit the capabilities of the tech, you can make that decision in the context of intention to make sure you aren't compromising what's most important about the process design.

Technology should be easy to use for your managers and employees

The days of needing to offer training classes to teach managers and employees how to use a technology tool should be gone. In today's technology marketplace, if you have to offer training to employees on how to use the tool, it's bad design. As you roll out your new performance management processes, you will need to offer training on a variety of things but one of them should not be the technology tool. When selecting tools, ask some employees to jump into the tool and navigate around to see what they think. If it's hard or confusing for them, keep looking.

Technology shouldn't be the default

There are a lot of ways to use technology to enhance and amplify your processes, but just because you can, doesn't mean you should. Does the technology amplify the impact of the process or does it just make it go faster? Does it help build relationship or does it possibly harm it? The example I shared above of the tool I used for one-on-ones is an example where technology actually amplified a process and helped build relationship. I had better and more meaningful conversations with my people as a result of that tool. The opposite example is the Menlo Innovations Feedback Lunch profiled in Chapter 11. For a technology company, they used a decidedly non-technical approach to feedback which is extremely effective for them.

When it comes time to look for technology to automate your system, the evaluation of options should be grounded in how the technology can help your process to be more effective and human-friendly. The abundance of technology products on the market today means that if you look hard enough, you are very likely to find a tool that is a great fit for your process and objectives.

Training

As you review your new performance activities and processes, it's important to consider the skills or abilities managers and employees will need to effectively utilize the process. While the technology should be usable without training, the human interactions involved are not likely to be as easy and intuitive.

For example, if you recall the Vistaprint story from Chapter 12, an important part of their new peer-to-peer feedback system was training for employees and managers on feedback. They were trained both on how to give and, perhaps more importantly, how to to receive feedback with empathy. Without improved capabilities around feedback, a good process and great technology might have little impact.

If your plan includes using feedforward approaches instead of traditional feedback, your managers (and employees) will likely need some training and coaching to make that transition. If employees are to play a collaborative role in goal setting, they may need some basic understanding of effective goals and how to set them. If your managers have never considered how to articulate behavioural expectations for a team, they will need some support.

It is vital to think about what kind of training is needed. Deploying a new process that employees are not equipped to use properly will only lead to further frustration and will not improve performance. As you think about where training might be needed, consider these tips.

Don't assume manager and leader competence

In any performance management system, there is a dependence upon managers and leaders to play a significant role in a number of ways. One blind spot in the implementation of new people management systems of any kind is our assumptions about the competence of managers on the fundamentals of management. If you recall the story I shared about the system we implemented where I worked, which resulted in my 'you suck' list, our biggest failure in the implementation of that system was caused by an assumption. We assumed that executive leaders knew how to give feedback in a constructive way. And, we assumed that those who reported to executive leaders could successfully receive and process feedback in a way that would fuel their development. We were wrong.

There are many managers and leaders who were never given the training and development to learn great people skills. And the longer they've been in management and the more promotions they get, the harder it is for them to admit (or recognize) that they lack these skills. It's not until something bad happens that this skill deficiency becomes painfully visible as it did in my story. The best approach is to make no assumptions. Start with the fundamentals and build from there. Even the best professional athletes in the world practice the fundamentals of their sport daily as part of their preparation. Managers can always benefit from reviewing and working on the fundamentals of coaching and leading people as well. By starting with the fundamentals, it allows even your executives to have access to some training and development that they may not have even realized they needed.

Use pilots to identify skills gaps

In the last chapter, we explored the value of using pilots to test and validate your processes. The pilot is also a rich source of insight into where the biggest skill and ability gaps might exist related to the expectations of the new system. As the pilot group(s) used the new process, where did they struggle? Where was there conflict or confusion? Investigating this friction in the process will lead you to either determine that you have a process design problem, or you have a skills gap on the people side of the process.

Let's use the feedback lunch process from Menlo Innovations as an example again. When you consider the dynamics of this process, it requires a lot of the individual participants. It requires those providing feedback to understand how to identify and share information that will be useful in a way that is constructive. The receiver needs to be able to listen to and process feedback for an hour without becoming defensive or distracted. And, for any of it to work, there has to be a foundation of trust and respect in place for everyone.

In a pilot of feedback lunches, a lot of things could go awry. If it doesn't work optimally the first few times (and it would be surprising if it did), the next step would be to talk to the participants in the process to understand their experience. If trust is the issue, that's obviously a bigger cultural challenge to address, but one you must address to proceed. It could also be a lack of skill in identifying what good feedback looks and sounds like. Or learning how to receive and process feedback in a way that minimizes emotional response. All of these discoveries point to the training interventions needed to ensure the successful implementation and use of your new system.

Create training to be available just-in-time

It is common practice when rolling out any new programme or process to train everyone right away when the new system launches. That seems like the right thing to do. Why wouldn't we want to provide all of the 'know-how' that employees and managers might need to use this new system right away?

The problem lies in the fact that using a new skill is important to our ability to learn and retain it. 'Learning by doing' has long been understood as one of the most important ways that adults learn (Reese, 2011). You can talk me through how to do something. You can show me how to do it. But until I have to do it for myself, the process of mastery hasn't even begun. I remember sitting through supervisory training classes and reading books about management that talk about how to confront difficult situations with employees. But reading about it is very different than sitting across from another human being and actually having the conversation. Until you've been through the experience a few times, you can't really internalize and begin to master the skills you need to do them well.

The challenge with designing training resources for a new performance management system is that the interactions or processes where training is most needed happen throughout the year and, in some cases, are unscheduled and unpredictable in terms of when they will be needed. It makes sense to train managers up front on how to set goals and conduct one-on-one meetings. They should have an opportunity to practice those skills right away. But for skills like providing critical feedback or confronting performance issues, they may not have an opportunity to practice that skill for months. By then, they aren't likely to remember much about the training.

We prefer just-in-time training. It's not until we are faced with a need that we become most motivated to learn. The hours or days before I'm scheduled to provide an employee with some important feedback are when I want the training on how to do it effectively. So, while it's not necessarily a bad idea to train managers up front in all the skills they'll need to succeed in the new system, it's important to also create some on-demand training they can access for a refresher when the need arises. Creating a library online of quick-read 'how to' resources is one way to help. It's also valuable to capture training or coaching sessions in short videos that are easy to find and access. Providing these resources is aligned with how we learn and solve problems outside of work. When in doubt, Google it. My 20-year-old son and his friend recently replaced the manifold on his diesel truck (neither are mechanics) using free videos posted by mechanics on YouTube. Make it easy for managers (and employees) to find some help and training when they need it.

Communication and roll-out

You are now ready to share these new processes with your organization. You've invested a lot of time and energy creating processes that will work better and feel better to both employees and managers. Ensure that your efforts have their greatest impact by crafting a solid communication plan.

Regardless of how much your old process was disliked, your new process represents an unknown change for employees and managers alike. A well-planned, robust communication effort can help decrease the resistance you will encounter during the roll-out.

Here are some tips to help guide your communication planning efforts.

Sell, don't tell. As you communicate, highlight how and why this new process is better than what you've done in the past. Even if your traditional performance management approaches seem to be universally hated, don't assume that means people will be instantly accepting of the new approach. It can be helpful to think about how you'd communicate about these new processes if it was optional for employees and managers to use them. How would you convince them that it will help them have a better experience and find more success? Sell the benefits of the new process – don't just tell them what's happening.

Share the why. Make sure your employees understand why the new process was created. If you've done the work to define and articulate the employee experience your organization is investing in creating, this is the time to share it. Use this opportunity to reinforce your commitment to employees. As you communicate about the new system, be transparent about the process that was used to include feedback from employees and managers. Make it clear that this new system emerged from the business as a way to strengthen the employee experience. Share with them the inclusive process that was used. This will help create buy-in and adoption more quickly.

Segment your communication. One size does not fit all when it comes to communication. Consider the different types of employees across your organization (hourly, salary, non-manager, manager, etc) and ask 'How does this impact me?' from their perspective. Make sure your communication plan is segmented to answer that question in detail for each distinct group of employees. As you consider these groups, also think about the best way to communicate with each. It's important that they hear and understand what's happening. In some cases, you might be dramatically changing their experience. Imagine working for a decade without having much communication with your manager and suddenly having weekly check-ins. Sending out an e-mail isn't going to do it. Meetings, videos, posters, mailings, and e-mails should all be considered. And it's best to communicate the message using multiple methods to account for individual preferences as well.

Overdo it. Err on the side of over-communicating about the change. The 'rule of 7' from marketing suggests we need to hear a message seven times before we truly retain it (Onibalusi, 2015). Advertisers understand this rule well. It's why we see the same advertisement, slogan or television commercial over and over again. The more we see a message, the more likely we are to retain it. The goal is to make sure everyone knows what's coming (and why) by the time it arrives. I don't know that I've ever seen an organization overdo it on communication. Our instinct with internal communication is to stop long before we should. When you think you've communicated enough, it's a good bet you've probably not even done half the communication you should. Keep going.

Make the time to create a robust communication plan to support the implementation and adoption of your new system. Then work your plan, even when you get sick of the message. It takes a great deal of time, resource, and effort to arrive at this point. Don't let a failure in communication diminish the impact of all that investment.

Track and celebrate progress

As I close this final chapter, I offer one last piece of advice. Once your new process is deployed and in use, make sure you have a process in place to track and highlight the impact of your new system. This should be an ongoing effort as it not only helps reinforce the effectiveness of the programme, but also provides an early warning when things aren't working ideally.

There are a variety of ways to track the progress of your new performance management system. The measures you use should connect to the intentions and aspirations you articulated in the design process. How well are you delivering on the employee experience you articulated?

Are people using the system? How have organizational measures of performance changed?

A well-designed and managed system should show some significant positive results fairly quickly. At the very least, managers and employees should be happier that the old, painful processes of the past are gone.

Identifying and sharing stories of success is the most powerful way to reinforce and support the new system – particularly early on. There will be stories, like the one in Chapter 8 from Baystate Health, of the very first online recognition shared by a physician to a groundskeeper. Years of appreciation never expressed until a new system made it possible. In sharing these stories, you can not only reinforce the purpose of the system, but also provide inspiration for others to participate.

Key takeaways

- Successful implementation of your new performance management system requires a developing a strategy for technology, training, and communication.

- The evaluation of technology tools should be grounded in how they can help your process to be more effective and human-friendly. Remember, just because you can, doesn't mean you should. It should have purpose and add value.

- As you review your new system, including the activities and processes involved, it's important to consider the skills or abilities managers and employees will need to effectively utilize the process. In considering what training is needed, don't assume competence, use pilot experience to identify gaps, and develop just-in-time training resources.

- Communication is critical to a successful implementation. Extensive time, resource, and effort are required to develop a new system, don't let a failure in communication diminish the impact of all that investment.

- Make sure to measure and share stories of the impact of the new processes. This will reinforce its purpose and fuel its use.

References

Onibalusi, B (2015) The rule of 7: skyrocket your business growth with this marketing principle, *Effective Business Ideas* [Online] https://www.effectivebusinessideas.com/the-rule-of-7/ [Last accessed 8 May 2018]

Reese, H W (2011) The learning-by-doing principle, *Behavioral Health Bulletin* [Online] http://psycnet.apa.org/fulltext/2014-55719-001.pdf [Last accessed 8 May 2018]

INDEX

4D Design Process 197–203, 204–13
    Define 198, 199–203
    Deliver 198, 207–13
    Develop 198, 204–07
    Discover 198, 199–203
360-degree assessment 108, 145–47, 148, 149

accountability
    in relationships 127–30
    meaning of 126–27
    see also performance accountability
Adidas 52
Agile methodology 97, 123, 149
Amazon 46–47
annual performance appraisal
    context of the broken appraisal process 21–22
    effects on the work relationship 34–35
    lack of consideration of employee experience 45–46
    origins and purpose 19–21
    shortcomings 19–21
Ansarada, personal values (case study) 83–84
Antis, Charles 99–101
Antis Roofing, journey to purpose (case study) 99–101
appreciation
    importance of giving and receiving at work 103–09
    operationalizing 108–09
Arbor Day Foundation, Food For Thought programme 118, 119
autonomy as an intrinsic motivator 95–96, 97–99

Baystate Health, employee recognition (case study) 106–08, 221
Behavioural Insights Team (BIT) 105–06, 210
behaviours versus goals 72–74
Best Places to Work programmes 11, 28, 31, 32
best practice
    annual performance appraisal 19–22
    avoiding the best practice trap 195–97
    context dependence 13–14
    impact of changing context 19–22

    shortcomings of 13–23
    understanding the reasoning behind 13–14
blogging 164
BMW 47
brand promise 46–47
Buckingham, Marcus 144
Burbage, Lee 96, 208
bureaucracy in management 17, 18
    influence of the government and military 21
Bureaucratic Theory (Weber) 17

Campbell, Lynette 113–14
Capelli, Peter 21
CARE International 52
Carnegie, Andrew 21
case studies
    Ansarada (personal values) 83–84
    Antis Roofing (journey to purpose) 99–101
    Baystate Health (employee recognition) 106–08, 221
    DirectPath (good to great behaviours) 75–76
    K&N Management (game films) 161–63
    Menlo Innovations (Feedback Lunches) 139–41, 147, 205, 216, 218
    Menlo Innovations (positive work experience) 50–51
    Merck (one-on-ones) 36
    NVIDIA (Post-Mortem process) 169
    South Dakota State University (Rocks) 69–70
    Vistaprint (feedback process) 149–50, 167, 183, 217
certainty, brain's need for 59–60
change, making the case for 189–92
CIPD (formerly WWA, Welfare Workers Association) 19
clarity
    definition 60
    reducing uncertainty 60–61
Clifton, Don 29, 34, 103, 104
coaching 86
cognitive bias 134–35
collective bargaining 22
Collins, Jim 76

communication
    new performance management processes
        219–21
    organizational culture 72–74
competence, tendency to overestimate
    134–35
contractual model of work 25–28
    compared to work as a relationship
        31–33
    contractual mindset 21–22
    effects of changing context 26–28
    origins of the HR function 19
corporate wellness programmes 111
creativity, motivating 94
culture, translating into behavioural
    expectations 74–75
customer experience design 44, 46

Davidson, Beau 169
Deci, Edward 93
Design Council (UK), Double Diamond
    design process 197–203, 204–13
DirectPath, good to great behaviours (case
    study) 75–76
dissatisfaction at work, drivers of 94–95
diversity at work, celebrating 117–19
Double Diamond design process 197–203,
    204–13
Druckenmiller, Rachel 114–15
Drucker, Peter 28
Dunning, David 134–35
Dunning-Kruger effect 134–35

efficiency focus
    impact on the work relationship 35–37
    time for reflection and 165
emotional connection with work
    impact of good and bad jobs 30–31
    impact on performance 28–30
employee engagement
    as driver of performance 43–44
    crisis of lack of engagement 6–7
    drivers of 28–31
    effects of the annual performance
        appraisal 34–35
    employee experience as driver 43–44
    feeling cared about 29–31
    feeling of belonging 29–31
    feeling valued 29–31
    impact of efficiency focus 35–37
    importance of giving and receiving
        appreciation 103–09
    origin of the term 28
    pursuit of 28
    recognition and appreciation 29–31
    trust 29–31
    what lack of engagement looks like 5–6

why it matters 7–9
work as a relationship 31–33
employee experience
    aligning with organizational purpose
        50–51
    as driver of performance 43–44
    characteristics of a healthy and positive
        work relationship 33–37
    high-stakes moments of truth 45–46
    impact on personal relationships 9–12
    performance management and 44–46
    research on the employee's experience
        28
    what people are looking for 31–33
    why engagement matters 7–9
    work as a relationship 31–33
employee focus groups 121, 125
    review of new performance management
        processes 208
employee performance issues
    choosing not to meet expectations
        175–77
    confronting 172–78
    five main reasons for 173–77
    inability to meet expectations of the role
        175
    lack of clarity of expectations 173
    lack of skill or ability to perform as
        expected 174
    relationship test 177
    unawareness of poor performance
        173–74
employee surveys
    emotional connection with work 28–30
    follow-ups 124–25
    identifying systemic obstacles 123–25
    importance of 49–50
    recognition of the need for 28
    types of question to use 49
employees
    equipping with the resources to succeed
        85–87
    individual expectations 76–79
    individual user manual 78–79
    input in goal setting 64–65
    personality/behavioural assessments
        77–78
expectations
    attaching meaning and purpose to goals
        81–88
    awareness of your own expectations
        63–64
    communicating the organizational
        culture 72–74
    creating clear expectations 63–66
    creation of an individual user manual
        78–79

defining behavioural expectations
72–80
document everything 65–66
effects of lack of clarity 173
individual employee expectations 76–79
influence on another's performance
63–64
invite input and feedback 64–65
need for clarity of 62–63
tools and approaches for achieving
clarity 67–70
unspoken expectations 72–73
experience design 44, 46
clarify your intentions 46–51
extrinsic motivation 93–94

factory system
influence on management thinking
14–17
'soldiering' problem 16
task specialization 16–17
Farm Credit Services of America
(FCSAmerica)
communicating the culture 74–75,
200–01
employee wellbeing 113–14, 117
positive work experience 74–75
Faulkner, Jennifer 106–08
feedback
360-degree assessment 145–47, 148,
149
abandon confidentiality and anonymity
148
approach to giving 136–41
ask open-ended, feedforward questions
147
ask permission first 136–37
building skills for receiving feedback
151–55
consequences of lack of performance
feedback 173–74
consequences of lack of quality feedback
134–35
discomfort of critical feedback 133–34
feedforward approach 143–56
give control to the employee 148–50
give feedback like a gift 137–38
group feedback 145–50
making feedback feel less threatening
136–41
making feedback work 135–41
making peer-to-peer feedback work
145–50
relationship test 136, 138–39
role in performance accountability 131,
133–41
sandwiching critical feedback 135
share a story 137
training for feedback delivery 151–55
type to avoid 143
Vistaprint case study 149–50, 167, 183,
217
why we hate critical feedback 134–35
feedback loops in the design process 200
Feedback Lunches at Menlo Innovations
(case study) 139–41, 147, 205,
216, 218
feedforward 143–45
fight or flight response 59, 134
flexible work arrangements 97–99
focus groups *see* employee focus groups
Food For Thought programme 118, 119
Fuller, Colleen 149–50

Gallup-Sharecare Well-Being Index
112–13
Gino, Francesca 104
goals
alignment with personal values 83–85
attaching meaning and purpose 81–88
contribution to organizational success
81–82
world and community impact 82
Goldsmith, Marshall 143
Golem Effect 64
Grant, Adam 104
gratitude, link with prosocial behaviour
104–05
group reflection 168–70

Hamel, Gary 15–16
Herzberg, Frederick 94–95
Hubspot
Culture Code 47–48, 169, 199, 200
Failure Forum 169–70
Hudl 98
human resources (HR)
compliance function 19
contracts of employment 19
Employee Relations function 172
enforcing the contractual model of work
25–26
evolution of the HR function 18–22
role in the evolution of management
18–22
Hurst, Aaron 78–79
hygiene factors (Herzberg) 94–95

Imperative (purpose-activation company)
78, 101
implementation of a performance
management system 214–22

inclusion at work
    celebrating diversity 117–19
    distinction from assimilation 116–17
    performance implications 115–19
individual user manual 78–79
Industrial Economy 28
Industrial Revolution 14
internet 28
interpersonal obstacles to performance 122
intrinsic motivation 93–94
intrinsic motivators 95–101

Jacobsen, Lenore 63–64
job satisfaction, link with giving and
        receiving appreciation 104–05

K&N Management, game films (case study)
        161–63
Kahn, William 28
Knowledge Economy 28
knowledge work 28
Kruger, Justin 134–35

learned helplessness 122
love, and work as a relationship 31–33

management practices
    bureaucracy 17, 18
    historical role of human resources (HR)
        18–22
    history of 14–18
    influence of the factory system 14–17
    influence of the Knowledge Economy
        28
    micro-management in the factory system
        16–17
    pursuit of employee engagement 28
    scientific management 16–17
    Taylorism 16–17
    Theory X and Theory Y approaches
        26–28
mastery as an intrinsic motivator 95–97
McGregor, Douglas 26–28
measuring employee performance 157–63
    assessment stage 160–62
    defining what will be measured 159–60
    employee concerns 157
    sharing of results 162–63
    three steps 159–63
Meek, Will 33–35
meetings, impact on performance 121–22,
        124–25
Menlo Innovations
    Feedback Lunches 139–41, 147, 205,
        216, 218
    Stand-up meetings 123

work experience design 50–51
mentoring 86
Merck, one-on-ones (case study) 36
micro-management
    in the factory system 16–17
    versus autonomy at work 95–96
mindset
    contractual mindset 21–22
    cultivation mindset 90–92
    learned helplessness 122
    obstacles relating to 122
Moody, Graham 84
motivating factors (Herzberg) 94–95
motivation 93–102
    Theory X and Theory Y 26–28
The Motley Fool 208
    handbook 199
    purpose and values 48
    recognition and appreciation 106
    tenets about work 83, 85, 96–97

Nesta, Randomized Coffee Trials
        (RCT) 118, 119
networking 86
NVIDIA, Post-Mortem process (case study)
        169

Objectives and Key Results (OKRs)
        68–69
obstacles
    anticipating 85
    'death by meetings' 121–22, 124–25
    disruptive effect on performance
        121–22
    types of 122
    ways to identify and remove 123–25
onboarding process
    as assimilation 116
    relationship test 37–38
Patke and Associates 98–99
pay, as a motivator 93, 94–95
peer-to-peer feedback 108
peer-to-peer recognition and appreciation
        104, 105–06
performance
    impact of lack of engagement 7–9
    individual wellbeing and 111–15
performance accountability 54–56, 126–32
    accountability in relationships 127–30
    confronting performance issues 172–78
    fostering mutual commitment 129–30
    impact of accountability 130–32
    meaning of accountability 126–27
    measurement and ratings 157–63
    meeting expectations 130–32
    new approach to feedback 143–56

power imbalance at work 129
role of feedback 131, 133–41
role of reflection 164–71
performance cultivation 54–56
cultivation mindset 90–92
identifying and removing obstacles 121–25
inclusion 115–19
lessons from farming 89–90
motivation 93–102
processes 92
recognition and appreciation 103–09
wellbeing 111–19
performance improvement plan (PIP) 172
performance management
accountability 129–30
arguments for a rebrand 51–53
clarify your intentions 46–51
employee experience aligned with organizational purpose 50–51
employee experience and 44–46
employee experience research 49–50
need for 52–53
new perspective on 46
origins of 21
redesigning 53–54
rethinking 41–56
scientific management 16–17
three processes 54–56
performance management system design
4D Design Process 197–203, 204–13
avoiding the best practice trap 195–97
building a sustainable and effective system 179–81
communication and roll-out 219–21
Define stage 198, 199–203
Deliver stage 198, 207–13
design process 188–89, 195–203
Develop stage 198, 204–07
Discover stage 198, 199–203
documentation of goals and expectations 185–86
focus group review 208
hacking your current processes 184–86
implementation 214–22
insights and practices 179–81
make feedback less painful 186
making immediate improvements 182–87
making processes optional 183–84
making the case for change 189–92
one-on-one meetings 184–85
pilot programmes 208–12
process mapping for a one-year cycle 212–13
recruiting you design team 192–94

relationship test 184, 193–94, 206
stopping the process 182–84
technology 214–16
testing and feedback 207–13
track and celebrate progress 221
training 216–19
performance planning 54–56, 58–61
anticipating obstacles 85
attaching meaning and purpose to goals 81–88
clear expectations and goals 62–70
collaboration for success 86
creating clarity 60–61
defining behavioural expectations 72–80
identifying resources needed for success 85–87
knowledge and skills required 86
learning/training needs 86
link between uncertainty and stress 58–69
new resources required 86–87
reducing uncertainty 60–61
performance ratings
inaccuracy of single-number ratings 158–59
relationship test 158
subjective nature 158–59
why they failed 158–59
personal relationships
impact of experience at work 9–12
moments of truth 41–44
personal values, alignment with organizational goals 83–85
personality/behavioural assessments 77–78
pilot programmes 208–12
identification of skills gaps 218
Pink, Dan 94, 95, 97
power imbalance at work 129
progress as an intrinsic motivator 95–96, 101
prosocial behaviour 104–05
purpose as an intrinsic motivator 95–96, 99–101
Pygmalion Effect 64, 68

Quantum Workplace 11, 31
Quiroz, Gini 161–62

Randomized Coffee Trials (RCT) 118, 119
Rath, Tom 29, 34, 103, 104
ratings *see* performance ratings
recognition, importance of giving and receiving at work 103–09

recognition programmes 106–08
reflection
    building into performance management
        167–71
    distinction from self-review 165–66
    group reflection 168–70
    role in performance management
        164–71
    versus efficiency 165
relationship test
    employee performance issues 177
    evaluating workplace processes or
        interactions 37–38
    giving feedback 136, 138–39
    goal setting 65
    onboarding process 37–38
    performance management system
        changes 184, 193–94
    performance management system design
        206
    performance ratings 158
Ressler, Cari 97
Rocks approach, South Dakota State
        University (case study) 69–70
Rosenthal, Robert 63–64
ROWE (Results Only Work Environment)
        97
Ryan, Richard 93

S.M.A.R.T. goals 67–68
Samaha, Mia 210
Santayana, George 13
satisfaction at work, drivers of 94–95
scientific management 16–17
self-review, distinction from reflection
        165–66
Seligman, Martin 122
servant-leader philosophy 83
Sheridan, Richard 50
shout outs 105–06
SIG (consulting firm) 97–98, 114–15
Silberstein, Richard 98
social worth as a motivator 104
South Dakota State University, Rocks
        approach (case study) 69–70
Stand-up meetings 123
strengths-based management approach 134
stress, link with uncertainty 58–60
strikes 15

Taylor, Frederick 16–17
teamworking 72–73
technology for performance management
        214–16
    as a tool not a solution 215

ease of use by managers and employees
        216
    evaluation of the options available 216
    select to fit your solution 215–16
Theory of Motivation (Douglas) 26–28
Theory X management approach 26–27
Theory Y management approach 26, 27, 28
Thomas, Kenneth 95
Thompson, Jody 97
time investment in relationship building
        35–37
TOMS Shoes 82
trade unions 15, 21, 25
traditional performance management,
        shortcomings of 13–23
training in performance management
        activities 216–19
    create training to be available just-in-
        time 218–19
    don't assume manager and leader
        competence 217–18
    identifying training needs 86
    knowledge and skills gaps 174
    online resources 219
    use pilots to identify skills gaps 218

uncertainty
    link with stress and anxiety 58–60
    reduction by performance planning
        60–61
user experience (UX) design 44, 46

value creation in the Knowledge Economy
        28
values card exercise 84
Vistaprint, feedback process (case study)
        149–50, 167, 183, 217

Warby Parker 82
weaknesses, tendency to underestimate
        134–35
Weber, Max 17
Wickman, Gino 69
Wistia 106, 117
work, contractual mindset 25–28
work as a relationship 31–33
    Merck one-on-ones (case study) 36
    see also relationship test
work experience see employee experience
workplace wellbeing, implications for
        performance 111–15

YouTube 219

CPSIA information can be obtained
at www.ICGtesting.com
Printed in the USA
BVHW020208260219

541186BV00019B/205/P